TRACING THE IMPACT OF FIRST-YEAR WRITING

Tracing the Impact
of First-Year Writing

Identity, Process, and Transfer at a Public University

LAURA WILDER

UTAH STATE UNIVERSITY PRESS
Logan

© 2024 by University Press of Colorado

Published by Utah State University Press
An imprint of University Press of Colorado
1580 North Logan Street, Suite 660
PMB 39883
Denver, Colorado 80203-1942

All rights reserved
Printed in the United States of America

 The University Press of Colorado is a proud member of Association of University Presses.

The University Press of Colorado is a cooperative publishing enterprise supported, in part, by Adams State University, Colorado State University, Fort Lewis College, Metropolitan State University of Denver, University of Alaska Fairbanks, University of Colorado, University of Denver, University of Northern Colorado, University of Wyoming, Utah State University, and Western Colorado University.

∞ This paper meets the requirements of the ANSI/NISO Z39.48-1992 (Permanence of Paper).

ISBN: 978-1-64642-656-0 (hardcover)
ISBN: 978-1-64642-657-7 (paperback)
ISBN: 978-1-64642-658-4 (ebook)
https://doi.org/10.7330/9781646426584

Library of Congress Cataloging-in-Publication Data

Names: Wilder, Laura, 1971– author.
Title: Tracing the impact of first-year writing : identity, process, and transfer at a public university / Laura Wilder.
Description: Logan : Utah State University Press, [2024] | Includes bibliographical references and index.
Identifiers: LCCN 2024008329 (print) | LCCN 2024008330 (ebook) | ISBN 9781646426560 (hardcover) | ISBN 9781646426577 (paperback) | ISBN 9781646426584 (ebook)
Subjects: LCSH: English language—Rhetoric—Study and teaching (Higher)—United States. | Academic writing—Study and teaching (Higher)—United States. | Education, Higher—Curricula—United States.
Classification: LCC PE1405.U6 W545 2024 (print) | LCC PE1405.U6 (ebook) | DDC 808.042071173—dc23/eng/20240329
LC record available at https://lccn.loc.gov/2024008329
LC ebook record available at https://lccn.loc.gov/2024008330

Cover photograph by eclipse_images/istockphoto.com

Contents

List of Figures and Tables   vii

Acknowledgments   ix

Introduction: Questioning the Impact of the First-Year Writing
Requirement   3

1. "They Write a Lot More Than I Am Writing at My School":
    The Role Writing Plays Across Curricula and Lives
    at an Institution Lacking Privilege   27

2. "If There Was a Class That Could Make Them Confident":
    Comparing the Writing Experiences of Students Who Took
    the First-Year Course to Those of Students Who Did Not   63

3. "In Every Part of Your Writing, You Should Be Inside of
    It": The First-Year Course Encouraged a New Mindset
    Toward Writing for Some (But Not All)   86

4. "You Should Write to Know What You Don't Know":
    Three Case Studies Tracing Affordances and
    Limits of the First-Year Course   113

5. "Being Able to Write Things Quickly, Easily":
    Low-Self-Efficacy Student Writers' Theories of Writing   151

Conclusion   180

Appendix: Open-Ended Interview Question Script   201
Notes   207
References   217
Index   229
About the Author   237

List of Figures and Tables

Figure

2.1. Percentage of students in junior year interview who identify as a writer. 72

Tables

1.1. Genres (identified by participants) of writing samples submitted each year by all participants. 33

1.2. Genres identified by participants in response to the question "What have you been writing recently?" 35

1.3. Statistics describing the page counts of writing samples submitted by participants each year. 37

1.4. Statistics describing the number of sources cited in writing samples submitted by participants each year. 38

1.5. Tallies of participant-offered reasons for why the experience they described as a successful writing experience was successful. 48

1.6. Tallies of participant-offered reasons for why the writing assignment they identified as useful was useful to them. 53

1.7. Tallies of participant-offered reasons for why the experience they identified as a failure or "less successful" writing experience was a failure to them. 56

5.1. Student 45's response to the question "How would you define good writing?" or "What does it mean to be a good writer?" during each interview. 157 viii : LIST OF FIGURES AND TABLES

5.2. Student 45's response to the question "When you get stuck when working on a writing assignment or experience writer's block, how do you overcome it?" 159

6.1. Participant responses to question "What advice would you give instructors who assign writing?" 195

Acknowledgments

As you will discover in these pages, many of the students I interviewed over the course of 5 years told me about the significant contributions others made to their thinking and writing: family members, roommates, friends, instructors, classmates. Their experience mirrored my own as I wrote these pages. While writing often seems a solitary act, no one writes alone. We not only seek out the responses of supportive readers and try out ideas in conversation but we also sit with and extend the words and ideas of those who wrote before us. The research presented in these pages would of course not have been possible without the willing and candid contributions of its volunteer participants. I am deeply indebted to the 58 young people who responded to my invitation and met with me to talk about writing, sometimes several times over a period of several years. Thank you.

I am also deeply grateful for the thoughtful and helpful responses of two anonymous peer reviewers and the supportive shepherding of the manuscript by Utah State University Press's Rachael Levay. By asking me to expand my frame of reference, their contributions beyond a doubt improved the conclusions and recommendations I offer here.

I also must acknowledge the sage, kind, and practical support big and small offered by colleagues such as Robert Yagelski, Bruce Szelest, Stephanie Hassan-Richardson, Joanna Wolfe, Elliot Tetreault, Tamika Carey, Derik Smith, Glyne Griffith, Eric Keenaghan, James Lilley, Erica Fretwell, Helene Scheck, Ineke Murakami, Vesna Kuiken, Karen Williams, and Bianca Hedges. Thanks also to Melissa Guadron for attentive help with early transcription. Graduate students in my course on longitudinal studies of college writers have my gratitude for helping me try out some initial ideas and better understand the terrain of this work; thank you Andrew Brooks, Katie Brown, Laura Dacus, Maureen Gokey, Andrea Guerrero, Audrey Peterson-McCann, Angelica

Schubert, Yan-Yun (Gloria) Wang, Robin Ward, and Joe Wozlonis. Noah Kucij was also in this class and many others; my memories of him motivate this work and the continued practice of reaching out with kindness to all those we cross paths with in our classrooms.

More than a COVID-19 pod, my friendships with Wendy, Jesse, Maia, and Sage Roberts and Paul, Megan, and Violet Stasi have kept me sane, grounded, and productive—thank you for that! Family near and far have done the same, so thank you to Robert, Nancy, Jeremy, Aki, and Izna Benjamin, Jaya Vasandani, and Tracey Burdick. Niki Haynes, Steve Rein, Jennifer Greiman, Barry and Harley Trachtenberg, Marci Nelligan, and Lee, Sonya, and Dahlia Franklin add up to the best extended, chosen family one could have. The memories of my parents, Michael and Ann Wilder, are forever warm and sustaining. For their warmth, sustenance, loveliness, and cleverness, Bret and Jolie Benjamin have my undying awe, appreciation, and love.

This research was made possible with the financial support of a CCCC Research Initiative Grant. These grant funds allowed me to compensate research participants and transcriptionists and acquire NVivo software. Without these funds this research would not have been possible. I am deeply grateful for this professional resource, and in particular for Kristen Suchor's assistance.

TRACING THE IMPACT OF FIRST-YEAR WRITING

INTRODUCTION

Questioning the Impact of the First-Year Writing Requirement

Perhaps no other postsecondary field has experienced the same sustained level of anxiety and curiosity about the impact of its teaching than composition. This may be because, on many campuses, a composition course (sometimes two) is the only requirement universally shared—though not universally loved—by all students. While there may be other general education requirements, they can often be fulfilled by a menu of courses from which students can select to match their interests.[1] Since its storied beginning in Harvard's English A (Crowley, 1998), the required composition course has been laden with high hopes and dread. Instructors' and stakeholders' expectations for the outcomes of this course have varied over time and synchronously, with some mix of goals from a dream of error eradication to the development of critical consciousness being more or less dominant at different times and in different programs and individual classrooms (Berlin, 1988; Faigley, 1986; Fulkerson, 2005). Critics of the requirement have called into question whether such outcomes are feasible in one semester in a generic course required of everyone, especially given the varied genres and contexts for writing that await those who complete the course (Petraglia, 1995; Russell, 1995; Smit, 2004), but also given the logistically daunting realities of staffing such a course (Crowley, 1998).

https://doi.org/10.7330/9781646426584.c000

As composition's teachers turned into researchers, they turned anxiety and curiosity about impact into disciplined inquiry using a variety of research methodologies. They have used ethnographic methods to conduct longitudinal research to trace the afterlives of a semester of first-year writing in students' subsequent years of college and beyond (Beaufort, 2007; Carroll, 2002; Haas, 1994; Herrington & Curtis, 2000; Johnson & Krase, 2012; McCarthy, 1987; Sternglass, 1997; Wardle, 2007). They have used pre- and post-test forms of experimentation to assess the immediate impacts of a semester of composition on students' attitudes, knowledge, and writing (Driscoll et al., 2020; Neely, 2014). They have used surveys and interviews to elicit students' retrospective accounts of what the course meant to them and what they learned in it (Bergmann & Zepernick, 2007; Jarratt et al., 2009; Yancey et al., 2018, 2019). And researchers have analyzed the texts students produced in and after a first-year composition course (Connors & Lunsford, 1988; Donahue & Foster-Johnson, 2018; Hansen et al., 2015; Haswell, 1991, 2000; Kitzhaber, 1963; Lunsford & Lunsford, 2008).

The news has not always been good, with early longitudinal studies, like those by McCarthy (1987), Haas (1994), and Beaufort (2007), finding that students tend to compartmentalize instruction, leaving composition behind in the composition classroom rather than drawing from insights on writing process and practice gleaned in the course when writing in other courses and contexts. Carroll (2002) demonstrated how students may transfer "basic" techniques practiced in a first-year writing class related to "research, style, audience, and analysis" (p. 74), but not the expert process strategies such as revision and peer review that a first-year writing course attempts to introduce when either motivation or conditions do not encourage the investment in time that they require. Hansen et al.'s (2015) investigation of college-equivalent writing courses in high schools found no statistically significant differences in the ratings of the writing students produced later in college between students who had taken a required first-year course and students who had not yet taken that course. Driscoll (2011) found students' faith in the transferability of knowledge from first-year composition to other courses and scenes of writing decreased from the start to the end of the semester. Retrospective student interview studies, such as those by Bergmann and Zepernick (2007) and Jarratt et al. (2009), which asked students to look back on first-year composition from a later vantage point, added further support to findings that students tend to compartmentalize or dismiss first-year writing instruction. In these studies students explained that they associated their composition instruction with English studies and questioned its relevance to their work in other disciplines.

Further studies complicated the earlier findings, however, offering some evidence of the efficacy of first-year writing instruction, though the nature of that instruction can vary considerably from institution to institution (Ruecker, 2014) and instructor to instructor (Carroll, 2002, pp. 64–65; Fulkerson, 2005). Subsequent studies of student writing have added more promising support to Carroll's (2002) finding evidence of transfer of learning from the first-year course. For instance, Johnson and Krase (2012) documented how students can transfer the use of claims and evidence practiced in a first-year writing course to courses in other disciplines, and Donahue and Foster-Johnson (2018) demonstrated that students carry over text features such as placement and type of thesis from a first-year writing course to a first-year seminar course. However, Johnson and Krase (2012), like Haswell (1991), Carroll (2002), and Beaufort (2007), found that students' writing skills may appear to have "stagnated" and even "regressed" (p. 42) when they later encounter new, diverse genres in the context of the disciplines. Thickly descriptive case studies such as those reported by Herrington and Curtis (2000) point to the entwined nature of "personal" and "academic" writing in students' lives and the role that a first-year writing course can serve in supporting students' developing identities.[2] Neely (2014) found that after a semester of a first-year writing course, students' beliefs shifted from an absolutist epistemology to a more contingent view of knowledge as they came to embrace a view of writing that was more process based and communicative and to see greater value in exploring and acknowledging multiple perspectives in their writing (p. 149–150). Such impacts for one course taken in the first year of college are not insignificant and could be life-changing for many, opening the doors to seeing oneself in the projects of academic writing. A number of studies demonstrated that students may come to understand writing as rhetorical and epistemic long before signs of these views emerge in their writing (Haas, 1994; Penrose & Geisler, 1994; Sommers & Saltz, 2004), suggesting that a first-year course can plant seeds that may not bear fruit until years later.[3]

Adding to our understanding of the complexity of investigating and designing learning experiences that promote high impact, recent important work has examined what students bring with them into a first-year writing course and how these dispositions, habits, and prior understandings contribute to shaping what is possible in that course and what students transfer from it. For instance, the students in Reiff and Bawarshi's (2011) study who embraced a novice identity were more successful "boundary crossers," more likely to engage in high-road transfer of knowledge from high school to college because they were less likely to assume that they had already fully mastered writing and more likely to meet genres new to them with curiosity. In contrast, the students in the study Reiff and Bawarshi describe as "boundary guarders" tried to fit new genres they encountered in their first-year writing course into what genres they already knew from high school; their assumption that they knew all the genres they would need encouraged only low-road transfer and actually inhibited their development as writers. Sommers and Saltz (2004) described similar findings as they began to track students' writing experiences from their first year at Harvard; those who embraced a novice identity early on grew more as writers. Additional work examining students' dispositions, such as their tendencies toward preferring (and their past educational experiences promoting) "answer-getting" versus "problem-exploring" approaches to knowledge acquisition (Wardle, 2012), or seeing their work in a first-year writing course as "connected" or "disconnected" to their future goals (Driscoll, 2011), or seeing themselves as capable of and valuing what they do in the course (Driscoll & Wells, 2012), or their ability to regulate their emotions around writing (Driscoll & Powell, 2016), further revealed the profound role dispositions play in shaping students' experiences in first-year writing courses and with writing beyond the course, likely regardless of their instructors' approaches to teaching writing.

The uneven findings from longitudinal and retrospective studies coupled with writing studies scholars' provocative calls for abolishing the course requirement have recently motivated calls to innovate and radically change the pedagogies and aims typical of the course (Adler-Kassner, 2012; Bawarshi, 2003; Beaufort, 2007; Downs & Robertson, 2015; Downs & Wardle, 2007; Hayes et al., 2018; Yancey et al., 2014). Some of the findings tracking the results of these innovations have shown promising initial results. For instance, Wardle (2007) found that students from her first-year course taught as an "introduction to writing studies" (or a "writing about writing" approach) carried with them a "meta-awareness about writing, language, and rhetorical strategies" (p. 81), though they did not subsequently engage this awareness primarily because they were not asked to write much in the years after their first-year writing course. Yancey et al. (2014) demonstrated how a first-year course curriculum focused on "teaching for transfer" by developing students' theories of writing through reading and reflecting on key terms in writing studies such as *genre, audience,* and *discourse community* supported students' productive use and adaptation of these concepts in different concurrent (Yancey et al., 2019) and later contexts (Yancey et al., 2018). A first-year course designed by Driscoll et al. (2020) to increase students' genre knowledge produced measurable improvements in students' written performances, with their reflective writing pointing to their increased genre awareness as a source of this improvement.

As the literature reviewed in the preceding paragraphs demonstrates, longitudinal studies examining the afterlives of a course in writing are characteristically interested in exploring the transfer of learning (Perkins & Salomon, 1988), what learning students appropriately (and inappropriately) transfer and fail to transfer from one context to another—even as the term "transfer" has been widely recognized as profoundly imperfect to describe the transformation, recontextualizations (Nowacek, 2011), repurposing (Wardle, 2012), integration (Smith et al., 2021), wayfinding (J. Alexander et al., 2020b), and negotiation (Baird & Dilger, 2023) that occurs when students draw from writing knowledge acquired, confirmed, or honed in one educational context and used in another. Further, rich case studies employing cultural historical activity theory like those conducted by Prior (2018), Roozen (2009b, 2010, 2016), and Rounsaville (2014, 2017) have shown us the complex, multilayered, and nonlinear nature of the writing knowledge that individuals draw upon and repurpose across their lifetimes. These studies importantly remind us that seldom is a writer's development a simple matter of transferring knowledge wholesale from one course or discourse community to another in a linear progression and as if starting from a tabula rasa. Individual experiences accumulate over lifetimes in ways that make generalizations about "transfer" experiences across different individuals and contexts difficult to make. I agree with these criticisms, such as the suggestion that the term "transfer" implies a wholesale, unchanged use of knowledge from one setting to another rather than a repurposing or integration that involves agency, creativity, and expansion of knowledge. And yet like so many others interested in documenting and analyzing this phenomenon, I use the term "transfer" throughout this book because it has clearly become the term scholars in writing studies use to signal to one another that we are in shared conversation.[4]

Comparison to a "Control Group" and Broadening the Writers Represented: How This Book Contributes to Longitudinal Research on College Writers

What previous studies investigating the impact of first-year writing have lacked, for entirely understandable, ethical reasons, is the ability to ask what would happen if their participants had not taken a composition class at all or a comparison to a control group.[5] For reasons I will explain below, I stumbled into a situation where such a study would be possible. Once I recognized that I was presented with a unique research opportunity, I moved to design, approve, fund, and conduct a study where I could compare the experiences with writing over time of students at the same institution, at nearly the same time and in otherwise nearly identical conditions, who had and had not taken a required composition course. Though new, the required composition course introduced at this institution was in many ways comparable to other first-year writing courses offered at similar institutions, drawing as it did on design principles articulated in several decades of composition scholarship while supporting instructor autonomy (but eschewing some of the more recent innovations that emphasized writing studies and rhetorical genre theory briefly reviewed above). Chapter 2 presents the results of my comparative study of the college writing experiences of students who took this new course and students who matriculated at this same institution before the initiation of this new course requirement.

Another gap in the longitudinal research of college writers has been the lack of representation of public institutions and the diverse student bodies they serve. Sternglass's (1997) early study stands out for its attention to students for whom attending college is a great challenge and sacrifice. The first-generation college students in her study of the student writing culture in CUNY's City College in the early 1990s juggled multiple jobs and family care obligations while attempting to navigate a writing assessment regime that held many of them back from progress toward their degrees.[6] Their experiences stand in stark contrast to those of the participants in the majority of the subsequent large-scale longitudinal studies set in institutions of marked privilege: Pepperdine (Carroll, 2002), Harvard (Sommers, 2008; Sommers & Saltz, 2004), Stanford (Fishman et al., 2005; Lunsford et al., 2013), Dartmouth (Delacambre & Donahue, 2012; Donahue & Foster-Johnson, 2018), MIT (Lerner & Poe, 2014), and University of Michigan (Gere, 2019). Though certainly not all the participants in these studies came from privileged homes and high schools, their experiences of writing in college were shaped by the expectations, traditions, resources, and support that encircled them at these institutions.[7] The story emerging from places like Harvard, Stanford, and Pepperdine, in the 30 years since Sternglass's study at CUNY's City College, is one of undergraduates writing a great deal, in a diversity of genres and media for a range of audiences, and conquering progressively greater writing challenges that stretch their abilities and produce real growth personally, intellectually, and in sophistication on the page. For instance, findings from the Stanford study of writing (Fishman et al., 2005; Lunsford et al., 2013) show us that while students' confidence in their writing may drop on entering Stanford, their experiences with writing for public audiences and in legitimate disciplinary contexts (often leading to publication) greatly legitimizes their identity as writers, which in turn enhances their willingness to commit to writing as a process and markedly improve as writers. While this is an inspiring and hopeful story for our field, we should be alerted by Melzer's (2014) nationwide study of assignments across the curriculum that not all college writing experiences are as interactive, rich, and productive of deep learning as these longitudinal studies have to date documented.

With my study, I set out to complicate our emerging story of students' college writing experience by selecting as a research site an institution of notably less privilege, notably fewer resources, and serving students who routinely juggle the kinds of competing demands and economic hardships that Sternglass (1997) documented in her groundbreaking study. My research site is a mid-sized public regional university that has experienced decades of cuts to its funding, which is set each year by the state legislature. It boasts an extremely diverse student body with many students the first in their families to attend college and most applying for financial aid. Most come from urban or rural home communities of lower- and lower-middle-income households. The research site for this investigation provides, then, a decidedly different, and I dare say more typical, educational context in which to consider the effects of a first-year composition course than recent longitudinal studies of college writers have provided. Chapter 1 presents my contribution to the burgeoning longitudinal studies of student writers and their transfer-of-writing practices and knowledge with examination of a population not often enough centered in this literature.

If longitudinal studies of college writers have tended to inform us about the experiences of students attending institutions of privilege, they have also tended to tell us about the experiences of students who feel some ease and pride in writing. While as teachers we may have a good deal of experience with students who are uncomfortable with or resistant to writing, as researchers we have found it very challenging to recruit such students to participate in our studies, especially longitudinal and qualitative studies that require a good deal of commitment and time from participants. As a result, most of our findings reflect the experiences of students with some facility and interest in writing. Concern that those who tend to volunteer to participate in this research are likely individuals "predisposed to appreciating the value of writing in their lives" led J. Alexander et al. (2020a) to call for studies that "seek to document and account for less positive affects about writing" (p. 588). In an attempt to do just this, I cast my net wide, did my best to signal an interest in hearing from all students, including those who dislike writing or have felt a lack of connection with writing assignments, and crossed my fingers. I had no reason to believe I would have any better luck in avoiding volunteer bias than previous researchers, and I suspect I have not entirely—most of the participants in this study feel some facility with writing and can express themselves in writing with relative ease. But I did have a chance to sit and talk with several students who distrusted writing teachers, sought to avoid writing, did not identify as writers, and sought out majors and professional paths that they hoped would ask them to do very little writing. Their candor with me was welcome and illuminating, and I pay special attention to what they have to teach writing instructors and administrators in Chapter 5, adding to the few smaller studies such as McCarthy's (1987) and Knutson's (2019) that listen to students who do not view themselves as efficacious writers.

Thus, the overarching research questions the study presented in this book set out to investigate are:

- How do the experiences with writing at a public, regional research university serving a diverse student body, with many first-generation college students who frequently come from economically disadvantaged backgrounds, compare to the experiences with writing documented in longitudinal studies of writing at institutions with far greater privilege and resources? In other words, how do class, race, and ethnic background and institutional prestige and resources affect students' experiences with writing in college? (Chapter 1)
- How do students at this institution who have taken a required first-year writing course experience, understand, and perceive writing as compared to students in the same institution who have not taken such a course? In what ways are their experiences with writing in college similar and in what ways do they differ? (Chapter 2)
- What are the immediate and long-term impacts of a first-year writing course on students' experience with writing in college? Do students transfer knowledge gained in the course to other appropriate contexts in the years after its conclusion? What are the long-term influences of the course, positive and negative, on students' experiences with writing? (Chapters 3 and 4)

- What can students who do not see themselves as strong writers teach us about their responses to writing instruction, their views on writing, and possible interventions that may support their development as writers? (Chapter 5)

Researcher Positioning

These research questions emerge in part from my acting upon the happenstance development of circumstances at my research site and in equal part as a progression from my previous scholarly commitments and perspectives. Those commitments include understanding writing as a complex sociocognitve phenomenon, a negotiation and dance between an individual's past experiences, identities, embodiment, and cognition and larger, contextual social expectations, histories, material spaces, and exigencies. This understanding drew me to (and was informed by) empirical research using methods suited to explore writing from multiple angles: the perceptions of writers and their readers, process tracing, the effect of process interventions, textual analysis, and tracing community textual practices over time. My previous research (Wilder, 2002, 2006, 2012) sought to contribute to writing in the disciplines (WID) research by studying a disciplinary discourse community's entrenched, expert textual practices and the experience of introductory students at the periphery of this discourse community where traditionally these practices play a significant yet implicit role in oral and written discourse and in evaluation standards. My perspective on writing is informed by writing studies' robust debates and research on theories of discourse communities, genre, rhetorical invention, tacit writing knowledge, transfer of writing knowledge, and the efficacy of explicit genre instruction.

Like many WAC and WID researchers, the questions I have pursued have been motivated by concern for those historically excluded from access to disciplinary authority and power through discursive gatekeeping: minority students, especially Black and Latinx students; students from lower-class backgrounds; students who are the first in their family to attend college; and women and gender-nonconforming students.[8] An imperative turn in writing across the curriculum (WAC) scholarship has called for not only more explicitly naming this concern but also more directly engaging racial, ethnic, class, and gender difference in WAC/WID scholarship. Indeed, I am as guilty as those cited by Anson (2012) and Poe (2013) in not foregrounding this concern in my past work, even as I felt it as centrally motivating. For instance, you won't find this rather muted articulation of the concern until page 111 of my book-length treatment of literary studies as a disciplinary discourse community:

> The sense that complex social circumstances likely support the development of some students' apparent special "knacks" for intuiting the implicit rhetorical instruction of the disciplines motivates many arguments in favor of explicit rhetorical instruction on the grounds of social equity. Recognition that the discourse practices of the community of school more closely match, indeed stem from, the discourse practices of the white middle class leads many to claim that students from other backgrounds are placed in distinct disadvantages in this context, especially when instruction makes no attempt to acknowledge and bridge different discourse community practices. (Wilder, 2012, pp. 111–112)

My concern that the privileging of white discursive practices is historically embedded in what we widely call "academic discourse" in its many variants animates this project as well. But as a white, cisgender woman whose parents both held graduate degrees, I have humbly learned in the interim so much more about how knowledge of Latinx and Black rhetorical and linguistic traditions might animate writing pedagogy and promote code meshing (Baker-Bell, 2020; Banks, 2011, 2016; Carey, 2016; Hinojosa & de León-Zepeda, 2019; Newman & García, 2019; Perryman-Clark, 2013; Richardson, 2004; Sánchez et al., 2019; Young et al., 2014) and heard Kareem's (2019, 2020) and Baker-Bell et al.'s (2020) criticism of composition and WAC's apparent silence on naming these as learning outcomes. I wish to take care now to foreground rather than murmur these concerns.

Research Site, or How I Am Able to Approximate a Control Group in the Study of the Impact of Required First-Year Writing

The research reported in this book was conducted at a regional state research university with an unusual history of writing instruction: In the mid-1980s it followed through on the provocations in composition's literature and abolished first-year composition. Beginning in the mid-1980s, many four-year colleges and universities opted to supplement their first-year writing course requirement with WAC programs that moved to distribute the site and responsibility for writing instruction across disciplines and across all years of students' classwork. This embrace of WAC came as a response to the growing understanding, supported by then burgeoning WID and longitudinal research, that writing is contextual and developmental and that one generalized course is insufficient (or incapable) for helping students meet all the challenges of writing in diverse majors and professional tracks. But in contrast to the trend of WAC programs then being built to buttress and build upon a first-year composition course requirement, in 1986 the faculty of the university where the research reported here takes place was persuaded by their writing program colleagues to rescind their first-year composition course requirement then housed in the English Department and replace it with a WAC structure of two required writing-intensive (WI) courses offered by many departments, one a lower-level course and one an upper-level course (Brannon, 1995).

This new approach to college writing instruction, devoid of first-year composition, was clearly intended to support students' development as writers over their years of study and to introduce them to writing conventions and practices in their major field of study. I understand that, when instituted, the structure was supported with faculty commitment, oversight, and WAC professionalization, features that were originally well-funded. But as has happened to WAC programs at other institutions (White, 1990), funding eroded over time, and subsequently so did the faculty outreach, oversight, and perhaps finally faculty commitment, which held on unevenly across departments and was no longer coordinated. This left the two-course requirement as something students continued to fulfill, but in courses where instructors' commitment to and training in writing instruction could vary widely. At a bare minimum, this meant that students could only reliably be said to have written a certain number of pages in their WI courses, and even this requirement received little oversight. A wide variety of courses fulfilled the WI requirement, from introductory creative writing to large lecture courses that allowed some students to enroll in a WI section that asked them to write some additional papers but provided no writing instruction. Anecdotally, I learned a number of students waited until their senior year to take the two WI courses, undercutting the developmental goals of the original WAC program. Some departments did not offer sufficient WI courses, sending their majors to fulfill the upper-level course requirement in other departments, undercutting the original goal of supporting students' acquisition of writing skills and knowledge in the context of their chosen field.

Growing recognition that the original goals of the WAC structure were not being met motivated a provost to institute a committee to investigate and propose an alternate approach to writing instruction. In a "back-to-the-future" development, the outcome of this committee's work was to propose a new first-year course requirement. The aim of this development was to ensure that all students had a similar early college experience with writing. A continuing but seemingly toned-down commitment to WAC was maintained in a further requirement that all major programs identify how at the upper level they support students' acquisition of writing practice and knowledge in their fields.[9] The first class of students to take this new, required first-year course matriculated at the university in 2013.

As I watched these curricular developments from the sidelines,[10] I realized I was witnessing a rather remarkable development in the early 21st century—the return to a required composition course after all the potent critiques this requirement has buffeted (Brooks, 2002). It also presented an opportunity not usually available in longitudinal studies of students' experience with writing in college—the ability to compare the experiences of students on the same campus in near identical circumstances with the one variable difference of participation in a first-year writing course.

Implementation of my hastily designed study faced some delays. After receiving institutional review board (IRB) approval, an initial attempt to recruit participants in spring 2014 failed to yield sufficient participation—only two students volunteered. After determining the culture of research participation on this campus led participants to (justifiably) expect compensation, I secured funding for this purpose (as well as for support with interview transcription).[11] Thus in spring 2015, 2.5 years after the launch of the new first-year composition course requirement, my study began. A downside to the delay in launching the study is that my longitudinal engagement with students who had not taken a first-year writing course was necessarily truncated to either their last 2 years of study as college students or their final year and 1 year post-graduation. In other words, by the time I started interviews, participants who had not taken the new first-year writing course were in either their junior or senior year of college. An upside to the delay, though, was that I ended up not tracking students emerging from the very first year of the new first-year writing course program but instead from the program's third year. This way the faculty who taught this course, all of whom were newly hired and most of whom were new to campus, had some time to establish the new course before I sought to track its possible afterlives.

This institution serves a very different population than those represented in many recent large-scale longitudinal studies of student writers. The public, regional research university where the present study was conducted enrolls annually approximately 13,000 undergraduates, most of whom come from the surrounding region in the Northeastern US, which includes large urban areas like New York City and rural areas like upstate New York. Approximately 40% are first-generation college students; 82% apply for financial aid and, of those, 46% come from families whose annual income is less than $50,000. In response to identified needs, in 2019, spurred by a faculty and professional staff union initiative, the university launched a food pantry open to students, faculty, and staff, and a free exchange for students to obtain gently used professional clothing. The student body is racially and ethnically diverse, with 43–45% of the student population described as belonging to a racial or ethnic minority. At the time of the study, the largest of these minority populations (17%) identified as Black, though in recent years the number of students identifying at Latinx has surpassed this figure.

In my own advanced undergraduate writing studies courses at this institution taught in the years before the new first-year writing requirement I had regularly assigned articles emerging from the large-scale longitudinal studies of writing at institutions of far greater resources and privilege, such as Harvard (Sommers & Saltz, 2004) or Carnegie Mellon (Haas, 1994). The reactions of many of my students upon learning from these articles how much students are asked to write and how seriously faculty in a wide range of disciplines engage with student writing at such institutions have included shock and even anger. They recounted their own early college writing experiences in very different terms, describing lower expectations in many ways, including simply lower expected page counts. It was evident to me that the anecdotal experiences of these students, in the time since Sternglass's (1997) groundbreaking work, were underrepresented in this line of research and begging to be heard. My research set out to offer a needed corrective at the same time that it set out to take advantage of a unique opportunity for comparative study.

Interview Methodology

I set out to conduct a longitudinal, interview-based study with a comparative component in the footsteps of previous longitudinal studies of college writers. I determined that interviews would be the primary mode of data collection because, as with other longitudinal studies of student writers, I wished to analyze and compare experiences with writing that would likely vary a great deal. Simply collecting students' writing from different courses and majors without the context of their experience would leave me to compare vastly differing genres and assignment goals that would not tell much about students' experiences with or abilities in writing. Perceptions of self-efficacy, motivation, and general dispositions have been shown to be tightly tied to student writers' performance of writing (Driscoll & Jin, 2018; Driscoll & Wells, 2012; Pajares, 2003), making them the root beliefs we need to study as much or more than any individual written performances. Further, a number of studies demonstrate that students come to understand writing as rhetorical and epistemic long before signs of these views emerge in their writing (Haas, 1994; Penrose & Geisler, 1994; Sommers & Saltz, 2004), meaning we may miss important learning about writing if we only focus on students' writing.

I wanted to hear from as many students as possible and recruit a large number of participants in order to consider diverse experiences and attempt to avoid volunteer bias, particularly as it relates to participants' willingness to discuss the sometimes-sensitive subject of writing. This can be an area where survey methodology is better than interviews, especially when the primary investigator has no research team or assistants. But I knew from conducting large-scale survey studies (Adsit & Wilder, 2020), and from reading and participating in them, that there was no way surveys could account for the nuances and complexity I hoped to be able to learn about. Furthermore, surveys suited for quantifiable analysis require that the researcher predetermine responses for participants to select from, and since the institution type and population I hoped to study were underrepresented in previous longitudinal studies of college writers, I wanted to allow participants the freedom to determine their own responses and work on the back end, in coding and analysis, to attempt to determine trends in findings rather than assume that trends in the existing literature applied to my research site.

Yet a limitation of interview as a research methodology is its ability to only document what participants consciously recollect about the subject at hand. Writing is a process that is notoriously difficult to fully and accurately recollect after the fact. Writing researchers have documented that a good deal of expert writing knowledge is tacit knowledge, which bearers do not recognize that they possess but which powerfully guides many of their regular writing practices (Flower, 1989; Freedman, 1993; Olinger, 2021; Rymer, 1988; Tomlinson, 1984; Warren, 2011; Wilder, 2012). And writing researchers have recently learned that a good deal of transfer of students' newly acquired writing knowledge and skill to new contexts is invisible to them and often unavailable for conscious reflection during an interview (Brent, 2012; Driscoll & Cui, 2021). Writing researchers have also learned that because emotions around the topic of writing can for some be strongly positive or negative, interview participants' ability and willingness to fully recollect their experiences with writing can be impacted. Jarratt et al. (2009) and Dipardo (1994) have reflected on this limitation, arguing that students' memories can become particularly cloudy or even repressive when asked to reflect on writing experiences they found uncomfortable. According to Jarratt et al. (2009), questions about writing present some students with painful reminders of previous "insecurities, and sometimes resentment about the writing requirement" (p. 63), and students' answers may only become vivid when recounting experiences that they see as pleasant or directly related to their own specific goals.

In an effort to diversify my sources of data and to lessen these limitations in interview methodology, I asked participants to bring to each interview a piece of writing they felt "represented their recent writing," a qualification that I asked them to explain their interpretation of each time. I collected copies of these samples and reread them as I coded interview transcripts. In addition to providing a window into the types of writing and assignments participants experienced, these samples played an important role during interviews when I used them in attempts to stimulate participants' recall of their process of writing them. I drew from composition research methods designed to prompt participants' memories and place them back in the position of making process-based decisions about their writing such as the discourse-based interview (Odell et al., 1983) and stimulated recall (Dipardo, 1994). The writing samples they brought to each interview were pieces we looked at together as I asked them questions about the process steps they took to write the sample. Wherever possible, we examined together specific portions of these texts, and I asked questions about choices made in composing them and sources of knowledge and experience they drew from while writing them. Thus, as much as possible, I aimed to move participants away from discussing "writing in general," which could produce vague, inaccurate, or wishful depictions of this complex phenomenon, to discussing particular and recent writing events. That said, readers should be aware that even so these writers' representations of their writing can be inaccurate, with the automaticity of many writing processes (Anson, 2015) making them inaccessible to writer's recollections. Further, our regular meetings to discuss their writing may have come to shape and inform the very phenomenon I set out to describe and understand. But inaccurate or not, I and many qualitative writing researchers argue that writers' representations of their process matter a great deal, perhaps as much as or more than what actually transpires during a writing session. Each time we met, participants and I reflectively coconstructed representations of their writing (Roozen, 2016), with my questions serving as prompts to help them make sense of what they already do and know. Their understanding of themselves as writers and their writing processes, even if not fully accurate, may inform their actions and choices the next time they sit down to write, like a working script, and this is why their own representations, or theories of writing (Yancey et al., 2014), matter and are important for us to study.

My interview protocols drew many questions from previous studies so that I could compare my findings with theirs (see the Appendix for the interview questions I used). In particular, because they were publicly available at the time I began my study, I drew questions from the Irvine (Jarratt et al., 2009), Pepperdine (Carroll, 2002), City College (Sternglass, 1997), Florida State (Yancey et al., 2014), University of Hawaii (Hilgers et al., 1995), and Stanford (Lunsford, 2010) studies of writing. I also reused some questions from my own smaller longitudinal interview study of students emerging from experimental and control sections of a writing about literature course because I had found them productive in encouraging students to discuss what they recalled from a writing course (Wilder, 2012). My questions were designed to elicit students' views on a wide range of issues related to writing. I asked about their recent writing, their positive and negative experiences with writing, their sense of themselves as writers, their previous experiences with writing in and outside of school, their advice for other writers and for their teachers, their writing processes and habits, their use of technology, and their preferences for environments in which to write. I asked nearly the same questions annually in order to compare their responses over time, though I sometimes did not have time to ask all questions every year, and the sequencing of questions could change as I attempted to follow participants in the topics they wanted to discuss or offer what seemed at the time like a logical follow-up question. As Gere (2019) did at Michigan, I set out to compare the experiences of two different groups of students. Whereas Gere (2019) and her collaborators compared the experiences of writing minors with students who did not pursue this minor but who still did fulfill a first-year writing requirement, I set out to compare the experiences of students who had never taken a first-year writing course with those who had. Students who did not take the new required writing course were asked to reflect on their experiences in courses they took to fulfill the lower- and upper-level writing-intensive course requirement in place for them. Students who took the required first-year writing course were asked at first to describe their expectations of the course and thereafter to describe their impressions and memories of the course. In the final interviews of this study, I asked students to reflect on what participation in the study had meant to them or how it affected them. Before each interview, I reviewed transcripts of previous interviews and planned follow-up questions to supplement the scripts that appear in the Appendix.

In total, 58 students participated in this research, and I conducted 143 interviews over 5 years. Generally, the racial and ethnic demographic distribution of these 58 participants reflect the larger population of undergraduate students attending this school, with 45% identifying as a belonging to a racial or ethnic minority. However, in comparison to the larger population at this school, Black students are overrepresented (26% of participants) and Latinx students underrepresented (5% of participants). I identified students to invite to participate from the two groups I wished to compare in slightly different ways. The campus Office of Institutional Research helped me create a randomly sampled list of students who had not taken the new first-year writing course and who were thus in their junior or senior year by the time I contacted them.[12] I emailed invitations to participate to 200 them, and 25 of them responded and arranged a first interview during the spring 2015 semester. In the following spring 2016 semester 19 of them returned for a second interview. With the assistance of the new writing program director, I created a random sample of 200 students enrolled in the new first-year writing course during the 2015–2016 academic year and sent them a similar invitation. Responding to this request, 31 students participated in an interview in the first days of the semester during which they enrolled in the first-year writing course (16 in fall 2015 and 15 in spring 2016), 22 returned for a follow-up interview during the final days of their first-year writing course semester, and 19 students returned for an interview during their sophomore year,[13] 13 for an interview during their junior year, 9 during their senior year, and 5 in the year following their graduation.[14] Nearly all interviews were conducted in person, digitally recorded, and transcribed.[15] However, as some students transferred, graduated, or studied abroad, some interviews were conducted by phone or video conferencing, and the final five interviews of graduates of the new writing course conducted in their post-graduation year were all conducted using video conferencing due to the then new COVID-19 pandemic. Thus, most interviews were conducted in person, in my campus office, which is across campus from the new writing program's offices. Students knew me, or grew to know me, as a white, cisgender woman researcher considerably older than them and interested in their experiences with and perceptions and feelings about writing. They recognized and sometimes commented on the fact that my office was in the English Department but that I used research methods they were familiar with from other disciplines. Each interview lasted around 45 minutes but ranged from 30 to 60 minutes depending upon the time the participant had available and their interest in talking at greater depth.

In presenting my analysis of the transcripts of these interviews throughout this text, I identify participants by a unique number, 1–58. When quoting a transcript, I indicate which student I am quoting by this number as well as indicate in what year of school the student is (first-year, sophomore, junior, senior, or post-graduation) and from which interview with them, 1–6 or 1–2, the quotation is drawn. I regret the impersonality of using numbers to refer to these very human, very lively and diverse participants. When I began interviews in some haste, I did not ask participants to select a pseudonym, and inventing pseudonyms for them seemed unwieldy and inappropriate. I used the numbers you see here in my record keeping to anonymize my data in keeping with IRB protocol and promises I made to participants in the consent process. The size of my participant pool proved a challenge to me not only during the intense years of arranging and conducting interviews but also in finding ways to share my findings that preserve the intimacy of their qualitative character while also discussing larger trends within groups big enough to support such claims. Please know that the numbers consistently refer to the same participants, and please excuse their impersonality.

Analysis and Coding of Interview Transcripts

Analysis of the interview transcripts was a recursive process and one for which I followed the guidance of writers on qualitative research methods in the arts and humanities (Saldana, 2015) and on grounded theory (Charmaz, 2006). In previous research I have used similar methods for coding interview transcripts (Wilder, 2012), but not at this scale in terms of number of interviews and number of participants. This project undoubtedly suffers by being the work of one researcher—as someone who has collaborated on research in past projects I know very well the benefits of collaboration, especially in the fuzzy, interpretive work of coding—but I do hope it may benefit in a consistent, single (though not always focused) mind making uncountable judgments from interviewing procedures to coding and interpretation. Initial coding followed closely the topics of the interview questions I imposed on our interactions, and thus could be described as deductive and largely aimed at organizing the data for purposes of comparisons across interviews that were loosely structured, and during which related topics could be circled back to many times. Subsequent coding is better described as inductive, with the recursive readings of sections of the transcripts on similar topics next to one another telling me what subtopics or sentiments I ought to keep track of through coding. In other words, in the second round of coding I let participants' responses guide the coding; I provided coding labels to facilitate clustering together and counting similar responses when participants would speak of similar experiences but often use different terms to do so. As much as this round of coding enabled me to see similarities and trends in responses, it also enabled me to see and tabulate all the different responses generated to the same question over time or by different participants.

For all this coding work I used NVivo software. NVivo proved invaluable in helping me keep track of responses from a large number of participants. While my analysis was primarily qualitative, with NVivo assisting me in tracking themes that emerged in interviews and allowing me to locate relevant responses quickly, NVivo also facilitated some quantitative analyses, making it possible to tabulate different types of responses and make quantitative comparisons of different groups of students or the same group of students over time. However, one important limitation of the quantitative data presented here is that my interviews did not always proceed as planned; sometimes I was unable to ask all my prepared questions during every interview because I ran out of time or because I departed from the planned order of questions to follow my sense of a participant's train of thought and then, due to human error, I forgot to return to all questions. Anytime I did not ask a question meant a topic I coded for may not have come up not because the participant didn't have anything to say on it but because I didn't bring it up.

The New First-Year Writing Course

A first-year writing course launched in 2013 had the benefit of decades of composition theory and research to draw upon in its design. But I don't think this made the task of design any less daunting. This body of knowledge provided compelling evidence for some pedagogical practices, such as peer and instructor interventions in students' writing processes, but left open to debate which from an array of overall objectives the course can and should pursue: Civic engagement? Development of writerly voice and agency? Rhetorical and genre awareness? Digital and multimodal literacies? And no new writing program administrator could claim ignorance of the critiques of labor practices in composition. On both pedagogical and labor fronts this new program faced daunting constraints. As a state institution receiving most of its budget from tuition rather than state funding, struggling to remain affordable to low-income families and individuals while buffeted by political will, the institution had obvious financial limitations. This presented immediate obstacles to easily implementing fair and ethical labor practices that are generally understood to be advantageous not only to faculty but to student learning. Adding to the already imposing pedagogical challenges of shaping a 21st-century introductory writing curriculum was the campus's immediate assignment of several general education requirements beyond but related to writing to the course, such as oral discourse and information literacy, each with a list of learning outcomes and assessment schedules in use across the statewide university system. And familiar though faulty stakeholder expectations for the course—that it eradicate student errors in writing or decrease the need to teach writing across the curriculum—arose with new gusto on a campus that had removed its first-year writing requirement so long ago that stakeholders could forget, or never knew, that such unrealistic expectations were reasons why.

Nonetheless, a director was hired and work begun to hire 16 full-time instructors. Some advantageous pedagogical and labor conditions were secured early: the class size was capped at 19 students and, while not tenure-track, instructors were full-time, teaching three sections of the course each semester, on three-year renewable contracts, working conditions modeled after the by-then well-established writing program at the University of Denver.[16] Though constrained by the expectations of the committee's vision, which proposed the course and numerous general education learning outcomes, the director had a fair deal of autonomy in designing the course's common curriculum.[17]

The director opted to draw most prominently from pedagogical theory and research on fostering student voice and inquiry, a line of thinking with expressivist roots in Macrorie's (1988) I-search papers but also framed by social and cognitive understandings of writing as epistemic, conceptions of writing sometimes painted as conflicting (Berlin, 1988; Faigley, 1986) but which the director's own scholarly commitments and contributions sought to braid together. Care was also taken to make the common elements of the course adaptable so that individual instructors could draw on their own expertise and approaches to pedagogy in shaping plans for their own sections of the course. The writing faculty had a great deal of autonomy in adapting common course objectives to pedagogical practices and exploration of topics and themes related to their expertise or interests. While individual sections of the course could explore different topics and themes and practice different genres, all were to share common curricular goals, methods such as conferencing and instructor and peer feedback on drafts, and three core assignments that instructors adapted to work with their chosen topics and themes. These writing assignments, adapted from the composition program at the University of Wisconsin, Madison (Weese et al., 1999), emphasized inquiry by supporting students' personal exploration of an academic issue, analysis, and original contribution to a scholarly conversation. For Essay 1, students wrote to explore their own experiences and to identify a relevant issue for close analysis in Essay 2; the focus of Essay 3 was to develop an argument that contributes to a scholarly conversation about the subject of Essay 2. Instructors were expected to treat Essay 3 as an analytic essay that engages with sources, a type of essay frequently assigned as a capstone to a first-year writing course as it brings together research and analytic skills practiced throughout the term. In practice, some sections focused on a common theme all semester while others explored a variety of topics or asked students to select their own individualized topics for inquiry across the semester.

The instructors of the course all had previous experience teaching first-year writing courses, but their experience and areas of expertise varied. Some had MFAs in creative writing and were active writers; others had MAs or PhDs. The vast majority of these were trained in English departments, with expertise in various areas of literary and cultural studies. Only one instructor specialized in rhetoric and composition. A few held PhDs in other areas such as history or anthropology. Coming together in this new writing program, all understood they were expected to participate in ongoing professional development activities focused initially on fostering a shared understanding of the course's learning objectives and the nature and purposes of the assignment sequence.

What I want to emphasize is the many ways the above description of the course and its teaching staff are typical of the way required first-year writing courses are taught in postsecondary institutions across the US, especially at public research universities similar to my research site. As a qualitative researcher, my first impulse tends to be to emphasize the particular and context-specific of situations I describe, and there are many important variables pertaining to the institution and experiences I describe in this book that are particular and not generalizable to other settings. But those interested in considering the ways in which my findings on the impact of first-year composition may be applicable elsewhere should look first to this description of this particular first-year course for the ways it may match similar courses elsewhere. Instructor expertise rooted in graduate training in creative writing or literary studies is very common for instructors of this course (see Adsit & Wilder, 2020; J. H. Anderson & Farris, 2007; Bergmann & Baker, 2006; Smit, 2004; Wolfe et al., 2014). Some degree of instructor autonomy in shaping such a course around shared objectives and assignment types is also quite common (see Carroll, 2002, pp. 64–65). And while I know the director of the course often described the course in opposition to "traditional composition," by which I understood him to mean a current traditionalist focus on grammatical correctness and formal features of writing, I think it is fair to say that many other first-year writing programs have moved away from this focus also, especially at research universities where rhetoric and composition has a scholarly presence, even as individual instructors and stakeholders also continue to uphold standards and practices labeled as current traditional.[18] Recent critiques of "themed" sections of first-year composition would suggest that this practice is widespread (Adler-Kassner, 2012). And Fulkerson (2005) has pointed out the ubiquity of treating writing as a process in the ways this program does with emphasis on peer review, draft feedback, and revision.

Overview of Chapters

Before attempting to describe the impact of this new-yet-familiar first-year writing course on students' experiences at this campus, *Tracing the Impact of First-Year Writing* begins by comparing students' experiences of the overarching culture of writing across the curriculum on this campus with those documented in longitudinal studies of writing conducted on campuses of notably greater privilege and resources. Chapter 1 aims to broaden and diversify the types of institutions and students documented in longitudinal studies of college writers. In doing so, it challenges generalizations that might otherwise be made from this literature about the prevalence of writing in students' college experiences. While this chapter continues to document the critical role writing plays in students' learning across time and across disciplines, it also shines light on concrete inequities across institutions. It reveals how access to writing as a means of learning is one way privilege is delimited rather than shared in higher education.

Chapters 2–4 offer my analysis of the impact the new first-year writing course had on students' experience of writing at my research site. These findings are summed up in the subtitle for this book, *Identity, Process, and Transfer*. While the course may not have all the lasting impacts its stakeholders would hope for, it does seem to have significantly affected the way many of its graduates see themselves as writers and engage in writing as a social and epistemic process while helping them carry these views and practices into future contexts appropriately. These impacts are far from trivial and stand to benefit students in years long after college. Chapter 2 specifically compares the experiences of and views on writing of students in their junior year who had previously taken the first-year writing course and students who had not, documenting statistically significant differences related to their reported identity as writers, their writing processes, and their moments of writing knowledge transfer. Chapter 3 traces the impact of the course over students' 4 years of college and beyond. And Chapter 4 presents more fully fleshed-out case studies of three students who in part are representative of others in their cohort and in part illustrate how each student's experience of the course and of writing across their years of college is unique and hard to reduce to generalizations. Specifically, these case studies seek to exemplify how the first-year course was powerfully enabling for some students but also how it left lasting negative associations with others, including impressions that it policed academic honesty in unfair ways and that it was overly intrusive into students' personal lives.

Lastly, Chapter 5 shares my findings from my years of interviews with participants who did not come to identify as writers and whose confidence in their ability as writers remained low across their years of college. For these students, the first-year writing course appeared to have little lasting impact—and even produced few lasting memories. My goal in listening intently to students whose affective response to writing is largely negative was not only to diversify the findings of longitudinal studies in which such views tend to be underrepresented but also to propose recommendations for first-year writing so that it may better reach other reluctant writers like them.

It is my hope that that the research presented in these pages contributes to broadening the representation of institutions and students in longitudinal research on college writers. I hope many readers recognize the experiences of the students recorded here as relevant and useful to the work they do as writing instructors, administrators, and researchers. I hope student writers find their and their classmates' hard-earned successes and their many frustrations accurately depicted and validated. The three key terms the title of this work highlights—identity, process, and transfer—emerged from what participants shared with me about how a first-year writing course affected them. These terms, which were among many I used to code interview transcripts, ended up denoting noteworthy differences between the ways students who had taken a first-year writing course and those who had not talked about their experiences with writing and the effects writing had on them. At my research site, a first-year writing course held the real potential to encourage students to embrace writing as part of their identity, to alter their writing processes in social and epistemic ways, and to transfer useful writing knowledge into new and appropriate contexts.

1

"They Write a Lot More Than I Am Writing at My School"

The Role Writing Plays Across Curricula and
Lives at an Institution Lacking Privilege

STUDENT 35: I see my friends from [other] schools . . . I find they write like a lot more than I'm writing at my school.

LAURA: So in your major it is just exams, I guess?

STUDENT 35: Yeah. . . . I did bring one paper. This is from my psych class, but this was like an extra credit thing. So this was literally the only writing piece I've done this whole semester. Yeah.

LAURA: How about even an essay exam? No?

STUDENT 35: No, no. Yeah, I wish I had more stuff like that.

LAURA: Yeah.

STUDENT 35: Yeah. When you emailed me, I was excited to talk to you about how like—I'm sad that I'm not writing as much anymore. (Student 35.soph.2)[1]

Many of the students I spoke with for this study reminded me of those in Sternglass's (1997) groundbreaking longitudinal study, *Time to Know Them.* Like the City College students Sternglass spoke with in the 1990s, many of the students who spoke with me were the first in their family to attend college. They juggled multiple jobs and familial obligations and still struggled to afford tuition, fees, books, computers, cell phones, housing, and food.

https://doi.org/10.7330/9781646426584.c001

Indeed, a number of the students I spoke with came from the same New York City neighborhoods as Sternglass's participants, while others came from rural and suburban working-class and middle-class families.

In this chapter, I would like to ask of the interview transcripts collected for my study what they can teach us today about students with backgrounds similar to those Sternglass studied 30 years ago: What are their experiences with writing in college now? How do their lives inside and outside college shape that experience? What are their perceptions of the expectations, traditions, resources, and support offered to them at a publicly funded, regional state school? And how do these experiences compare to those reported in longitudinal studies of student writing conducted at institutions of considerably greater privilege such as Ivy League institutions? To explore these questions, I draw from my interviews conducted 2015–2020 with all 58 participants, those who took the new first-year course and those who did not. The responses across both of these groups discussed in this chapter did not vary in any significant or noteworthy ways, so their description of the overall writing culture at this institution is presented here collectively. In Chapter 2 I present the ways in which the responses of these two groups did vary significantly on other issues, and in Chapters 3 and 4 I focus on the experiences of only those who took the first-year course, describing the ways they spoke of the impact of this course in the moment and in reflection years later.

Experience of Writing in High School

The inequities my participants experienced of course did not begin when they set foot on campus. Their earlier education and preparation for college likely differed a good deal from the students from affluent neighborhoods who make up the typical enrollees of institutions like the University of Michigan and Harvard. Thus, I began interviews by asking students to look back on their earlier experiences with writing and compare them to the experiences with writing they are having now. The participants in this study were almost evenly split in their assessment of the quality of their prior preparation for writing in college while in high school, with roughly half describing rather rich experiences (often in AP or dual enrollment courses taken during their senior year) with guided practice treating writing as a process and the other half describing predominately perfunctory experiences, with writing instruction geared toward passing a timed exam (such as the Regents, SAT, or AP exams) and focused on practicing forms such as the five-paragraph theme through the use of worksheets with no revision and few or no multi-page papers. Those who saw their high school writing instruction as inadequate preparation supported their claims with memories that resonate with the findings of Applebee and Langer's (2011) national study of secondary writing, which showed that students were very rarely asked to write more than one to two pages in their assignments (p. 15) and very rarely experienced explicit writing strategy instruction (p. 21). Applebee and Langer (2011) point to the increasingly extensive experience of standardized testing in high school as having these impacts and more: "Given the constraints imposed by high-stakes tests, writing as a way to study, learn, and go beyond—as a way to construct knowledge or generate new networks of understandings . . . is rare" (p. 26).

Here is a senior reflecting on his experience writing in high school (the Regents exams acts as a gatekeeper to successful graduation in New York): "In high school I felt like everything was centered around training for the Regents" (Student 26.sr.1). Student 58 concurred that writing instruction centered on timed essay exams:

> I remember writing a little bit in high school, especially, like, my freshman year, early on. Closer to my senior year we didn't do much writing because, after the Regents, they didn't really have anything to prepare you for. Yeah, so I feel like it was more, like, prepare for the Regents, and then you're good to go. Like, we don't have to do this ever again. (Student 58.post.6)

The students I spoke with also pointed to excessive focus on preparation for the SAT and ACT exams as steering attention away from preparation for other more rhetorically demanding occasions for writing:

> I don't think I was prepared as well as I should have been. Most of my preparation in high school was preparing to write a five-paragraph essay for the SATs or ACTs. It was just learning how to crank them out for that, and not necessarily for preparing me for college. . . . When timed you're not really thinking about how to make something concise, you're just more concerned about getting all the information you have onto the paper, whether it sounds good or not. (Student 6.jr.1)

The emphasis on high-stakes test preparation came for these students at the expense of exploring other purposes for writing beyond graduation.

Some students described feeling unprepared for college writing because they simply were not required to write very often or very much in high school: "Usually, the most we would have to write is like, two, three pages, four at the most. I just wrote an eight-page paper. I still can't believe that I did that" (Student 43.first-year.2). Student 9 similarly felt a stark contrast in the amount she was asked to write in college:

> I wasn't so hot at, because I think I didn't really write that long of papers in high school. . . . I think more like probably the max was three pages, stuff like that, and never too crazy. Meanwhile, when I have every three weeks a 15- to 20-page lab report, like I had never experienced anything like that. (Student 9.sr.2)

Some described what little writing they recall doing as excessively constrained with prescriptions or forms such as the five-paragraph form. For instance, Student 57 looked back on worksheets and formulas used in high school as inadequate for the writing she is doing now:

> In high school we were just given worksheets, like you have to write about this. This is—they kind of told us, you know, five paragraphs, introduction, conclusion, three in the middle. Whereas now they let you do as many paragraphs as you want as long as it just makes your point. So getting out of that structured, you know, what was it, TTQA, is that what the? We used to do this thing and it was like, yeah, *turn that question around*. And that's how you'd make a thesis. . . . Whereas now, I did that on my first—my second essay and she was like, "Well you need to add more information." (Student 57.soph.3)

Student 52 described a focus on superficial knowledge-telling (Bereiter & Scardamalia, 1987) in his high school papers that differed notably from what his professors expected in college:

> In high school, it's basically like if you go, "Here, just list facts about a topic." But in college, more like what are the facts? Where do the things that are making this happen, and you're like what are the deeper meanings behind it, like the concepts of the actual things that—and topics you're writing about? (Student 52.first-year.2)

Some students described the focus of their high school writing instruction centered on literary analysis, sometimes commenting that they felt unprepared for the genres they are asked to write now as a result. They described a repeated focus on MLA citation style that left them surprised and confused to discover in college that some instructors required different citation formats such as Chicago or APA. However, even students who went on to take literature courses in college often told me about having to learn to switch from mere plot summary to critical analysis in this genre they mistakenly thought was familiar to them.

In contrast, and highlighting the diversity of prior educational experiences of students at this institution, others reflected on rich experiences with writing in high school, sometimes claiming they wrote more and longer papers in high school than they had so far in college or that the research process they engaged in during high school was more intensive. Exceptional individual teachers or supportive parents were credited with providing them meaningful occasions for writing and useful feedback on their texts and processes that they carried with them. For instance, Student 30 described her senior year English teacher working with intention to prepare her for college-level writing with lots of writing:

> For senior year we had to do a bunch of research papers. And I feel like we did it intentionally because like my teacher told me that in college you do a lot of research papers, so we had to do like eight of them throughout the whole year, and they were hard in the beginning but then by the end of the last one, you knew at least what you were supposed to be doing. (Student 30.first-year.1)

And Student 57 described learning to navigate greater autonomy in her writing through the experience of being given it:

> Even in the most basic classes, you had to write so many papers. And then when I got to my senior year, my teacher told me I'm going to treat you like college students, so here's a book, write whatever you want about it. And we could just do whatever we wanted, and it was hard at first, but I'm kind of used to it now. (Student 57.first-year.1)

Suffice it to say that their prior educational experience with writing varied greatly according to their own recollections of it from the vantage point of college. Some felt more confidently prepared, even if in later years they told me about experiences that shook this confidence, and an equal number felt ill-prepared and highly critical of the dearth of writing instruction they experienced in high school.

Amount of Writing and Range of Genres Encountered in College

Several of the studies of writing at institutions of relative privilege sought to collect all or representative portfolio samples of writing their student participants produced each year of college, allowing them to corroborate their participants' accounts of the amount of writing they produced in college. For this study, to reduce impediments that might deter continued participation, I collected only one writing sample during each interview, two during the first year and one annually thereafter. I asked them to bring in a piece of writing they felt represented the kinds of writing they were recently producing, which they frequently interpreted as bringing in a piece they were proud of but sometimes meant bringing in the only piece they recalled producing in the past year. I also asked them about other writing they did recently in addition to the writing sample. In this way, this study can speak to the amount and types of writing participants produced in college, though with greater reliance on participants' memories.

Table 1.1 presents a tabulation of the genres of the writing samples participants submitted during each interview, and Table 1.2 presents a tabulation of the genres students named in response to my question about the kinds of writing they had been producing recently. For both I use the terms the participants used when labeling a genre or type of assignment or text. As a result, the tables may need to be read as separating some genres that a reader might not see as distinct, such as an "argument essay" and an "opinion essay." Often a generic "paper" or "research paper" served as participants' label of choice, a choice that masked significant disciplinary differences among these texts (for example, an anthropology paper in this corpus followed different genre conventions and served different rhetorical purposes than a philosophy paper in the corpus), emphasized the school-based nature of the work in students' eyes, or signaled instructors' assignment of a "mutt genre" existing in school and not within an authentic activity system (Melzer, 2014, p. 43; Wardle, 2009, p. 774). To add to the amorphous unhelpfulness of the term, "paper" is the term used to describe professional academic genres in some fields. Student 39, for instance, deliberately used the term as the label for published scientific papers in biology in our final interview the year after he graduated (see my case study of Student 39 in Chapter 4). As for recent writing, I understood students to emphasize the writing they did for school, though I did press them to ask if they did writing outside of school for personal reasons, work, or extracurricular activities. This emphasis on school assignments in their answers can be seen most vividly in the tabulations for text types like email and social media postings. I suspect participants wrote in these forums more frequently than Table 1.2 suggests. What Table 1.2 instead likely records is the times participants used these tools when required for work, internships, or a class assignment. The deliberate requirement outside of personal social contexts seemed to strike participants as worth mentioning to me when describing

TABLE 1.1. Genres (identified by participants) of writing samples submitted each year by all participants.

Students were asked to submit a writing sample that in their eyes represented the kind of writing they had been doing recently.

Genre of writing sample named by participants	First interview first year (N = 31)	Second interview first year (N = 22)	Sophomore year (N = 19)	Junior year (N = 27)	Senior year (N = 32)	Post-graduation (N = 12)	Total over all years
Paper	7	11	6	10	10	1	45
Research paper	6	4	2	2	3	2	19
Personal statement	10	0	0	0	2	1	13
Literary analysis	2	3	1	1	0	0	7
Compare and contrast	0	0	2	3	2	0	7
Memo	0	0	0	0	3	2	5
Reflective journal	0	0	1	2	0	2	5
Exam	0	1	3	0	0	0	4
Argument essay	2	2	0	0	0	0	4
Literature review	0	0	0	0	3	0	3
Opinion paper	3	0	0	0	0	0	3
Ethnography	0	0	1	0	1	0	2
Short story	0	0	1	1	0	0	2
Summary	0	0	1	1	0	0	2
Book review	0	0	0	2	0	0	2
Letter	0	0	0	0	2	0	2
Critical lens essay	1	0	0	0	0	0	1
Parody	1	0	0	0	0	0	1
Editorial	0	1	0	0	0	0	1
Free write	0	0	1	0	0	0	1
50-page business thesis	0	0	0	1	0	0	1
Court observation	0	0	0	1	0	0	1
Hypothesis	0	0	0	1	0	0	1

continued on next page

TABLE 1.1. *(continued)*

Genre of writing sample named by participants	First interview first year (N = 31)	Second interview first year (N = 22)	Sophomore year (N = 19)	Junior year (N = 27)	Senior year (N = 32)	Post-graduation (N = 12)	Total over all years
Website	0	0	0	1	0	0	1
Lab report	0	0	0	0	1	0	1
Case report	0	0	0	0	1	0	1
Features piece	0	0	0	0	1	0	1
Issue statement	0	0	0	0	1	0	1
Moral code	0	0	0	0	1	0	1
Policy brief	0	0	0	0	1	0	1
Report	0	0	0	0	1	0	1
Presentation speech	0	0	0	0	0	1	1
Grant implementation paper	0	0	0	0	0	1	1
Total different genres named	9	7	10	12	15	7	

their recent writing, whereas their use of these media for purely personal reasons was discounted as "not writing."

These tables show us that collectively participants wrote in a wide range of genres over their 4 years of college, 61 distinct genres named by participants in describing their writing samples and their recent writing. Additionally, each year a noteworthy number, some years around 50%, of students reported using visual elements in their recent writing, elements such as images, charts, or graphs, and a casual glance at the list of genres in Tables 1.1 and 1.2 would reveal the appropriateness of such visual elements, many of which depict quantitative data, for many of these genres. This is an amazing diversity of genres, though as can be seen in the low frequency of mention of most genres, no one student wrote in all these genres. The diversity of genres students may encounter across the curriculum is a finding that instructors of first-year writing courses may find surprising and complicating to the goals for this course related to preparing students for their future writing tasks. In students' first year alone, they named 16 distinct genres to describe their

TABLE 1.2. Genres identified by participants in response to the question "What have you been writing recently?"

Genres named by participants in describing recent writing	First interview first year (N = 31)	Second interview first year (N = 22)	Sophomore year (N = 19)	Junior year (N = 27)	Senior year (N = 32)	Post-graduation (N = 12)	Total over all years
Academic paper or essay	6	19	15	8	12	3	63
Research paper	3	1	6	10	7	3	30
Lab report	0	1	3	6	4	1	15
Journal reflection	0	0	2	3	3	2	10
Close reading literary criticism	0	2	2	4	2	0	10
Blog post	0	0	0	3	4	1	8
Email	0	0	1	2	3	0	6
Creative writing: poetry, memoir, short story	1	0	1	0	1	1	4
Personal statement	0	0	1	0	2	1	4
Summary	0	0	1	1	2	0	4
Writing for self	0	0	3	0	1	0	4
Presentation	0	0	0	2	1	1	4
Scientific writing	0	0	0	1	3	0	4
Memo	0	0	0	0	3	1	4
Opinion paper	0	1	1	0	1	0	3
50-page thesis for business	0	0	0	0	3	0	3
Comedy material	0	0	0	0	2	1	3
Scientific article for publication	0	0	0	0	0	2	2
Discussion post	0	0	0	1	1	0	2
Movie review	0	1	0	1	1	0	2
Website	0	0	0	0	2	0	2
Policy paper	0	0	0	0	2	0	2
Debate paper	0	0	1	0	0	0	1
Observation	0	0	0	1	0	0	1
Personal experience essay	0	0	0	1	0	0	1

continued on next page

TABLE 1.2. (*continued*)

Genres named by participants in describing recent writing	First interview first year (N = 31)	Second interview first year (N = 22)	Sophomore year (N = 19)	Junior year (N = 27)	Senior year (N = 32)	Post-graduation (N = 12)	Total over all years
Treatment plan	0	0	0	1	0	0	1
Advocacy letter	0	0	0	1	0	0	1
Zine	0	0	0	1	0	0	1
Case study	0	0	0	1	0	0	1
Letter	0	0	0	0	1	0	1
Movie analysis	0	0	0	0	1	0	1
Resume	0	0	0	0	1	0	1
Case report	0	0	0	0	1	0	1
Cover letter	0	0	0	0	1	0	1
Ethnography	0	1	0	0	1	0	1
Incident report	0	0	0	0	1	0	1
Lesson plan	0	0	0	0	1	0	1
Press release	0	0	0	0	1	0	1
Social media post	0	0	0	0	1	0	1
White paper/ executive summary	0	0	0	0	1	0	1
Abstract	0	0	0	0	0	1	1
Template form	0	0	0	0	0	1	1
Argumentative paper	1	0	0	0	0	0	1
Case brief	1	0	0	0	0	0	1
Field project	0	0	0	0	0	1	1
Plan	0	0	0	0	0	1	1
Report	0	0	0	0	0	1	1
Not much or not writing now	1	0	2	4	2	1	10[*]
TOTAL	12	26	8	48	71	22	
Total different genres named	5	7	12	18	32	16	

[*] Of these 10 claims to not be doing much writing, four were made by students pursuing majors in the social sciences and four by students pursuing majors in STEM fields.

"They Write a Lot More Than I Am Writing at My School" : 37

TABLE 1.3. Statistics describing the page counts of writing samples submitted by participants each year.

Year	Mean length	Range of page lengths	Median page length	Mode paper length
First interview, first year (N = 32)	3.27	1–8.5	3.00	1.50
Second interview, first year (N = 23)	5.09	2–8.0	5.00	5.00
Sophomore (N = 18)	3.50	1–7.0	2.75	2.00
Junior (N = 28)	8.74	2–114.0	5.00	3.00
Senior (N = 36)	5.43	1–14.5	4.00	2.00
Post-graduation[*] (N = 11)	5.27	1–20.0	3.00	2.00

[*] Often these were papers from participants' final year of college. Occasionally they were from graduate classes.

samples and recent writing.[2] This range of genres compares favorably with those reported for the Stanford Study of Writing, for which 18 distinct genres were reported as encountered in students' first year of college (Addison & McGee, 2010, p. 155).

The writing samples provide an opportunity to make broad comparisons over time in two easily quantifiable descriptors, their length and number of sources cited. Table 1.3 shows the average page count of the writing samples submitted during each interview for all participants in this study. However, the average lengths may not provide a full picture of the typical samples submitted because, as shown in the column providing the range of paper lengths submitted each year, the lengths of the writing samples varied widely, most notably in the junior-year samples when a student submitted her 114-page capstone paper for her business management course but also in every other year where the range of paper lengths could vary from one page to 20. Therefore, median (the paper length at the midpoint of the range) and mode (the most common or frequent paper length) may be more revealing in producing an image of the typical writing samples students submitted. These measures of central tendency suggest that writing assignments of two to five pages were typical throughout students' 4 years of college. This is noteworthy because while these samples do not represent all of the writing participants produced, they tended to represent what participants were proud of or had invested effort in. The typical length of papers crept up just a bit from the first

38 : "THEY WRITE A LOT MORE THAN I AM WRITING AT MY SCHOOL"

TABLE 1.4. Statistics describing the number of sources cited in writing samples submitted by participants each year.

Year	Mean number of sources	Range number of sources	Median number of sources	Mode number of sources
First interview, first year (N = 32)	2.78	0–12	1.0	0
Second interview, first year (N = 23)	3.48	0–17	3.0	0
Sophomore (N = 18)	2.72	0–10	1.5	1
Junior (N = 28)	3.93	0–31	2.0	1
Senior (N = 36)	3.03	0–11	3.0	0
Post-graduation (N = 11)	3.45	0–17	3.0	0

writing samples submitted, which often were papers written while participants were still in high school.

While source citation would not be appropriate for all of the genres submitted as writing samples, the range, mean, median, and mode of number of sources, as shown in Table 1.4, gives us some sense of students' collective engagement in research writing over their years of college. Here, too, these figures point to little change in source use over students' 4 years of college, with many sharing samples that use no or very few sources each year, but with a minority submitting samples that cite considerable numbers of sources.

Tables 1.3 and 1.4 can be read as the length of participants' papers and number of sources cited in them, on average and with notable exceptions, not varying greatly from their final year of high school to their final year of college. Of course, as demonstrated in the Council of Writing Program Administrators (CWPA) collaboration with the National Survey of Student Engagement (NSSE), the sheer amount of writing alone is not determinate of higher-order, integrative, and reflective learning; the nature of the writing tasks matters a great deal more than simple number of pages written in cultivating such deep learning experiences for students (P. Anderson et al., 2015). For example, the personal statements that many participants submitted during their interview as they began college and that some students submitted in later interviews as they prepared to apply for graduate programs are necessarily short texts, tightly confined to one to two pages, with no source citations. However, though brief, these texts were often composed with extensive drafting, feedback, and revision processes that participants reported were personally meaningful and high-stakes opportunities to develop their rhetorical understandings of audience and purpose. For determining students' perceptions of the nature of their writing tasks assigned to them, my interview questions about their writing samples, their recent writing, and their experiences of writing instruction are far more revealing than simple page and citation counts. Though of course limited to students' perceptions and not of instructors' intentions, I specifically probed students to recollect the kinds of "interactive writing processes" associated with deep learning, such as inventive brainstorming, peer review, and instructor feedback (P. Anderson et al., 2015, p. 219).

Quality of Students' Experiences With Writing in College

Setting aside for the moment roughly half of the participants' experience of the new first-year writing course, which will be discussed in Chapters 3 and 4, experiences of writing across the curriculum and across their years of college varied greatly for my participants and seemed to hinge a good deal on the major they selected, with some majors providing in their eyes very richly interactive and meaningful experiences with writing regularly over the course of several years of study and others providing infrequent, disconnected, and impersonal writing experiences.

RICH, INTERACTIVE EXPERIENCES OF WRITING

Multiple participants majoring in political science, criminal justice, public health, journalism, sociology, philosophy, history, English, and biology described repeated, interactive experiences with writing for which they received constructive feedback from instructors and peers, opportunities to apply that feedback in in-progress drafts, and sometimes collaborative experiences of generating ideas and structures for their writing. These students generally started writing regularly for their courses in these fields from their first year on campus with assignments increasing in length and complexity over time. This is to say that these students appear to have written a great deal and frequently in courses that used interactive teaching tools that support seeing writing as a process. Student 11, a journalism and political science double major, told me that the institutional designation of "writing intensive" courses was meaningless in his majors since

> they all end up being writing intensive. I feel even some classes that weren't 'writing intensive' I did a lot of writing in. Even if it's small stuff like, oh, just, you know, write your reaction to this in a page. But if you do that

twenty times that's twenty pages, and I believe that's the requirement for a writing intensive. (Student 11.sr.1)

For him and for others, writing assignments not only prompted writing a lot frequently but they were also often opportunities to interact with instructors and peers in developing ideas and learning genre conventions. Student 3 noted the difference this made for him in helping him learn to write in the field of criminal justice:

> Most professors just say, "Oh, here's the due date. Turn it in." But my criminal justice professor right now is requiring me to have a draft for each three parts of the paper, so I really appreciate her feedback and stuff and it really helps improve my writing skills. (Student 3.jr.1)

Student 21 described for me how writing was an interactive experience for her in multiple ways throughout her courses in public health. When we last spoke, she was enrolled in a course designed to support a capstone project which she described as breaking down the process of writing a "big paper" this way:

> What we do is we have one big paper which is our final grade, but throughout the entire semester we do steps. Like we have our literature review, which is three to five pages, we have our introduction, which is two pages, so they break each section down and describe to us what they expect, how you're supposed to write this part of the paper. Now we're starting the intervention part, which is a little more free-range for us to figure out how we would implement a program. (Student 21.sr.2)

While she saw this "big paper" and its component parts as a new genre to her, she had completed lots of writing assignments in her public health coursework leading up to this moment:

> I mean I'd say a good at least 80 percent of my public health classes require at least some form of writing, whether it be just a page or two or a big paper, but yeah. Almost all my public health classes have required some sort of paper or writing. (Student 21.sr.2)

Research she had done in previous classes exposed her to genres like literature reviews, which she claimed helped her understand how to write such a section in her current "big paper."[3] Previous public health classes also exposed her to considerable collaborative work on writing and research:

> I think the only classes I've done collaborative writing was in my public health classes. I did one in my promoting healthy people class last spring.

I think that was the last time I did one, but I did three or four collaborative pieces last year. (Student 21.sr.2)

She explained that public health likely requires so much collaboration because

if you continue on with public health you do a lot of collaborative work with people because it takes a lot more than one person to implement an intervention program or something to that extent. At some point you're going to have to work with people in order to figure out your problem at hand; it's not going to be only you. Especially if you're asking for grants or something for funding to some extent. (Student 21.sr.2)

The biology majors I interviewed began writing lab reports in their first year of college, but these early lab reports they described as being very short, sometimes exercises in completing worksheets. In later years I saw these majors producing long, complex lab reports that mimicked professional scientific genres (see my discussion of Student 45's senior-year writing sample in Chapter 5). So, while these majors experienced repeated practice in writing lab reports from their earliest semesters, they often discounted their early reports as "not writing," a tendency Driscoll (2011) noted of the science students in her study as well (p. 15). It also seems likely that my participants' biology professors and TAs varied in their teaching of lab reports as part of a process of discovery and meaning making in labs pursuing genuine new inquiry or as mere reporting of verification lab results that provide practice in lab procedures but whose outcomes are predetermined (see Baird & Dilger, 2018). As a result, I sometimes heard biology students claim they did no writing even as they told me of the many lab reports they produced and sometimes told me of all the insights into writing they were experiencing in their labs, especially among those who worked in labs outside of class as part of a professor's research team pursuing authentic, publishable research (see my case study of Student 39 in Chapter 4).

INTERACTIVE WRITING OPPORTUNITIES
DELAYED UNTIL LATE IN COLLEGE

However, some of the majors that provided rich experiences with writing withheld these experiences until the final year of college in upper-level courses. Many students pointed to the lack of interactive experiences with writing in their first 2 years of college because most of their introductory-level classes were taught as large lectures. As a result, students who were required to take the new first-year writing course often pointed to it as the only course that asked them to write in their early years of college. Those who matriculated before the new first-year writing course was required claimed they did no or very little writing in the large lecture courses they took in their early years of college. These students were required to take a lower-level writing-intensive course, but some delayed taking this course and others told me they fulfilled this requirement by enrolling in writing-intensive sections of a large lecture course and completing only a few additional writing assignments. For example, a sociology and economics major described an introductory African American history course she took as a writing-intensive course, which meant she wrote two "book reports" that others who enrolled in the course without the writing-intensive designation did not have to complete. The course was a large lecture course, with about 150 students, but in comparison to her other courses Student 20 considered this course size "medium sized—uh, medium for [my university], at least" (Student 20.jr.1). The writing of these two book reports seems not to have involved interactive instruction. When I asked if the students enrolled in the writing-intensive version of the course ever met separately to discuss writing, she told me:

> No. Because with the writing-intensive section he would just say, "If you're people in the writing-intensive section, just have your citation"—first you have to give him a MLA format of the two books you have to do, so that he knows what books we're reading, or we're going to read, and then, . . . he said by like Thanksgiving you had to actually give him the book reports. And then after that we just had the final [exam]. (Student 20.jr.1)

She did receive some clarification that these reports should differ from what she understood as a "book report" in high school; however, "I remember I love how he called them a 'book report' even though it was really analyzing the book" (Student 20.jr.1). Student 27, a communications major, explained to me after she graduated that a challenge in learning the new genres and citation styles expected of her in college was the long pause in writing she experienced in the transition from high school to college: "Your first two semesters are usually your gen ed courses, and they're huge classes, so paper writing is not as much as until you get to your 300 level classes" (Student 27.post.2).

LIMITED, IMPOVERISHED OPPORTUNITIES FOR WRITING

The descriptions of encounters with writing by participants pursuing other majors could dramatically vary from those richly interactive learning experiences described above in ways that never did seem to change over students' years of study. In every round of interviews with the exception of the interview conducted with participants as they completed the first-year writing course some participants responded to my question asking about what they had been writing recently with the claim that they had not done any writing of note in the year since we last spoke. The majority (80%) of these responses came from students majoring in social sciences or STEM fields. While the amount of writing alone may not be indicative of the quality of deep learning students experience through writing, surely if students cannot recall being asked to do any writing in recent months then they are shut out from even the possibility of learning through interactive writing experiences.

Two participants were quite vocal about their sense that students pursuing their majors at other institutions of greater privilege were asked to write a great deal more. They claimed they knew this because they compared their experiences with acquaintances at these other institutions. In our interview during her sophomore year, Student 35, a psychology major, was very invested in speaking with me about these observations of writing inequity, bringing it up several times. She compared her current writing experience with her memories from high school, when she recalls writing a great deal more, and with what her friends studying psychology at other colleges told her, as you can see in the transcript excerpt that prefaces this chapter. She explained that she longed to write about what she is learning because it helps her to understand the material or, as she put it,

> if you just put stuff in Excel, you're just going to get the answer, you know? But if you write *why* you put this in Excel, *why* you did this, you'll understand stuff a lot more by the time it comes to the test. (Student 35.soph.2)

Student 14, an accounting major, similarly compared her writing experiences with those at institutions of greater privilege when I spoke with her during her junior year. Majoring in accounting but with past experiences writing creatively and more recent experiences writing comedic material collaboratively with friends for fun, she longed for feedback on her writing and support in exploring publishing her work. When I asked her what she would recommend to the university to better support writers like her, she turned to comparing her experience with her sister's at Tufts University, finding the support and expectations for writers varying notably between their two universities and longing for the kinds of resources and connections an institution of greater privilege could provide:

> I know that some schools, like I know my sister at Tufts, like obviously they're all geniuses, so there's a—they have a connection right in Boston

that can edit and tell them how their writing is. So maybe that kind of thing. (Student 14.jr.1)

Taken with the comparisons participants frequently made between the quality of high schools they and their classmates attended, these comparisons left me with the impression that a number of students sensed differences that impacted their educations between institutions with greater and lesser resources and prestige.

The 11 business students I interviewed presented a rather unified picture of a writing path that delayed intensive writing until their senior year. With little writing asked of business students in the first 3 years of college, this junior accounting and business major's declaration to me was not atypical during those years: "I have not written one paper this year" (Student 8.jr.1). Students 8 and 57 were the only business students who described writing assignments in business courses prior to their senior year. However, Student 57 shared her sinking feeling in her sophomore year that her business professors might not actually read her writing, a feeling she believed was supported by her submission of a paper in which she expressed what she thought were controversial views and which received no response. But in business students' final year of college, they all faced a management course that required a 50-page paper, a capstone assignment about which I heard a lot over the course of this study.

While students pursuing other majors experienced a similar delay in not being asked to write substantively until their senior year, their delayed experiences could still be rather dynamic and interactive. In contrast, the business students described this final push for writing as an onerous, anxiety-producing hurdle with few supports or interactive opportunities. I heard their curiosity and anxiety about the 50-page paper in their years leading up to it and their bitterness and cynicism about it when they could look back upon it. When I spoke with students currently in the course that required the 50-page paper or looking back later on the experience, they indicated to me that the course did not provide much interactive support for writing in this new and intimidating genre. While the class required a couple shorter papers prior to the 50-page assignment, students indicated they sensed that these were for the purposes of collecting writing samples that could be used to determine if they wrote the later 50-page paper. For these they often submitted papers they had previously written for other classes. They did not get feedback on these shorter papers, and class time was not used to explain how these papers could prepare them for the 50-page paper.

Students were not asked to submit rough drafts of the 50-page paper at any point, making peer or instructor feedback within the context of the class impossible. The resources students relied upon to navigate this enormous writing challenge with minimal instructor scaffolding were surreptitious, unsanctioned peer review; surreptitious, unsanctioned examination of prior students' successful completed papers; and sanctioned assignment templates or outlines. While I do not know for certain if the course's instructors viewed the outside-of-class peer-review activities and sharing of past assignments as unsanctioned, I describe them as such because the students I spoke with described feeling as if they were working secretively around sanctioned practices to get the information and feedback they needed. For instance, Student 2 used a conspiratorial tone to tell me, "I'm gonna be bluntly honest with you, just about every kid that's taken it [the business capstone course] had somebody else's paper to look at from the years before" (Student 2.sr.2). In looking back on the experience after he graduated, Student 10 told me that while no peer review was conducted in the class,

> there were a bunch of my friends that were in the class and who had had the class prior. So they kind of gave some feedback, and we wanted to make sure that it wasn't necessarily if we knew what we were doing was right, but at least if we all did it the same kind of way we were all going down in the same boat. (Student 10.post.2)

Note how the initiative to seek out this form of self-sponsored yet clandestine peer review makes this a practice that students are invested in,[4] but also how the lack of instructor guidance in the practice leaves them wondering if they are helping or hurting one another's drafts.

The writers of these 50-page papers also reported to me what it felt like to write for a reader they were convinced would not read their text in its entirety. When several students, including those who were more positive in acknowledging some learning experiences associated with the 50-page paper assignment, told me their capstone instructor specifically told them he does not read their papers, I took seriously their descriptions of how writing for such an audience affected their process. Student 10 told me when he was enrolled in the course his instructor "even said, he's like, 'I don't read every page.' . . . So, yeah, but you never know what pages he's checking so it's all gotta be there" (Student 10.sr.1). Student 57, a highly conscientious student who graduated early, responded to my asking her if she had any recommendations for the university to help students become better writers, this way:

46 : "THEY WRITE A LOT MORE THAN I AM WRITING AT MY SCHOOL"

> Probably stronger professors in these business classes. You're expected to write *all* this. And they don't care about writing at all. And so there'd be a couple times I would ask the professor instruction. Like, "Oh, am I doing this right?" And he's like, "Whatever. As long as you write fifty pages, I don't care what's in there." (Student 57.sr.4)

Then, in a conspiratorial tone, Student 57 leaned in and said,

> I don't know if anyone told you how they grade it. They check the entire document for like structurally, like if you have a heading, making sure it's not at the end of one page and your paragraph starts in next. And they check to make sure this is required and you have to have it like this. But other than that, they flip randomly in the beginning and read like two or three pages. They flip randomly in the middle. And the end. (Student 57.sr.4)

I asked if she understood her paper would not be read linearly or completely as she wrote it, and she said she did and that, like Student 10, she felt pressure to make sure her text was clear for a reader to pick up at any point. When I asked what they understood to be the rationale for this reading practice, Student 57 and Student 10 were positive it was because the instructor didn't have time to read all the 50-page papers in a section of approximately 30 students. While we know professional reading practices for certain genres include skimming (see, for example, Charney, 1993), I sensed from the business students I spoke with some disappointment that the longest paper they ever wrote would be unlikely to be read by anyone in its entirety.

Despite the cynicism students expressed about the assignment, Student 10 and Student 57 did see positive aspects of the assignment. Student 10 found the way the capstone course asked students to analyze two currently existing corporations to be "the most realistic" course he ever had "in terms of it's not just textbook stuff and learning about old theories from the last century. It's looking at current stuff, you know, looking at stocks, looking at how businesses operate" (Student 10.sr.1). He also agreed with the professor's claim that writing the capstone paper would make him a better critical reader of financial statements. Student 57 claimed writing the capstone paper helped her synthesize her learning from across the business curriculum: "I would definitely say it helped me collect all my thoughts from the classes I've taken. Before, they were all kind of on their own, but I was able to pull from everything and be able to write one paper itself" (Student 57.sr.4).

Meaningful Writing Experiences

In every interview I asked students to tell me about a recent time when they had an experience with writing that they would describe as successful and an experience that in comparison felt less successful or like a failure to them. I also asked them separately to describe any writing assignments they experienced recently that they found useful to them. Together their answers to these questions invite comparisons to Eodice et al.'s (2016) *Meaningful Writing Project*, though *successful* and *useful* were not interpreted as *meaningful* by all my study participants. Nonetheless, their answers to these questions provide another window to the moments in the curriculum when some had interactive and meaning-making experiences with writing as well as times when writing was treated perfunctorily or meaninglessly by students and instructors.

In response to my asking them to tell me about a successful experience with writing, student responses concentrated around two very different explanations for their success that I coded as "received good grade" and "engaged in process," as can be seen in Table 1.5. While students suggested a range of reasons for their success, and a few students most years indicated they had no successful experience with writing to tell me about, these two responses were the most frequently invoked over all the years of the study, and while sometimes a student's response could be coded as encompassing both of these reasons, more often they demarcate two different clusters of participant responses. The "received good grade" responses can be further subdivided to demarcate those who took the good grade they received as a sign of having a desired impact on an audience member with their writing (a reason for success a few other students brought up without mentioning a grade), and those who took the grade as itself the sole goal and sign of success. In responses where the grade was presented as the sole sign of success, it struck me that the definition for the success of their own writing was surrendered by the student to their instructors. In such responses the grade received was very often the first or second descriptive element the participant listed about the "successful" paper. For instance, student 58's response to my request for a description of a successful writing experience was typical of the "received good grade" responses: "I had a four-page research paper to write. And I feel like that was pretty successful. I ended up getting like an 85 on it. So I thought that was pretty good" (Student 58.first-year.2). Student 30's response demonstrates how sometimes the instructor's positive evaluation could supplant the student's negative evaluation:

TABLE 1.5. Tallies of participant-offered reasons for why the experience they described as a successful writing experience was successful.

This table combines all participants; those who took the first-year course and were invited to be interviewed six times over five years and those who did not take the first-year course and were invited to be interviewed two times starting in either their junior or senior year. Some participants offered more than one reason for the success of their successful assignment, and so their responses were double coded.

Why was successful writing experience successful?	First interview first year (N=31)	Second interview first year (N=22)	Sophomore year (N=19)	Junior year (N=27)	Senior year (N=32)	Post-graduation (N=12)	Total
Engaged in process	11 (35.48%)	6 (27.27%)	5 (26.32%)	7 (25.93%)	12 (37.50%)	4 (33.33%)	45
Received good grade	7 (22.58%)	3 (13.64%)	5 (26.32%)	12 (44.44%)	14 (43.27%)	2 (16.67%)	43
Learned something	4 (12.90%)	6 (27.27%)	5 (26.32%)	4 (14.81%)	8 (25.00%)	0	27
Impact on audience	6 (19.35%)	1 (4.55%)	3 (15.79%)	3 (11.11%)	7 (21.88%)	3 (25.00%)	23
Room to make assignment own	5 (16.13%)	6 (27.27%)	0	4 (14.81%)	5 (15.63%)	0	20
Topic or assignment interesting	6 (19.35%)	3 (13.64%)	0	5 (18.52%)	5 (15.63%)	0	19
Personal expression	6 (19.35%)	6 (27.27%)	1 (5.26%)	1 (3.70%)	3 (9.38%)	2 (16.67%)	19
Grammar	1 (3.23%)	0	1 (5.26%)	3 (11.11%)	0	2 (16.67%)	7

Enjoyed writing	1 (3.23%)	0	0	0	4 (12.50%)	0	5
Fulfilled a requirement	0	0	1 (5.26%)	1 (3.70%)	0	0	2
Style	0	0	1 (5.26%)	0	0	0	1
Lack a successful writing experience	0	4 (18.18%)	2 (10.53%)	3 (11.11%)	2 (6.25%)	0	11

When I handed it in, I was, like, "Okay. I don't know if I'm that happy with this," but when I got my grade back, I was pretty happy with my grade, so, I mean, I guess I did the assignment to the full extent that *he* had wanted us to do it to. (Student 30.jr.4, emphasis added)

The way Student 30 describes the instructor's sense of what completing the assignment successfully means as contradicting her own sense of success also illustrates the tendency of attributing luck and good fortune for the good grade and thus the success. As discussed in Chapter 5, luck was often attributed when participants described not investing much in the writing process. As a result, the students in this subgroup of "lucky to receive good grade" defined their successful experience in terms completely opposite of those whose description was coded as "engaged in process." For example:

STUDENT 44: There is one paper I was like pretty cutting it pretty close to the deadline and I didn't think it was that good, but I gave it in, and I guess the professor was pretty lenient with the grading because it was okay. And I got a decent grade. I don't really count that as a good experience, more like a lucky experience. Yeah.

LAURA: Okay. [Laughs] Like a thank your lucky stars experience?

STUDENT 44: Yeah, that was definitely a pretty bad paper by my standards. (Student 44.soph.3)

Here Student 44 elected to present as a success a paper he defines as "pretty bad" but which his instructor assigned a "decent grade." He suggests it was "pretty bad" in his eyes because he did not invest in the process of writing it, "cutting it pretty close to the deadline" to get started on it. When students like Student 44 shared such anecdotes in response to my asking about a successful experience with writing, it showed how far they surrendered their own judgement and relied on the instructor to determine success, thus redefining "a good experience" into "a lucky experience." This surrender is of course not surprising given how little agency many described feeling in relation to a writing assignment—they did not design the assignment, the instructor did, and thus evaluation of the assignment as a success or not they left for the instructor to determine.

This perceived lack of agency in the descriptions of their successful writing experiences stands in sharp contrast, however, to the descriptions offered by participants who stressed their full engagement in the processes of prewriting and writing as the defining feature of their successful experience. Many of these participants stressed the length of time they worked on a piece of

"They Write a Lot More Than I Am Writing at My School" : 51

writing, often saying they spent several weeks or months on a project and several describing becoming deeply involved in primary research in some form, whether ethnographic observations, archival finds, interviews, or scientific experimentation. In describing the writing stage, these participants said repeatedly that starting early, writing multiple drafts, and seeking out feedback to consider during further revisions were key to their finding the experience successful. This is what struck me as interesting about responses coded as "engaged in process"; sometimes the engagement itself, and not the impact this engagement had on the final written product, was what respondents stressed in explaining their success. For example, Student 28 described the personal statement he wrote in high school to apply for college as important to him for many reasons:[5] He wrote about his mother, "It was the first assignment I really took seriously in high school" because he viewed the stakes of college admission as high and he cared about the subject matter, and because "I did about four or five revisions to that and that was the first time I actually really took care of my paper and I was really proud of it" (Student 28.firstyear.1). Sometimes these process steps, such as drafts and peer review, were mandated by an instructor, but rather than take away students' agency because the assignment design and grade were out of their hands, these instructor-initiated interventions seemed to increase these respondents' sense of agency and ownership of their process and product. For instance, Student 27 described writing a paper for a music class that had not been her first choice of class to enroll in, making her all the more surprised to find herself so engaged in the process of writing her first 10–15 page research paper about a topic she selected, the history of tap dance in film: "To find something that I was very passionate about in a class that I wasn't really looking forward to taking and then doing really well at the end, I thought it was probably one of the most rewarding feelings ever" (Student 27.sr.2). Her instructor required students to submit process-step components of their work "every couple of weeks" and present their work to the class. At first Student 27 found these requirements reminiscent of high school in ways that may have reduced her sense of agency: "It did feel like going back to high school," but she found "it was good" because this upper-level course in her later years of college was "the first time" she had ever written a research paper in college, and the required length was much longer than any papers she had written in high school (Student 27.sr.2). Her presentation pushed her to prepare her research and think about structuring her findings far in advance of the deadline for her paper, something she found extremely fortuitous. She shared this paper with me as her writing sample, with instructor comments in the margins cheering on her good work, correcting a few factual errors, and pushing her to clarify and extend the implications of some of her claims—the instructor seems engaged with her words at a level that matched the engagement of the writer in the process. In other words, she knew her words had been read, giving the high grade she received on it more meaning than simple "luck" in a professor not noticing a rushed process.

Grades and luck were absent from participants' responses to my separate question asking them to identify a recent writing assignment they found useful. As can be seen in Table 1.6, their responses here overlap a good deal with student responses to Eodice et al.'s (2016) *The Meaningful Writing Project*, with learning (both about the topic of the paper and about the process of researching and writing), future applicability, and personal connections and interests central among the reasons my and their participants offered for why a writing assignment was useful or meaningful. Several participants spoke of learning to write in genres that will be useful to them in graduate school or future career paths, especially during interviews in the later years of college when they were immersed in their majors. For instance, Student 23 in her senior year looked back and said, "A good portion of the writing I did here was related to my passion, my career choices, and so I would say that I found purpose, yeah, I found purpose in a lot of it" (Student 23.sr.1). Some of these responses may signal what Driscoll and Jin (2018) termed a "unidirectional" disposition focused solely on career preparation and seeing little purpose in college requirements that they could not connect to this preparation. On the other hand, those few who told me all their writing assignments were useful to them may indicate what Driscoll and Jin (2018) termed an "omnidirectional" disposition willing to see purpose in all writing experiences in the way Student 51 described in her first year of college: "I mean, I always get something out of every writing experience because when you write you're literally thinking, and you're writing, you're learning more things" (Student 51.first-year.1). Those whose responses I coded as "opportunity for self-examination" described reflective writing from the new first-year course that facilitated their learning about themselves as writers and personal writing that was therapeutic in that it helped them sort out their own emotions and thinking on aspects of their lives. As Student 56 put it, "it helped me as a person figure out how I was feeling" (Student 56.first-year.1).

Participants' responses to my question asking them to contrast their recent successful writing experience with a less successful experience stress again

TABLE 1.6. Tallies of participant-offered reasons for why the writing assignment they identified as useful was useful to them.

This table combines all participants; those who took the first-year course and were invited to be interviewed six times over five years and those who did not take the first-year course and were invited to be interviewed two times starting in either their junior or senior year. Some participants offered more than one explanation for why an assignment was useful to them, and so their responses were double coded.

What made the useful writing assignment useful?	First interview first year (N=31)	Second interview first year (N=22)	Sophomore year (N=19)	Junior year (N=27)	Senior year (N=32)	Post-graduation (N=12)	Total
Learned	17 (54.84%)	6 (27.27%)	6 (31.58%)	5 (18.52%)	7 (21.88%)	1 (8.33%)	42
Relevant to future	1 (3.23%)	2 (9.09%)	1 (5.26%)	7 (25.93%)	5 (15.63%)	4 (33.33%)	20
Opportunity for self-examination	6 (19.35%)	6 (27.27%)	1 (5.26%)	2 (7.41%)	1 (3.13%)	0	16
Own interest explored	3 (9.68%)	1 (4.55%)	2 (10.53%)	1 (3.70%)	2 (6.25%)	1 (8.33%)	10
It was difficult	2 (6.45%)	0	0	0	3 (9.38%)	2 (16.67%)	7
All assignments useful	1 (3.23%)	1 (4.55%)	1 (5.26%)	2 (7.41%)	0	0	5
Lack a useful experience	1 (3.23%)	6 (27.27%)	5 (26.32%)	4 (14.81%)	3 (9.38%)	1 (8.33%)	20

the role of deep engagement in the writing process in their definitions of success. While collectively participants named a great many reasons for their perceived failure, as can be seen in Table 1.7, they often claimed ownership of their experience of failure and were less likely to name the grade the assignment received as the sole sign of failure, in contrast to responses describing their success. For instance, Student 20 defined as a failed experience a research proposal that she "didn't do the best job that I could, even though I got a good grade in the paper" (Student 20.jr.1). The all-nighter she pulled to write that paper left her feeling she "could do a much better job" (Student 20.jr.1) if she had engaged more fully in the process of writing over time. She felt stinging shame that comes through in her description even after she learned she received a "good" grade:

> Because of the time I just wrote what I felt was necessary, and I wrote it in like nine hours. I went to sleep at 7 o'clock that morning and when I submitted it later that day I was like, here you go, and then just kept walking. I just—I didn't even want to think about the paper. I'll take whatever grade she gives me because I was like I'm so done with writing this right now. (Student 20.jr.1)

Participants often named procrastination as a reason for failure, but some took a step further to explain what such a truncated writing process sacrifices. For instance, several students recognized rushing their writing left them with no time for editing, and they were painfully aware this meant instructors read their work with errors they would have caught if they had time, as Student 51 explained:

> And then I'm doing it last minute, and I really typically write what I'm thinking, so I just feel bad about it when I don't read over—because I don't have time to read over it, because I usually make grammatical errors, so that makes me feel bad about the writing, because I'm like, dang. Now the teacher has to read a bunch of—it's not going to be a lot, but it's going to be, like, she's going to have to read some grammatical stuff that might make me seem like I don't know anything. (Student 51.soph.3)

Student 53 felt acutely the loss of time for planning activities when he rushed writing the paper he identified as his failure when we spoke during his sophomore year:

> The early paper, where I wasn't really planning. I was kind of just reading the prompt or the question and expecting myself to just, like, free-flow or come up with something—and that wasn't really how it worked, because I

"They Write a Lot More Than I Am Writing at My School" : 55

didn't have all the information. A lot of this, I had to do background information and then kind of pull my ideas out and see where I was going to argue from. (Student 53.soph.2)

Procrastination may be a fact of life in the college experience regardless of which college one attends, and several participants describe it as a difficult experience from which they learned about more effective writing processes. But lurking behind many of their descriptions of investing too little time in the writing process were the many conflicting obligations students at this university typically juggle, making procrastination not always the result of immature decision making but of being genuinely overwhelmed. For instance, Student 16's writing experience that "wasn't my shining moment" occurred when he "was god-tired because I was also working" and tried to write a 20-page paper using "twenty-some odd sources" in one night and found himself "just citing just to cite" (Student 16.sr.1) without really using sources to understand his topic. Student 3 told a similar story of his failure occurring when the clock was against his obligations:

I did it the night before it was due because I had my internship, and I just didn't get to it—and then I had eight-hour—I had my internship from 8:00 to 3:00. Then I had to go to class at 5:45—a three-hour class. Then I had to get up and go to my internship again from 8:00 to 4:00, and then it was due Friday at noon. So I had from 4:00—and I was so exhausted and I should not have left it, but I did, and it was just it was three pages. It was based on an anti-youth gang program. I would have—I had to find one online and research it, and I didn't do a good job. It was very bad. (Student 3.sr.2)

While students at all universities are encouraged to experience internships in their final years of college, the hours of Student 3's unpaid internship with the NYS Department of Corrections and Community Supervision (the state prison system) approach full-time employment and I suspect exceed those of internships arranged for students at institutions of greater privilege. Student 25's description of what she juggled in addition to an internship may give voice to the unnamed reasons many participants were unable to engage as fully in the process of writing as they may have ideally liked to:

I think it was just because—again, I procrastinated, but it was because of outside things I had going on, like I was working a lot. I was still doing well, I had another internship at the time. I was just doing a lot, and then on top

TABLE 1.7. Tallies of participant-offered reasons for why the experience they identified as a failure or "less successful" writing experience was a failure to them.

This table combines all participants; those who took the first-year course and were invited to be interviewed six times over five years and those who did not take the first-year course and were invited to be interviewed two times starting in either their junior or senior year. Some participants offered more than one explanation for why an assignment was a failure to them, and so their responses were double coded.

Why was failed writing experience a failure?	First interview first year (N=31)	Second interview first year (N=22)	Sophomore year (N=19)	Junior year (N=27)	Senior year (N=32)	Post-graduation (N=12)	Total
Invested too little time or effort	5 (16.13%)	4 (18.18%)	4 (21.05%)	7 (25.93%)	9 (28.13%)	1 (8.33%)	30
Lack of interest	9 (29.03%)	2 (9.09%)	0	2 (7.41%)	4 (12.50%)	2 (16.67%)	19
Too little guidance	2 (6.45%)	6 (27.27%)	1 (5.26%)	0	7 (21.88%)	0	16
Lack of genre knowledge	0	3 (13.64%)	5 (26.32%)	2 (7.41%)	1 (3.13%)	0	11
Regurgitated course or source content	1 (3.23%)	1 (4.55%)	0	4 (14.81%)	3 (9.38%)	1 (8.33%)	10
Too many rigid guidelines	2 (6.45%)	1 (4.55%)	1 (5.26%)	2 (7.41%)	3 (9.38%)	1 (8.33%)	10
Made mistakes	1 (3.23%)	1 (4.55%)	2 (10.53%)	3 (11.11%)	2 (6.25%)	1 (8.33%)	10
Received bad grade	1 (3.23%)	0	2 (10.53%)	5 (18.52%)	1 (3.13%)	0	9
Dislike genre	3 (9.68%)	1 (4.55%)	3 (15.79%)	0	1 (3.13%)	1 (8.33%)	9
Don't understand content or subject	0	1 (4.55%)	0	3 (11.11%)	4 (12.50%)	1 (8.33%)	9
Research difficult	3 (9.68%)	0	1 (5.26%)	0	2 (6.25%)	0	6

Category							
Stressed out	1 (3.23%)	0	1 (5.26%)	0	3 (9.38%)	1 (8.33%)	6
Citation trouble	0	0	3 (15.79%)	1 (3.70%)	1 (3.13%)	0	5
Difficulty level	1 (3.23%)	3 (13.64%)	1 (5.26%)	0	0	0	5
Timed exam	2 (6.45%)	0	3 (15.79%)	0	0	0	5
Unwilling to ask for help	1 (3.23%)	2 (9.09%)	0	1 (3.70%)	1 (3.13%)	0	5
Topic too personal	1 (3.23%)	1 (4.55%)	0	1 (3.70%)	1 (3.13%)	0	4
Felt compelled to conform to instructor's views	2 (6.45%)	0	0	1 (3.70%)	0	0	3
Lack of confidence	0	0	1 (5.26%)	0	1 (3.13%)	0	2
Lack of resources	0	1 (4.55%)	0	1 (3.70%)	0	0	2
Out of practice	0	0	1 (5.26%)	0	1 (3.13%)	0	2
Teacher expertise on topic intimidating	1 (3.23%)	0	0	0	1 (3.13%)	0	2
Didn't revise	0	1 (4.55%)	0	0	0	0	1
Dislike teacher	1 (3.23%)	0	0	0	0	0	1
Overly focused on vocabulary	0	0	0	1 (3.70%)	0	0	1
Can't think of a failure experience	3 (9.68%)	0	0	2 (7.41%)	5 (15.63%)	1 (8.33%)	11

of that, I had personal things like family and, like, relationship issues that was stressing me out. (Student 25.sr.2)

For Student 25, "working a lot" meant working two retail jobs at two stores in a nearby mall and a regular babysitting engagement. When I commented it seems she worked a lot of hours, she simply offered "I need money" as an explanation (Student 25.sr.2).

These students worked on top of internships because of financial need. And financial need can sometimes serve as an underlying cause of a student's full lack of engagement in the writing process. For example, Student 31 explained how her lack of access to important course resources she could not afford produced her failure, a failure that was compounded by her reticence to reveal her lack of required materials to those who could help her:

STUDENT 31: Most of my lab reports for chem lab, I would get, like, Cs and stuff on, and, I'm not really sure—to be honest, I wasn't sure why but I didn't ask anyway. So I was just, like, okay, I should probably do something better.

LAURA: Did that lab provide any instruction on writing lab reports, on how to go about writing them, or was that something you had to figure out on your own?

STUDENT 31: I kind of had to figure it out, because I was under financial constraints in the beginning of the se—for most of the semester. So, I got most of my supplies late. So, in the labs, when people were doing lab reports and stuff, I was trying to make my way through it. I got better. I started getting up to Bs and stuff, but in the beginning, this semester, I was getting, like, Cs and Ds.

LAURA: Oh, so by not having equipment, were you not able to even do the lab—is that what you're saying—that you were supposed to be reporting?

STUDENT 31: I was able to do the lab, but it's just, like, the lab manual has a specific way to write the lab reports.

LAURA: And you didn't have the manual.

STUDENT 31: Yeah. (Student 31.first-year.2)

Student 31 ultimately decided to change her major from biology to English because of her lack of familiarity with the conventions for writing in biology, which the prohibitively expensive lab manual would have helped demystify, and her greater familiarity with the conventions for writing in the English major, which she had been practicing since high school.[6]

Not all failure to engage in the process of writing can be attributed to financial hardship. The second most frequently named reason for failure, lack of interest in the topic or assignment, very likely motivated many participants to put off starting writing projects. Like the participants in Eodice et al.'s (2016) *The Meaningful Writing Project*, participants in this study highly valued the opportunity for choices they could make within an assignment's parameters for selecting a topic that intersected with their interests in and out of academic work and, more rarely experienced, a choice of the genre to write in or the audience to address. Eodice et al. (2016) claim such choices foster students' agency, and I agree, though, as J. Alexander et al. (2020a) note, this is an agency working with incomplete control of many writing constraints (p. 581).

The prominent role of emotional connection that J. Alexander et al. (2020a) document in participants' definitions of meaningful writing (p. 577) is one my findings also support. For instance, the word "passion" (or its variants such as "passionate") came up frequently in participants' descriptions of their successful and less successful writing experiences (20 times total). Engagement in the process of writing often meant an emotional engagement, and lack of engagement was often described as lack of emotional investment. As J. Alexander et al. (2020a) write, understanding the important place of emotion in meaningful writing expands traditional notions of *pathos* to value an emotional connection "between the writer and the writing process" and not only "the writer and a reader" (p. 580). Caring deeply, investing time, effort, and emotion, marked the difference between participants who cede defining their success to instructor's grading and participants who owned their own definitions of success and failure. But sometimes the withdrawal of caring seemed an act of self-preservation. When overwhelmed with obligations and work beyond school or struggling with a learning disability, there is often little room or resources for caring very deeply about a writing assignment or an instructor's evaluation of it.

Conclusion

The results of my interviews with 58 college students attending a racially diverse, public university serving many first-generation college students resonate strongly with Sternglass's (1997) findings from CUNY students 30 years prior. Like the students Sternglass (1997) interviewed, the students in my study spoke of the powerful learning that writing could afford them—how their knowledge of a subject matter and their knowledge of writing and research as dynamic processes could be enriched when they affectively and agentively engaged in writing. But also like the students Sternglass (1997) studied, the class status of the students in my study interfered with all writing's affordances. The family lives, work schedules, and challenges of being the first in their families to attend college (see Penrose, 2002) of participants in both studies stand out as factors that complicated their steady application and development of writing processes. The institutions they attended also set up barriers to their using writing to learn, such as large class sizes and writing-intensive designations that may have inadvertently discouraged writing in courses without that designation. The only difference of note that strikes me is that my participants did not face the writing assessment regime that demoralized and held back so many of Sternglass's (1997) participants from advancing toward completing a degree.

What my findings reveal about the amount of writing and interactive writing instruction my participants encountered in college is that these are areas of pivotal difference between their experience of college and their peers at more prestigious institutions. Sommers and Saltz (2004) generalized about the amount of writing all first-year Harvard students produced this way:

> Harvard freshman, for the most part, have multiple opportunities in almost every course to write a great deal. Most find themselves writing anywhere between fourteen and twenty papers their freshman year, in addition to lab reports, response papers, and a range of writing produced outside of class for their extracurricular activities. (p. 128)

They share as an illustrative, seemingly typical example, an anecdote about how much a student claimed to learn "in-depth" by writing a 25-page paper on a topic she "knew nothing about" before the semester began (p. 129).[7] I cannot find my participants' first-year experiences in these descriptions. Nor can I do so in those of the Pepperdine students Carroll (2002) recorded, for which "Carolyn" is presented as "a good example," a student who wrote 79 pages in her first semester for four different classes (p. 51). While Carolyn experienced a bit of a slump in writing when she took more large lecture classes in her second semester that my participants could relate to, she still produced 21–32 pages each semester through her sophomore year, climbing back up to 80 pages a semester in her junior year (pp. 53–54).

As also demonstrated in Arum and Roksa's (2011) *Academically Adrift* and Beyer et al.'s (2007) *Inside the Undergraduate Experience*, a student's major course of study can affect the amount of writing college students are asked to do. In both Arum and Roksa's (2011) nationwide study and Beyer et al.'s

(2007) study of the student experience at the University of Washington, students pursuing majors in the humanities and social sciences tended to report numerous writing experiences over all their years of college (p. 211). In several instances it seems students in these fields in the present study had experiences with writing that approximate those of their peers at institutions of greater privilege. However, students' experiences of social science disciplines at this institution could vary greatly. In the study of the University of Washington, social science majors were asked to write the most (Beyer et al., 2007, p. 211). Rachel, a psychology major whose experiences with writing in college Herrington and Curtis (2000) extensively documented, found that "writing was central" (p. 238) to all the psychology courses she took at the University of Massachusetts from sophomore year to senior year, with the number of papers and length of papers increasing each year. Her experience with writing entwined with her learning in psychology differed markedly from the psychology majors I spoke with; one psychology major's complaint that her friends studying psychology at other institutions were asked to write in ways she never was still rings in my ears. In contrast, the biology students I spoke with, while frequently discounting their writing for labs as "not writing" (see Driscoll, 2011, p. 15), seemed over time to be asked to deepen and extend their disciplinary genre knowledge, perhaps more than students at the University of Washington (Beyer et al., 2007, p. 211).

Melzer's (2014) nationwide study of writing assignments given across the college curriculum suggests that the relative dearth of "interactive writing processes" associated with deep learning (P. Anderson et al., 2015) in my study should not be surprising. Of the assignments Melzer (2014) analyzed, only 12.5% indicated that an instructor wished to collect and offer feedback on an in-progress draft to facilitate revision (p. 107). But when instructors built in scaffolded steps of the writing process for important writing projects, they typically helped my participants engage more deeply in this process, perhaps in part because the hurdles to starting early and luxuriating in exploratory writing, peer feedback, and substantive revision were otherwise activities too expensive to impinge on their overfull course and work schedules.[8] Such scaffolding tends to exist primarily in courses this institution designates as "writing intensive," of which students who matriculated before the first-year requirement was initiated had to take only two and now students typically take only one in their major after completing the first-year writing course. For instructors, building in such scaffolding is likely too high a cost on their time when teaching courses with large enrollments. But this difference in number of papers assigned and amount of support and feedback received during the writing process between institutions of privilege and resources and institutions for the have-nots is likely one area where the college experience is at its most consequential (see Arum & Roksa, 2011, pp. 60, 122). As a matter of equity and social justice, I believe publicly funded universities and colleges should work toward true parity in course size and in teaching loads with private institutions of greater privilege. I cannot otherwise in good faith ask instructors to do what WAC consultants have repeatedly advised and what instructors must already know would improve the education of their students—assign writing projects of steadily increasing length, difficulty, and rhetorical sophistication and respond to them constructively, with an eye toward encouraging revision.

Lerner and Poe (2014) encourage us to "investigate failed initiation into discourse communities—how and why students leave disciplines," and the decision Student 31, a Black woman, made to change her major very much mirrors the experiences of the three Black women Lerner and Poe followed through a change in their majors motivated "in part, because they do not identify with the discursive practices of the discipline" (p. 58). Financial hardships kept Student 31 from a course resource that could have helped demystify some of these discursive practices, so indeed Lerner and Poe (2014) are correct in asserting we need not only understand overtures on the part of disciplines to initiate but also "surrounding structural difficulties" (p. 58). What I am trying to argue in this chapter, and what the data I collected helped me to see more clearly, is that such financial hardships—class barriers—present structural difficulties to learning within this institution, making one major more affordable to Student 31 than another. Even more insurmountable divides exist across institutions, with the longitudinal studies of writing showing us that students who attend institutions of greater privilege and resources experience the rich learning that writing affords more frequently, more deeply, and with greater support regardless of their major than students who attend the kind of comparatively impoverished and always struggling financially institution my participants attended—an institution that is public largely in name only, with the state making up only a small fraction of its budget. Writing ought not to be an expensive luxury students cannot afford and thus forego. All college students, not only those attending Tufts, Harvard, and Pepperdine, deserve to experience writing as a central component to thinking, learning, communicating, and becoming in all fields of knowledge.

2

"If There Was a Class That Could Make Them Confident"

Comparing the Writing Experiences of Students Who Took the First-Year Course to Those of Students Who Did Not

LAURA: If you were advising the university on how to assist students to become better writers, is there any kind of classes or experiences you would recommend we try to design for students?

STUDENT 9: Um, I feel that creative, a creative writing course or something like that should be like a freshman mandatory thing. I feel I would have liked to take that class, I just didn't have time. But if it was part of a gen ed or something like that, I think it that would definitely be beneficial.

LAURA: Ok.

STUDENT 9: Yeah, especially first semester—aren't there some freshman—there's freshman classes, right, that people have to take? I feel like there should definitely be just a writing course to prep them for college 'cause I had a lot of trouble writing papers, especially my freshman year, and into my sophomore. But I feel like if I had a class that kind of like laid it out for me, like this is how it's different than high school, that would have been really beneficial.

LAURA: Ok. So you did have to have two general education requirements that were writing-intensive courses, right? A lower level and an upper level? Those your two bio labs fulfilled, or?

https://doi.org/10.7330/9781646426584.c002

64 : "IF THERE WAS A CLASS THAT COULD MAKE THEM CONFIDENT"

STUDENT 9: Um, I think I—I'm not sure if I got some of that fulfilled in high school. I'm not sure.

LAURA: You may have.

Later in the interview:

LAURA: So really the only other thing I want to ask you is that you know my intentions and goals are to produce knowledge that would help people teach writing to college students. So is there anything that I didn't ask about that's on the tip of your tongue that you wanted to share about that?

STUDENT 9: No, I mean the only thing, um . . . that was—it was a question—was about how it can be improved, and I just think that it would be really beneficial to have that like a writing-intensive course. Not necessarily writing intensive, but just like a writing course that's mandatory for freshman just because I definitely had some trouble and if that was something I did my first semester here that would have taken a lot of pressure off for further semesters.

LAURA: Yeah.

STUDENT 9: That definitely would be beneficial. (Student 9.jr.1)

A distinguishing feature of this study is the opportunity it affords us to compare the experiences of students at the same institution who have taken a first-year writing course with those who have not. Recent research has turned to comparing two groups of students in an approximation of quasi-experimental research seeking to explore the effects of a particular approach to teaching first-year writing. For instance, Yancey et al. (2014) compared outcomes and students' experiences between a traditional and an innovative version of the first-year course, which sought to increase students' metacognitive awareness of theories of writing, and Gere (2019) and her research team compared the experiences of students specializing in a writing studies minor with students who didn't elect this option, but with both groups still sharing a first-year writing experience. In both these studies the interventions and increased attention and time spent on writing and knowledge about writing (such as genre and discourse community knowledge) led to important gains for students that facilitated their transfer of writing knowledge to new contexts. But a finding from Hansen et al.'s (2015) investigation of college-equivalent writing courses in high schools found no statistically significant differences in the quality of the writing that students produced for a general education course between students who had taken a required first-year course and students who had not yet taken that course. In this chapter I present my attempt, afforded by the unique opportunity presented at my study site, to parse out the impact of a single, rather typical first-year writing course on students' knowledge and practice of writing and transfer of this knowledge and practices to other contexts.

This chapter presents a comparison of interview responses students gave in their third year of college between two groups: students who took a required writing course during their first year of college and students who did not. Their interview responses allow us to compare students' perceptions of themselves as writers and their experiences with writing in college, their attitudes and feelings about writing, and their conceptions of their own writing processes. Perceptions of self-efficacy, motivation, and general dispositions have been tied to student writers' performance of writing (Driscoll & Jin, 2018; Driscoll & Wells, 2012; Neely, 2014; Pajares, 2003), making them the root beliefs we need to study as much as or more than any individual written performances, each composed under unique constraints and circumstances and each one arguably not representative of all an individual writer can do given other constraints and circumstances. Indeed, while students shared a recent writing sample with me during each interview, their genres and purposes were so varied as to make comparisons of quality of the type Hansen et al. (2015) attempted inappropriate.

Data collection did not begin until the final class of students at this institution to matriculate without the new first-year writing requirement were in their junior year, so the fairest comparison my data allow is in the junior year of both groups. Thus, in this chapter I compare the responses to the fourth interview, the interview conducted during their junior year, of students who took the first-year writing course with the first interview, conducted during their junior year, of students who did not take the first-year writing course. My asking students in their advanced college years to reflect upon their experiences with writing instruction is similar to reflective interview studies by Jarratt et al. (2009) and Bergmann and Zepernick (2007), which asked advanced students to reflect on their experiences with writing in and beyond a required first-year writing course, and Hilgers et al. (1995, 1999) and Thaiss and Zawacki (2006), which asked students to reflect on their institution's sequence of writing-intensive courses as well as a first-year required course. As such, it shares in the limitations of these studies, such as the reliance on students' memories. Jarratt et al. (2009) reflected on this limitation more fully than most such research, claiming students' memories can become particularly cloudy or even repressive when asked to reflect on writing experiences they found uncomfortable. According to Jarratt et al. (2009), questions about writing present some students with painful reminders of previous "insecurities, and sometimes resentment about the writing requirement" (Jarratt et al., 2009, p. 63), and students' answers may only become vivid when recounting experiences they see as pleasant or directly related to their own specific goals. While I, too, encountered students who claimed only 2 years later to be unable to recall experiences from a specific writing course, whether the required first-year course or a writing-intensive elective, what I think the results presented in this chapter have to offer us is less the vivid recollections of students looking back on a particular course and more the notable differences and commonalities in experiences and perceptions between these two groups in their junior years: Might differences speak to possible long-reaching impacts of the first-year course? Might similarities help us better understand other sources of students' rhetorical and writerly educations beyond a first-year course?

The findings presented in this chapter offer a comparative element that past reflective studies could not. However, one clear limitation I must acknowledge is that this is a comparison of interactions with students I had developed some minimal rapport with over three previous interviews conducted in the past 2 years (students who took the first-year writing course) with students I was meeting for the first time (students who did not take the first-year course). Previous reflective interview studies concur that the reflection prompted by the interviews themselves produced for participants an increased awareness of their writing processes and transfer of learning, so it is reasonable to expect that my past three interviews with students who took the first-year writing course may have primed them to recollect and connect their writing experiences to a greater degree than the students who didn't take the first-year course whose first interviews with me I discuss in this chapter. Another limitation is that my group sizes are small and merely present possibilities worth further investigation rather than results generalizable to all student writers. This is in part due to my insistence on labor-intensive individual interviews (over surveys and focus groups) to collect thick qualitative data representing a diversity of minimally inhibited views and, for the students who took first-year writing, the inevitable attrition of participants in longitudinal studies. I can thus compare the experiences of 15 juniors who did not take first-year writing with 13 juniors who did. I used NVivo's cross-tab feature to compare the codes I assigned to these two groups and locate the trends reported in this chapter. In a few instances, as reported below, chi-square tests revealed statistically significant differences between these two groups, but more often, given the group sizes and the complexity of their interview responses, I am only able to describe trends in the data.

Similarities

It is noteworthy how indistinguishable these two groups are from each other in a number of the ways they talked about their experiences with writing. The ways these juniors collectively described their previous preparation for the writing they are doing now, their views on the purposes for writing in college, and aspects of their writing processes are similar. On these topics, members of both groups equally express a range of views with no one master narrative defining a group's position.

VIEWS ON PREVIOUS PREPARATION FOR WRITING DOING NOW

Looking backward from their junior year, both groups described their previous preparation for the writing they are doing now in similar terms, which is to say both groups were almost evenly split on the question of whether they felt adequately prepared or not. In fact, more of the students who did not take the first-year course reported feeling adequately prepared (60%), with only 31% of those who took the course reporting a similar view, though in the previous three interviews similar numbers of students who took the first-year course reported feeling prepared (68% in Interview 1, 59% in Interview 2, and 63% in Interview 3). It could be that as they entered their junior year and did more writing in their majors these writers' confidence took a dip that those who did not experience the first-year course did not experience, or perhaps the first-year course attuned some writers to what they did not know about writing in new contexts.

And while both groups clearly had different experiences in their first year of college, they both described their previous experiences writing in high school in similar terms, which is to say almost evenly split between describing rather rich experiences (often in AP or college-equivalent courses taken during their senior year), with guided practice treating writing as a process, or predominately perfunctory experiences, with writing instruction geared toward passing a timed exam (such as the Regents, SAT, or AP exams) and focused on practicing forms such as the five-paragraph theme through the use of worksheets with no revision or very little writing at all. However, a minority in both

68 : "IF THERE WAS A CLASS THAT COULD MAKE THEM CONFIDENT"

groups said they wrote more during high school than they did in college, saying the research process they engaged in during high school was more intensive or that they simply were required to write more and longer papers in high school than they are now. Their views on these experiences are more fully discussed in Chapter 1. Coming from the same communities around nearly the same time, the similarities in these ranges of experiences are to be expected, though it is noteworthy that those who took the first-year writing course were not more likely to report feeling prepared for writing in the junior year.

WRITING IN THEIR JUNIOR YEAR

There are also similarities in the ways these two groups describe the writing they are currently doing as juniors in their majors. The majority of both groups describe the writing required of their major as familiar to them by junior year and they could cogently describe differences in genre preferences and practices across at least a few of the disciplines they had encountered either through double majors, minors, or general education electives. For instance, when asked what writing advice she has for entering college students, one student who had not taken the first-year course told me:

> Oh. I have so much advice for this, specifically history. But I just say . . . try to make it as un–high school as possible. Because I feel like in high school you're given the five-paragraph structure system, and you're told to stick to it, and you're told that it's expected of you in college, to be rigidly structured in this format, and you get here and you realize that in some classes you don't have to do that. You don't even have to add in specific things that you were told that were necessary in high school. Or I know that I have MLA strictly memorized in my head, but I came to college and I'm a history major and now I have to use Chicago. So I have to learn that all over again. (Student 4.jr.1)

In their descriptions of recent writing, both groups described a range of genres: seven distinct genres for the students who had not taken the first-year course[1] and 15 for those who had.[2] Similarly, the writing samples they shared with me represented seven distinct genres for the students who had not taken the first-year course[3] and seven for the students who had.[4] While the most frequently named genre for both groups was simply a "paper," students brought in or described recently writing in genres such as case studies, blog posts, advocacy letters, treatment plans, and lab reports (See Chapter 1 for a list of the genres students named in response to my questions asking them to describe their writing samples and their recent writing experiences).

The writing samples of both groups were also similar in typical lengths and number of sources cited. The tallies of page counts and sources presented in Chapter 1 reflect the norms for the writing samples shared in the junior year interviews for both groups.

VIEWS ON WHAT MAKES A WRITING EXPERIENCE A SUCCESSFUL ONE

My discussion in Chapter 1 of the two competing explanations offered by participants for their successes in writing—either seceding definition of success to an instructor's grade or owning success through deep engagement in the process or writing—applies equally to members of both groups. Those who explained that their writing was successful because the process of writing the piece was elaborate and engrossing, with the writer engaging over time in steps of the writing process, were just as likely to have taken the first-year course as not (named by 33% of students who did not take the first-year course and 38% of those who did). Likewise, participants who identified the high grade they received on a writing assignment as the reason they designated it as successful were also just as likely to have had the first-year experience as not: this was the reason named by 40% of students who did not take the first-year course and 46% of those who did.

This finding may better help us understand the role of individual dispositions that scholars like Discoll and Wells (2012) and Baird and Dilger (2017) have recently advocated as necessary to a full understanding of writing transfer. These comments from students about successful writing are very similar to those made by students in Baird and Dilger's (2017) study of internship and practicum students. Using their terms, we may see that students who define their successful writing experience by their full engagement in its writing process as having strong "ownership" of this writing, while the students who allowed their instructors to define success in writing for them with a grade valued "ease" over ownership (p. 704). The comparison my data allows suggests that students' dispositions may have much more to do with the development of these views of successful writing than whether or not they have taken a first-year writing course.

VIEWS ON PEER FEEDBACK

In the same way, both groups expressed a similar range of views on the value of soliciting peer feedback on their own in-progress drafts. First, it is important to note that the majority (67%) of those I spoke to who did not experience the first-year course reported experiencing peer review as an activity required in at least one of their classes. While the students who took the first-year course all universally reported experiencing some peer review in high school, and all but two (91%) reported experiencing peer review in their first-year writing course, this group reported a dramatic falling away from this experience in the courses taken after their first year (only 42% reported experiencing peer review in their second year in courses outside of the first-year course, and no one mentioned peer review being required in courses beyond that year). Among the students who did not take a first-year writing course but who did experience peer review in a course, most of these experiences similarly occurred in their early college years and were not common in their courses. This is to say that in terms of experiencing peer review embedded within coursework, the experiences of both groups are not that different, with the required first-year writing course indeed increasing the likelihood that students will have this experience in their first year, but with the larger campus culture of writing unchanged by this requirement—many, but not all, students experienced peer review embedded in classes outside of first-year writing in other early general education courses.

It also does not appear to be the case that completion of the first-year course leads students to seek out feedback on their in-progress writing from others at a higher rate than those who have not taken such a course. The majority of respondents in both groups claimed they routinely solicit feedback from others on their in-progress writing projects; only 13% of students who did not take the first-year course and 31% of those who did claimed in their junior year that they regularly do *not* seek out feedback on their writing. Most of this solicitation for both groups is what Keating (2019) calls "self-sponsored" and sought voluntarily from peers like roommates and classmates (with parents and instructors serving as far less popular but possible sources of feedback) rather than "school-sponsored" and required as part of a class. One graduate of the first-year course attributed his continued self-sponsored solicitation of peer discussion of writing in his junior year as inspired by seeing the usefulness of the required activity in his first-year writing course:

> I definitely liked the peer review in the past. That's always good to sit down, get everyone's ideas out. Just to see what everyone else in the class is doing. Because honestly, I still do that in class. I'll walk in, you know, the week that the paper's due, let's say, if it's due Friday. Monday, Wednesday class, I'll walk in and I'll talk to a couple of the kids around like, "Hey, how's your

paper? What do you do? What did you find?" You know, like, "Did you find some way that went good for you? Did you find something you liked?" Then just talk about it a little bit and see what other people are thinking about the papers at the time. (Student 37.jr.4)

But students who did not take the first-year course also talked about their appreciation for self-sponsored collaborations with their peers as they brainstormed or revised. Student 17 spoke of her preference to talk with close friends early in her writing process:

I have two good friends that I have most of my classes with and we usually talk about our topics or say, you know, what we're doing our paper on, and what criticism we're going to use, and what argument we're making, and kind of help each other a little bit just figure that part out—just like the initial stages. (Student 17.jr.1)

Student 15, who did not take the first-year course, routinely asked an older brother whose writing and knowledge of history he holds in high regard to read a draft of his history papers because "it's always good to have a good other person's point of view" (Student 15.jr.1). The value for seeking out other perspectives and reader response was shared apparently equally across both groups.

Differences

Because so many aspects of the interview responses between the two groups were indistinguishable, with both groups sharing a similarly broad range of views on their prior preparation, their understanding of success in writing, and the utility of peer review, the few differences in their views and experiences may point to impacts the first-year course can have regardless of the vastly different dispositions and prior experiences and knowledge students bring with them to the course.

WRITER IDENTITY

One of the most striking differences in the interviews across all the years of this study were in the responses to my asking about participants' sense of themselves as writers: Do you identify as a writer? Is being a writer a part of who you are? Is writing a component of your sense of self? Consistently, across all the years of this study, the students who took the first-year writing course were far more likely to answer such questions affirmatively than those who did not take the course. The differences between the responses of the two groups to this

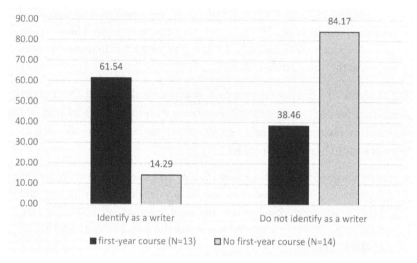

FIGURE 2.1. Percentage of students in junior-year interview who identify as a writer.

question was at its greatest contrast in the junior-year interviews that form the basis of this chapter's comparison. As Figure 2.1 illustrates, eight (61.54%) of the students who took the first-year writing course 2 years prior responded affirmatively to this question, while only two (14.29%) of the students who had not taken a first-year writing course similarly responded. A chi-square test of independence showed that these differences between groups on these views are significant, $X^2(1, N = 27) = 6.4542, p > 0.05$.

My discussions with participants about this question, as well as conversations I have had with students outside of this study, have taught me that for undergraduates the concept of "a writer" can be weighted with cultural expectations. While everyone I spoke with may on occasion write, or may even write regularly quite a lot, they often understood the identity of "a writer" as one who writes literary genres and perhaps also earns a living doing so or, even further, one who has been given the title "writer" as an honorific in praise of the high quality or popularity of their published literary writing. Considering the weight of regard given to the term, then, we can see why many students out of humility declined to describe themselves with this term. Some distinguished the act of writing voluntarily, outside of class or work requirements, and writing with personal intention, even if ultimately unpublished, as the mark of a writer. In this, these participants invoke the commonplace distinction between "people who write" and "people who are writers" that Hesse and O'Neill (2020) describe as potent among creative writers:

> While of course everyone writes, not least because school and work compel them, there is a difference between people who write and people who are writers. The difference is expressed in the need and desire to write when not compelled. By this way of thinking, writers have a particular allegiance to cultivating a writerly persona, to developing regular work habits, and so on. The identity of a writer needn't (and generally can't) be manifested in making a living as a writer. What matters is manifesting passions and commitments (and perhaps insights and abilities) beyond those in people for whom writing is an aspect of their identities—but not a centrally defining one. (p. 84)

This understanding meant my definitional question about an aspect of their identity and behaviors was likely interpreted as an evaluative question about their stature as a writer.

I am sure writing instructors will not be surprised to find I encountered with this question a number of students proclaiming an identity as "more a math and science person" and firmly "not a writer" (Student 22.jr.1). But this denial of a writerly identity could extend to students majoring in the humanities and social sciences, too. For instance, Student 37, a history major who took the first-year course, explained that he is more accepting of the "writer" label when he writes to present academic research, but not when he writes in genres he identified as "creative" and hadn't practiced since "freshman year. I don't think I've had to do one since" (Student 37.jr.4).

This common refrain of reluctance makes the responses by the majority of the students who took the first-year course all the more remarkable, then. They simply were far more likely to tell me that yes, they are a writer, it is a part of who they are. I cannot fully know why this striking difference exists, and it is true that a number of the students who took the first-year course gave an affirmative answer to this question each year when asked, with the proportion being greatest during this junior year.[5] The interviews point to being asked to write regularly, more than anything else, as a likely cause for students to embrace this identity. Students from both groups who claimed an identity as a writer would point to the amount of writing they were asked to do in college when explaining their answer. For instance, a student who took the first-year course stressed that for her now the exigency of school writing informs her identity as a writer, even more than her past as a writer of poetry:

> I guess right now where I am in life, I would consider myself as a writer. In the future, I mean, I don't know because if I'm not doing these essays and stuff, will I continue writing, is the question. Like, poetry I still enjoy. It's just finding a time, and as of now, it hasn't been a time right now . . . so, I

have stopped doing it as of right now. And in the future, who's to say that I'll keep writing more, even if I want to, so, like, will I find the time to do it? . . . So right now, I guess because I'm in school and this is what I'm supposed to do right now, I see myself as a writer, but in a long run, like, story, career-wise writer? I'm not sure. Then I guess I'll see. (Student 38.jr.4)

Students who took the first-year course were asked to write regularly and often to reflect on their writing in that course, and this early college experience may play a role in this significant difference in responses between groups. Several students in their junior year who did not take the first-year course often commented on how little writing they were asked to do in their early years of college when, without a required writing course, they mainly took introductory courses in large lecture formats where the main means of evaluation were examinations.

Recent research has helped us understand how consequential assuming an identity as a writer can be for students' sense of agency when writing and willingness to sustain the time-consuming and often frustrating processes of writing in school and beyond (J. Alexander et al., 2020a; Cleary, 2013; Lammers & Marsh, 2018; Roozen, 2009b). This finding, then, provides strong support for the important role even just one first-year required course can have on the development of a self-perception with profound consequence.

VIEWS ON COLLABORATION

Similarly, my asking about students' experiences with collaborative writing revealed greater enthusiasm for collaborative writing from students who took the first-year course than among students who did not take the first-year course. This comparison is not statistically significant and must be made tentatively because of the small group sizes—since not every student reported experiencing collaborative assignments, I am comparing two smaller subgroups of already small groups. But of the four students who took the first-year course and reported recently experiencing a collaborative assignment, three (75%) spoke very strongly of the value of this collaboration, even if they recognized they did not generally previously feel warmly about such assignments. One such student described the valuable contributions a transgender student brought to a zine she worked on collaboratively for a class project, acknowledging the project was made better for the diversity of perspectives among collaborators (this experience is discussed further in Chapter 4). Another student described intricate, ongoing collaborations in an education

"If There Was a Class That Could Make Them Confident" : 75

class to design teaching materials, while a third student described his impression of working together successfully in a small group to lead class discussion in a science class.

In contrast, of the 12 students who did not take the first-year course who shared experiences of collaborative writing with me, only three (25%) describe the experiences as positive ones. Because this was our first interview, these students often reflected back on several years' worth of collaborative experiences, rather than only reflect on the past year as the students who took the first-year course were encouraged to do with me. Their descriptions of these experiences recurrently recounted dividing collaborative projects up, working separately and individually, and patching together their different pieces which, while a legitimate form of collaboration, differed from the substantive intertwining of perspectives during brainstorming and composing the students who took the first-year course described. One student described the process of her only experience of collaboration as one in which she and her collaborators "crammed that together and made it flow and kind of copied and pasted our information into one paper" (Student 13.jr.1). The four (33%) students who described their collaborative experiences as negative experiences and who did not take the first-year course universally described malfunctioning group dynamics as the reason the experience was a bad one for them. Most of these students recalled just one single collaborative project during their college years, though one student majoring in accounting and business said the majority of his writing assignments after his first year have been collaborative. They all spoke of unfair work distributions or unreliable classmates not fulfilling their promised contributions. One student with some recent collaborative writing experience in a professional context characterized a sharp difference between this experience and collaboration for school assignments:

> Oh, god, yeah, it sucked. . . . I just feel like in the collaborative writing there's very little accountability, . . . it's just like how group work is, especially in an academic setting. You know, if you're doing it in a professional setting there's obviously more accountability, but personal accountability and academic group work, I guess that's just something that's known. . . . I didn't like it. I don't think it—like I was happy that we had to do it once. (Student 6.jr.1)

The first-year course included a required collaborative component, often an assignment for a group presentation related to one or more of their writing assignments or reflecting on those assignments in some way. While undoubtedly encountered in diverse ways, and not always remembered by students, this assignment and the many other ways the first-year course encouraged collaboration (through required peer-review work and small-group exercises) may have set up a foundation for students to build on when asked later to collaborate by other teachers. They may have been better prepared to see its benefits and practiced in navigating group dynamics, perhaps with some previous guidance from their writing instructor.

DESCRIPTIONS OF WRITING PROCESSES

It will likely come as no great surprise that some of the writing process steps that a typical first-year writing course emphasizes and requires practice in are not maintained by all students as they face assignments later in college. Students in both groups described tendencies to procrastinate, which made following such process steps impossible. Revision, in particular, both groups describe as truncated to mere editing, using descriptions of revision much like those used by the student writers in Sommers's (1980) study on student writing processes, even as the technologies for writing and revising have changed dramatically since her study.[6] Error and repetition detection remained primary goals for reviewing their texts rather than substantive revision.

But given these tendencies, the differences between the ways these two groups describe their typical writing processes emerged as an interesting finding that may indicate a lasting impact of the first-year course in shaping students' attitudes toward writing in ways that truly helped them generate new insights and new knowledge as they embarked on writing tasks. The students who took the first-year course were more likely, 2 years after that course, to describe at least one exploratory step in the early stages of their writing process than students who had not taken the first-year course. None of those who did not take the first-year course described using freewriting as an invention strategy, while three (23%) of those who did take the course described using open-ended, exploratory writing strategies to help them generate ideas and get started on a writing project. These students described writing exploratory drafts in ways similar to the experienced writers in Sommers's (1980) project. But the students in the present study used technology to facilitate this exploration in ways likely unavailable to Sommers's writers. For instance, Student 38 explained:

> I'll just have, like, 15 Word documents just opened up, and just a bunch of ideas. I'll start writing as though I think I'm going to write my paper now,

"If There Was a Class That Could Make Them Confident" : 77

but it won't even end up being that the first 10 times. It'll just be a random paragraph, just me talking to the laptop and writing out what I want to talk about. . . . And then slowly, it gets into more and more of an idea that I can make a thesis from. And sometimes I just—I write my paper without even a thesis. I don't even know what I want to really focus on until I'm done. I'll have ideas about my previous paper for my one English class about post-colonial lit. We read *The Sun Also Rises* by Hemingway and *Banjo* by Claude McKay, and we had to compare the two texts. And there's a lot of stuff to compare in them. However, the paper could only be five to seven pages, so you [had to make] . . . a specific argument, I guess, that could not be made by just looking at one text. You had to bring the both of them together to make one. And so I had a lot of ideas, and I felt—I knew I wanted to focus on the women in the text and how they're portrayed, but I didn't know what I wanted to talk about. And so I started out—one of my Word documents was just a page open that said Lincoln, who is the main woman in *Banjo*, and just all the characteristics and all how she's portrayed in the book. And then underneath that, it was Brett, who was the one in *The Sun Also Rises* and just all her characteristics. And then slowly, I would be, like, "Okay." In a new Word document, I'd make a paragraph in both Brett and blah, blah, blah. The women portray similar characteristics in this way, and then I would just bring those two together. Slowly, that would become a new document and on and on. So it's like a whole process. It's slow, and it takes a while, but it's a big trial and error, I guess, process of just writing until, eventually, I have enough documents that I can pull them all together and write my final one. (Student 38.jr.4)

The way Student 38 writes her way into a thesis and feels free to start writing before she knows what that thesis will be is an approach to writing only echoed by other junior-year students who took the first-year course.

In addition to using freewriting for epistemic exploration, these students were also more likely to describe a tendency to not write their text sequentially. By this I mean, they felt free to begin writing at points other than the start of the paper. Five students (39%) described their usual practice to me of starting "in the middle" (Student 22.jr.1), developing and figuring out an "argument itself" (Student 22.jr.1) before writing an introduction: "The introduction . . . I'm going to do that last just because I think that would be easiest" (Student 48.jr.4). Only one student who took the first-year course described consistently starting papers with the first word readers will ultimately read. In contrast, only one of the juniors who did not take the first-year course claimed to routinely begin writing papers in locations other than the introduction. This student said she routinely begins writing her texts in the middle because "I always struggle with the introduction" and shared how one of her high school teachers released her from the rigid faux rule of needing to begin her writing there:

> I guess in eleventh grade, my teacher, I remember him telling me you don't have to write your introduction first, and no one ever told me that before. My tutors were always like you have to start with an introduction, very formatted, and my brain just doesn't work that way. I think I'm very—I always have thoughts in my head, so this teacher was like write down what you're thinking first, and someone to tell me that I could do that was all I needed to really spark that, I guess. (Student 13.jr.1)

Two juniors who did not take the first-year course (13%) described starting with the introduction as the self-evident way to proceed, as if there were no other option: "I mean, you know, you always start with an introduction" (Student 8.jr.1).

Not feeling compelled to always start writing a text from the beginning can powerfully impact one's writing process. Rose (1980) documented how belief in a false but rigid rule that one must always begin by writing the first words one's readers may read can produce crippling writer's block. That the juniors who took the first-year course were more likely to describe feeling comfortable starting elsewhere than the first words of a text's introduction suggests their greater familiarity and comfort with letting flexible heuristic plans guide their writing, which Rose (1980) shows facilitates greater productivity and efficacy in writing. Rose (1980) suggested that helping a writer overcome such a block produced by adhering to a rigid rule could be as easy as informing the writer that the rigid rule, in this case of starting the writing process by writing the first words readers will encounter at the start of the document, is not actually a rule and that writers have permission to start writing elsewhere—where one already has ideas or where one finds it easier to begin. Perhaps at least some of the juniors in this study who took the first-year course learned they could follow looser heuristics in their first-year course the way Student 13, who did not take the first-year course, learned from her 11th-grade English teacher.

Students' responses to my request for what advice they would offer to students just beginning a first college writing assignment often revealed specifics of their own writing processes. Students who took the first-year course suggested a wider range of resources writers might consult beyond the professor. While five (33%) students who did not take the first year course recommended consulting with the professors about their assignments in contrast to only two (15%) students who did take the first-year course, five (39%) students who took the course recommended consulting a wider range of resources, such as models of the target genre and exploratory research, while only two (13%) students who did not take the first-year course recommended such resources.

These differences in descriptions of their processes are likely not without consequence and may point to a lasting impact of the first-year course in encouraging students to approach writing inquisitively, even playfully, with a willingness to allow it to be open-ended and being open to discovery. This certainly matches the goal of developing writing as a form of inquiry that is an explicit learning objective of the writing program offering this first-year course.

TRANSFER OF WRITING-RELATED LEARNING

During these junior-year interviews, students who had taken the first-year course narrated more instances of transfer of learning related to their current writing knowledge and practice than did students who had not taken the first-year course. Eight (62%) participants who had taken the first-year course reported instances of writing-related transfer of learning, with reports including six incidents of transfer occurring from their first-year course and three from high school coursework.[7] Only two (13%) participants who did not take the first-year course recounted incidents of writing-related transfer of learning; one incident originating in earlier college coursework and two originating in high school.[8] A chi-square test of independence showed that this difference between groups is significant, $X^2(1, N = 28) = 7.0487, p > 0.05$.

The types of writing knowledge and practices students reported transferring were diverse, including things such as strategies for using databases for research, strategies for writing conclusions that do more than merely summarize, and strategies for reducing anxiety when tackling longer writing projects. A first-year course graduate quoted above describes deliberately carrying with him the practice of peer review encountered in his first-year writing course into other classes, initiating the practice himself when the course plans or instructor do not. Likewise, a student who did not take the first-year course was quoted above explaining how she continues to practice loose heuristics for starting papers at points other than the beginning, a practice a high school instructor taught her.

Of course, transfer of learning about writing may have occurred for other students, too, they simply may have forgotten about it during our interview, I may not have prompted recollection with my questions, or their acts of transfer may be "low road" (Perkins & Salomon, 1988) or "invisible" (Driscoll & Cui, 2021) acts of which they are unaware. But if the experience of the first-year course helped foster in students a disposition more inclined to seek out transfer, or even to just have a baseline college writing experience from which to draw in later semesters, then it would seem to be an important experience to have at the start of college, meeting the hopes and expectations that many stakeholders place upon it. In Chapter 3 I describe the kinds of knowledge participants claimed they gained in the first-year course and drew on in later contexts across all their years of college and beyond.

RECOMMENDATIONS FOR THE UNIVERSITY

In every interview I asked students, after reflecting on their experience of writing in college, if they had any recommendations to offer the university. I also asked them for recommendations for their teachers, but when asking them about their recommendations for the university I asked them to step back, play "king for a day," and imagine potentially larger structural changes to the curriculum, requirements, facilities, resources, and so on that could help support student writers like themselves. In their responses noteworthy differences emerged between the two groups. Across both groups during this year's interviews, I coded 11 different types of suggestions. But what was striking was how frequently the students who had not taken the first-year course brought up that they would have liked to have taken, or recognized that they could have benefited from, an introductory writing course.

No one in their junior year recommended that there was no need for changes or that things should stay the same (this code I labeled "maintain the status quo"), though in the previous two interviews six students who took the first-year course offered such a response, with the greatest number, four (21%), during the sophomore year interviews conducted during the year after completing the first-year course. On the contrary, 10 (67%) of the students who did not take the first-year course recommended the university require more writing courses of students. Six (40%) specifically recommended an introductory course that they described as helping to make the transition from high school to college-level writing. Four (27%) recommended more explicit writing instruction within existing classes. Further, two (13%) recommended a writing course addressing the specific context of writing within the disciplines of their majors, while one (7%) recommended requiring a creative writing class, a class that many took to fulfill their lower-level writing-intensive course requirement, and one (7%) recommended the university require more general education courses, in which many of the students in this group described experiencing their only writing assignments in their first 2 years of college.

While some of these students may have gotten the idea to suggest a required introductory writing course when comparing their experiences with peers who attended college where such a course is required (one specifically compared her experience with her sister who attended Tufts), it sounded to me as if a few of the students I spoke with were inventing the idea as we spoke, drawing on high school memories and identifying a drop-off in attention devoted to writing on starting college. For instance, in reflecting on how to help writers generalize knowledge about their writing from feedback on a specific draft rather than merely focus on improving the one draft, one student found the term "writing in general" to describe a course that focuses on developing process knowledge:

> I would say getting a lot of feedback is good, but . . . you know, I feel like sometimes people. . . . are dependent on feedback and they don't actually consume it, they'll just use it for that short period of time, like, "Ok, this is how I should change *this* paper." But they don't really adapt it to their writing. So maybe a writing course that would try to give you feedback on writing in general like a long-term writing, not just for this paper. But how you should be writing in general or . . . or how you should be writing for different topics because you—there is a different writing style depending on whatever you're trying to write. (Student 21.jr.1)

Another student found her way from a concern for students' boredom with writing assignments to dreaming up a class that could help increase students' confidence as writers: "I feel like if students—not were excited about it, maybe excited about it, but if they were confident, if there was a class that can make them confident" (Student 27.jr.1). In my exchange with Student 9 that opens this chapter, you can see her bringing our conversation back to her suggestion that the university require an introductory writing course what would help students like her discern how writing in college differs from writing in high school. In response to this dream-big request, several students in this group reflected on the fact that they had never had a course devoted to writing as its focus while in college, noting that the writing-intensive requirement can mean a class requires writing but not that writing is a focus for discussion, reflection, and knowledge building.

Conclusion

The findings presented in this chapter afford us the rare opportunity to compare the junior-year writing experiences of students who had taken a first-year course with those who had not in circumstances that are otherwise very similar: the same university setting at very close periods of time, in spring 2015 for those who did not take the first-year course and in fall 2017 for those who did.

In many ways, the writing experiences of these two groups in their junior year were indistinguishable if by this we mean members of both groups had diverse experiences and held diverse views on these experiences. Some members of both groups felt well prepared for the writing they were doing in their later college years, some felt ill-prepared and struggling. Some were asked to write a great deal in their junior year, some were not. Some wrote long papers using multiple sources, some wrote short papers and cited no sources. Some wrote in a diversity of genres and media for diverse audiences, others mainly wrote "papers" with their professors as the only audience. Some valued and sought out peer feedback on their writing, some discounted it as unhelpful because either overly novice or dishonest due to peer social pressures. Some understood a successful writing experience as a process they engaged deeply in and learned from, others understood a successful writing experience as one they managed to earn a passing grade for while expending minimal effort and time. Having taken a first-year writing course 2 years prior did not seem to change the likelihood of some of these views over others. In Chapter 1 I explain that the major a student pursued may have greatly impacted the amount and types of writing they were doing at this juncture at this university. Their diverse views on the value of engaging in the process of writing may be impacted more by students' dispositions (Driscoll, 2011; Driscoll & Jin, 2018; Driscoll & Powell, 2016; Driscoll & Wells, 2012) or other unknown factors than by their taking the first-year course this university offered.

Yet for all these indistinguishable views and experiences, some striking differences are apparent in the ways members of these groups discussed their sense of themselves as writers, their early stage writing processes, and their awareness of transferring writing knowledge and practices from earlier educational experiences to the writing they are doing now. Participants who 2 years prior had taken the first-year course were more likely to claim "writer" as a part of their identity than participants who had not taken the first-year course. The consequence of embracing such an identity could be profound. The ways nearly all participants discussed this identity contained an evaluative component, so that to be a "writer" was in a sense to also be a "good writer." If the first-year course helped nurture their sense of writerly competency and self-efficacy, this sense of self may help sustain them through difficult writing challenges, supporting the persistence they need to complete challenging writing projects and to continue into coursework and fields where they see writing plays a role, especially fields where their earliest experiences may not have included much writing, such as the sciences. Embracing writing in this way may have encouraged them to try some of the invention techniques such as freewriting and starting writing projects out of textual sequence that support using writing as a generative, epistemic practice but which break from the tidy yet rigid rules earlier writing instructors may have emphasized. In this way, their writing process developed aspects of expertise in writing documented in studies like those by Sommers (1980) and M. Rose (1980). Likewise, the course may have made them better able to trace the origins of aspects of their writing knowledge and practice they employ today because of its heightened and explicit attention to aspects of the writing process that are often kept tacit in other courses that call for writing.

While what graduates of the first-year course reported transferring from the first-year course to their present writing were often skills such as learning to navigate university research databases that Carroll (2002) described as "basics" and also saw her participants transfer from their first-year course (p. 74), the prewriting and peer-review techniques some also reported transferring would seem to be at another level of complexity. They suggest the course fostered in some a deeper social and epistemic engagement with writing. Indeed, they were generally more open to and appreciative of collaboration in writing than their peers who had not taken the class. These findings lend further support to Neely's (2014) findings that a first-year course may impact students' attitudes toward using writing to explore multiple perspectives and to see writing as a process.

Of course, occasionally students who did not take the first-year course discussed collaboration, their transfer of writing knowledge and practice, and their identity as a writer with as much enthusiasm as students who did take the course. Likewise, not all students who took the first-year course embraced collaboration, saw themselves as writers, or traced writing knowledge and practices they use now back to that course. Students who did not take the first-year course often experienced peer review and some attention to writing as a process in other courses, especially general education courses they took early in college, and generally learned rhetorical and writing-process knowledge where they could. But my findings here suggest that the first-year course impactfully increased the likelihood of students taking on epistemic and social stances toward writing, claim "writer" as a part of their identity, and alter their practice to be more like established and experienced writers.

I think it is important to note that writing knowledge transfer was fostered in a first-year course whose curriculum did not set out to foster it as thoroughly as recently devised curricula (see Downs & Wardle, 2007; Driscoll et al., 2020; Yancey et al., 2014). The composition program studied here emphasized using writing as inquiry and using writing to bring together students' identities and interests with academic inquiry, research, and writing. Different curricula and teaching methods may produce different results. But I think it is important to see that a rather traditional composition program using commonly used teaching methods such as peer review, instructor conferences, comments on drafts, portfolios, and so on may have had these effects. And by "traditional" I do not mean "current-traditional," which does continue to inform writing instruction in many ways and places (Fulkerson, 2005; Ruecker, 2014). Rather, I aim to signify that the approaches taken in this composition program, and the training of their instructors, are similar to (and informed by) approaches taken in other university composition programs and have long-standing roots in expressive and process traditions of writing instruction (Tate et al., 2014). In this sense I see these results providing some response to the questions of efficacy and impact raised by "abolitionists" such as Smit (2004) and Russell (1995). The course for some, but not all, students may help foster general-purpose mindsets and habits related to writing that they continue to draw from and use in their later years of college, finding ways to repurpose practices and knowledge in new writing contexts. In response to Russell's (1995) famous ball-handling metaphor, it does seem that some general ball skills—and useful ways of generally understanding ball play and believing in one's ball playing abilities—can be picked up in a first-year course.

Of course, the size of the groups I was able to compare were rather small, 13 and 15 students each, and ideally one would like to see this study repeated with more participants. However, the conditions that supported my being able to make these comparisons may be unique or at least hard to come by again—I jumped on an opportunity one institution's curricular change provided and was limited by the number of students in their junior year who opted to participate. So, while similar conditions may not be possible again, this study provides some qualitative descriptions of possible signposts (writerly identity, epistemic and social processes, transfer) to use to look for the impact of a first-year course elsewhere, perhaps in larger-scale and quantitative research such as surveys.

Later chapters present thicker descriptions of students' experiences with the first-year course in the moment of taking it and in looking back on it each year all the way to 1 year after graduation for those students who stuck with this research project to its end. Some of these findings provide greater clarity on how the course had the impacts described here. Others shed light on the experiences of students who did not take up changes in their writerly identity, writing processes, or see anything of value in the course to transfer. While the news I share here of a traditional approach to the first-year course having long-term influences on students is news I believe proponents of the course can find heartening, the larger study from which these data are drawn provides the opportunity to listen more closely to students who did not find or actively rejected these influences. These are voices we should listen to as we continue to think about how to best teach this course.

3

"In Every Part of Your Writing, You Should Be Inside of It"

The First-Year Course Encouraged a New Mindset
Toward Writing for Some (But Not All)

LAURA: What are your expectations for that course? What do you think you'll do in it, what do you think you'll learn?

STUDENT 47: Uh, a lot of reading, a lot of writing [laughs]. Definitely going to have . . . I feel like I'm going to be a little bit tested. Like I've taken something like this in high school before, but this is college, everything's different. Everything's—uh, you have more expected of you. So, I'm intrigued. I'm intrigued by it, I'm definitely excited, my teacher seems awesome.

LAURA: Oh, good, you've already met the class?

STUDENT 47: Yes, I just met with her yesterday and we had our first class. It's like sixteen kids, fifteen now, one of my friends transferred, but it seems like it's going to be a pretty awesome class. I'm already done with the homework.

LAURA: Do you think you'll get anything out of the class? Learn anything?

STUDENT 47: Um . . . not sure yet. I'm excited to find out. (Student 47.first-year.1)

In fall 2015 I began interviewing students who responded to my email invitation just as they began taking the newly required and newly invented first-year

https://doi.org/10.7330/9781646426584.c003

writing course on campus—the course and requirement had only been in existence for 2 years. After asking a number of questions about their prior experiences with writing in high school and elsewhere, I settled into some questions about their first-year writing course. What were their expectations for the course? Some I spoke with had not yet attended the course, only seeing it on their schedules and imagining what it might be like, while others had attended the first few course meetings before we spoke. Their expectations mixed excitement with nervousness, with some expectations already being upended after only the first few class meetings.

Naturally, participants described their expectations for the first-year course in comparison to their high school English language arts (ELA) experiences. Students 45 and 31, who had yet to attend a class meeting when I first interviewed them, expected the course to be similar to their AP English Language and Composition course. Student 32 thought maybe the class would be on Greek mythology and "a lot of literature is what I'm thinking. I don't know" (Student 32.first-year.1). He noted that the class is certainly smaller than the ELA classes he took in high school, so he anticipated "a better teacher/student connection than a lecture hall" (Student 32.first-year.1). But Student 52 was surprised in the first class meetings to discover the class was "not like it's going to be like a lecture about how to write a paper" (Student 52.first-year.1). Student 40 reported detecting that the five-paragraph form that was emphasized in high school was not going to work now, and he felt a little adrift and anxious about what that would mean he should do now to structure his papers. Student 35 sensed the class wasn't going to treat what she called "actual essays" or "academic writing like that we're used to seeing in high school" (Student 35.first-year.1), but instead she thought the class would treat writing that is "modern. Like in today's media, like how writing influences us in our everyday lives. . . . Like more just like how every day how you use language, how you use writing" (Student 35.first-year.1).

Student 57 also detected a strong shift in the style and tone of writing this new course might ask of her. She described reading some of the essays that were recognized with writing awards by the program the previous year in the first few days of the semester, and she described the experience as being "really weird—like in my senior year we were told in college you're just gonna have freedom, but they were *very* informal" (Student 57.first-year.1). She pulled the essays out of her backpack to show me what she was having a hard time explaining about what made them "informal":

STUDENT 57: This one, like it has list of actors.

LAURA: Oh, ok, almost like a drama or something.

STUDENT 57: Yeah, it was more like almost a script where to the point . . . I'm trying to find . . . she's almost talking to herself, so more than just like trying to prove a point, it's . . . almost like a journal entry.

LAURA: Uh huh. Ok.

STUDENT 57: Where I've never done that. Where she's just literally talking to herself right here. And making notes of what people have called her. So it's weird to be that informal. (Student 57.first-year.1)

She went on to explain that the text she retrieved from her backpack to show me was "more telling a story, but very, very informal. So I don't know how I'm going to transition" (Student 57.first-year.1). She was used to the academic conventions for essay writing that were stressed in her high school ELA instruction and the stark differences in style and formatting before her in the award-winning essays made her "nervous that they're going to think that's high school" (Student 57.first-year.1). But Student 43 greatly appreciated the tips on brainstorming strategies that the peer mentor in her section had already shared because it was the first time she could recall ever being encouraged to consider her own passions when selecting a topic to write about:

> I thought that was really interesting because nobody's ever taught us how to brainstorm like that before. They're usually just like, ok, draw a circle with the idea, and then just branch off ideas. But I thought that was really interesting because he was like, "Write about things you're passionate about," and I've never heard anyone really say something like that to me. So I thought that was really cool. (Student 43.first-year.1)

In this chapter, I aim to describe students' sense of the impacts, positive and negative, that this course had on their first year of college and beyond. As on most campuses, students' experiences could vary a great deal across sections of the course. While all sections shared objectives, pedagogical techniques, and overarching purposes for four major assignments, instructors had a great deal of autonomy in designing their sections, with some focusing on a singular theme all semester and others asking students to select their own topics for inquiry across the semester. Additionally, as discussed in the previous chapters, students' past experiences with writing varied a great deal. So, too, did students' dispositions (Driscoll, 2011; Driscoll & Powell, 2016) and attitudes toward writing and toward being required to take the first-year course. Thus, while no one student's experience is generalizable, I can represent what a sizable number of students on one campus told me about their varied experiences: 31 students participated in the first interview at the start of their first-year course, 22 returned for a second interview at the end of the semester, 19 returned during their sophomore year, 13 in their junior year, nine in their senior year, and five in the year following their graduation. While I will focus my claims about students' longitudinal development as writers on the smaller number of students who participated over all the years of the study, in an effort to hear the most diverse voices I have not eliminated from analysis interviews by participants who elected not to participate in further interviews but did not request to be removed from the study. I chart tendencies and changes in participants' responses to my interview questions across their years of college. Read in concert with Chapter 2, which compares the experiences of college writing in students' junior year for students who took the first-year course with the experiences of those who did not, this chapter helps us understand the impact of the new first-year course on this campus, a campus whose writing culture is described in Chapter 1.

As can be seen in Student 32's comments above, a key difference nearly all participants who took the first-year course noted that set this course apart from almost all their other courses was its class size. When the course began in 2013 the class was capped at 25 students, but a new provost quickly moved this to a 19-student cap, and the intimacy of this size was commented on by so many participants. When I asked them if the first-year course was similar to or different from their other courses, class size was regularly seized upon as a big difference. As Student 30 put it, her "other classes are lectures" (Student 30.first-year.2). And those lecture halls could hold considerably more students; Student 32 estimated most of his other classes had 150 students in them (Student 32.first-year.2). The smaller class size also meant noteworthy differences in teaching styles. Student 41 said the first-year course was her "only class that focused on writing. All my other classes were lecture style. It was kind of like learn these facts and then take your test and that's it" (Student 41.first-year.2). Student 45 noted this meant "the teacher knew me by my name" (Student 45.first-year.2). The following year Student 35 looked back to note how different the course was in terms of the learning outcomes being much more individualized than in other courses dominated by textbook coverage of material and exam verification of learning:

It was more sort of like every student had different sort of take from the class. What I took from the class was definitely different than another student. And whereas bio was . . . different. Like every student sort of takes away, if you all do the work, you take away the same material. But in that class, it's, oh, very different than other classes. It's like every student had a different take. Every student experienced a different thing in the class because it was your own, personal sort of like journey in that class. (Student 35.soph.3)

The presence of this small, intimate course in everyone's first-year experience stands in marked contrast to the descriptions provided by students who did not take the first-year course in Chapter 2 of a college experience dominated by large lecture courses until students reached courses in their majors, often not until junior year. The smaller class size meant students in their first year of college were asked to participate in class discussions. Many noted it was the only class that required writing in their first year, and the only one to treat writing as a process by assigning projects in stages that they received feedback on from instructors and peers and included guidance on conducting research using the college's resources. Only in interviews in later years of the study did participants start noting similarities to the courses in their majors in these regards; in the first several interviews, my question asking them to compare the first-year course to their other courses elicited predominately these differences in pedagogy and class size.

Purpose for Writing in College

In each interview I asked participants why they thought their instructors asked them to write. I coded nine distinct responses to this question, including a rarely invoked "I don't know" response. A response that was frequent across all years of the study was that writing served the purpose of testing students' knowledge of course material or, as Student 58 put it, "To show that you read the book" (Student 58.first-year.1). Students offering this response to why they thought they were asked to write in college or high school thought of papers as merely an alternative assessment from exams, perhaps one better suited to assessing some forms of comprehension than multiple-choice questions. I coded such responses as "testing for knowledge of course material," and each year a noteworthy number of participants offered such responses, ranging from eight (26%) of participants in the first interview[1] when they referred to the purpose of writing in their high school to over half the participants (or three) I spoke with after they graduated and reflected back on their college experiences. The findings of Melzer's (2014) nationwide study of college writing assignments across the curriculum help us see why students would feel this way, with the vast majority of assignments he analyzed asking for an informative purpose (p. 22) for an instructor as examiner audience (p. 28).

However, while this response was frequent across all years of the study, participant responses to this question did change in other ways over time. Most notably, the number of participant responses I coded as "to earn a grade" as the reason why instructors require writing plummeted after the first interview, and the number of responses coded as "to express own ideas" increased in the third interview. During the first interviews, as participants began their semester of the first-year course and were reflecting back on their high school experiences, seven, or 23%, of respondents indicated that the need to earn a grade was the reason their instructors assigned writing. Responses coded this way were the second most frequent responses after "to test knowledge of course material." Coding these responses was uncomplicated because participants were direct. I asked why they thought their instructors required writing and they responded with some variation of what Student 48 said: "To get a grade" (Student 48.first-year.1). The purpose was to have something to assess, not to assess that something in particular was learned, but assessment for assessment's sake, because schooling produces grades. Student 46 suggested his high school English teacher "needed" some assignments to "supplement" test scores to justify their grades, so she gave writing assignments (Student 46.first-year.1). Student 36 seemed baffled why her high school instructors assigned writing, finding only the need to assign a grade as the purpose: "I honestly don't know because I felt like I would write something, give it to the teacher, they give it a grade, and then they give it back. So I was like, what was . . . it didn't contribute to anything bigger than that. It was just for a grade" (Student 36.first-year.1).

These types of responses declined dramatically in the second interview at the end of participant's first-year course and beyond. Only three participants, or 14% of those who participated in the second interview, offered a response I coded as "to earn a grade." This is notable because students were just completing the only course required of every student on campus (other general education requirements could be fulfilled from an array of courses students could select from), and thus one it would be understandable for some students to see the purpose of the writing assigned as Student 48 did, "to fill the credit"

(Student 48.first-year.2). But instead, the number of participants who gave such responses remained low across all the rest of the years of the study.

A type of response that increased after the first year of college was "to express own ideas." Five participants (16%) gave a response I coded this way in the first interview, and four (18%) in the second, but eight (40%) offered such a response in the third interview during their second year of college and were able to look back upon high school and their first-year course after its completion as well as consider other courses, whether general education or introductory courses in their major. Student 30's response exemplifies this reflection and change in perception for the purposes of writing:

> I feel like a lot of the time, professors are asking you to write almost like asking you about your own feelings on something, which, personally, like before—I almost said high school—before college, I was never really used to something like that. I feel like college is more based on your own analysis and perceptions and feelings on certain issues or what you read and stuff like that. Instead of just writing about exactly—like re-writing it to tell a story almost of exactly what happened. So, yeah. Yeah, I definitely feel it's more like you writing to share your opinion or make a statement or make an argument or something like that. It's different. (Student 30.soph.3)

Student 30 described high school writing feeling to her more like "re-writing" what others think, and college writing as being asked to insert her own views and arguments, informed by what she's read and analyzed—a dramatic development for her and other respondents. While Student 50 responded to this question in her sophomore year by saying that the reason she was assigned writing was "to see that you understand a topic," she went on to qualify this "testing knowledge" response by saying, "not that necessarily you think the same way as the professor, but that you could at least think a certain way and then argue how you think reasonably" (Student 50.soph.3). The number of respondents who felt this way about the purpose of writing in college notably grew from the first year to the second. It seems reasonable to infer that the one required writing course they took in that first year played a role in this shift to seeing writing as a means for developing one's own thought, expression, and argumentation. This is to say, some participants were coming to see a place for their own views and voice in their academic writing, more than who felt this way coming into college.

Descriptions of Writing Processes

While the full accuracy of self-reports of writing processes should be taken with some skepticism due to the tacit nature of our awareness of such complex processes (see, for example, Rymer, 1988), some stark differences over time emerged in participants' responses to my questions asking them to describe their typical writing processes and the processes they followed in composing their writing sample and other recent texts as well as advice on the writing process they would give to others. I developed 12 codes to capture the ways participants described their writing processes. Outlining and rereading a draft to edit it were the two most frequent ways of describing writing processes in both the first and second interviews, with 18, or 58%, indicating they outline and 27, or 87%, indicating they re-read to edit. Frequently participants indicated these were practices insisted upon by high school instructors, with some outlines following formal conventions a teacher specified and others functioning much less formally as a list of reminders of ideas and their arrangement. Re-reading to edit was often presented as the only form of "revision" participants engaged in, with "a lot of punctuation and a lot of spelling" (Student 28.first-year.1) and "maybe more sophisticated vocabulary" (Student 49.first-year.1) being the focus of their concern as they re-read.

However, other aspects of writing processes appear to have consciously changed between the first interview at the start of the first-year course and the second interview at its conclusion. At the conclusion of this course, more participants described practices that I coded as "substantive revision" and "start elsewhere" (in contrast to starting at the beginning of a text). At the start of the semester, only two respondents (6.45%) claimed to revise substantively as part of their typical writing processes. Student 54 indicated her initial drafts might veer "off track" and she would revise to "cut" what became "pointless," rearrange to keep similar content together, or "elaborate" to make "confusing" content work (Student 54.first-year.1), while Student 58 seemed to mainly rearrange to ensure she got "the point across before moving on to the next" (Student 58.first-year.1). The number of participants similarly describing substantive revision practices jumped up to eight (36%) in the interviews held at the end of their semester taking the first-year course. All eight of these students described their substantive revision practices as taking place within the context of their work for their first-year course. They described their instructors building the practice into the course with draft submission deadlines, peer review, individual conferences with their instructor, and portfolio submissions that required substantive revision. Student 50 described how peer review motivated some of her substantive revision: "Kids would write back to me about things that they noticed that I hadn't really thought about. And it would make me kind of think deeper about maybe one certain piece of my essay. And I'd focus on that more, and I think it made the essay better" (Student 50.first-year.2). Student 41 discussed how the Rogerian-style argument her instructor wanted from her was a new approach to argumentation for her, and fulfilling this approach's insistence on finding "common ground" rather than the "debate style" that was more familiar to her motivated her revisions: "When I was revising, had to make sure I kept doing that instead of talking about the two different sides" (Student 41.first-year.2).

Additionally, the interviews suggest that some participants made greater efforts to avoid procrastination as part of their writing processes, a change that would allow more time for invention and revision. In the first interviews, eight participants (26%) told me that they typically "procrastinate" (the term they used) when they have a writing assignment. For instance, Student 50 told me, "I do procrastinate with writing a little bit, so there's usually never time for a second draft" (Student 50.first-year.1); Student 41 said, "I mean usually I do procrastinate" (Student 41.first-year.1); and Student 47 declared, "I'm a procrastinator" (Student 47.first-year.1). But in the third interviews held the year after completing the first-year course, more participants described intentionally avoiding procrastination in their writing processes than they had in previous interviews: Only two students claimed they actively sought to avoid procrastination in each of the first two interviews, but four (21%) made such claims in the third interview. These claims tended to mark starting earlier on writing assignments as a new practice. For instance, Student 42 told me her typical writing process includes tricking herself into thinking the due date is earlier than it truly is. When I later asked if there were any changes she'd like to make to her current writing process, she responded:

STUDENT 42: Not that I can think of. I think that I've kind of made a lot of changes that have helped me so far.

LAURA: Oh, good. What would be some changes that you'd say you made?

STUDENT 42: Again, haven't been waiting till the last second to start writing it. I found a place; I go to the library. So I have a space to write. And peer review, I didn't realize how important that was until I had to do it.

LAURA: Yeah. So when would you pinpoint these changes beginning for you? Where did you start making them?

STUDENT 42: Probably the middle of [the first-year course].

LAURA: Okay. And what prompted them? What made you do it?

STUDENT 42: We had to. But then I realized that it was really helpful, so I continued to do it for other classes. (Student 42.soph.3)

Another aspect of the writing process that the first-year course may have had an impact on is students' willingness to begin their writing elsewhere other than the beginning of the text they are producing. The reason such a shift is important is because it signals a fuller understanding of writing as governed not by rigid algorithmic rules but instead by looser, pragmatic heuristics, a distinction that can make a tremendous difference in a writer's productivity and ability to overcome blocks to writing (M. Rose, 1980). At the start of the semester, seven participants (23%) indicated they always started at the beginning, writing the first sentence of their introduction first before proceeding to any other parts of their text. These participants described understanding the five-paragraph paper format they practiced in high school as not only a form but a sequence they must follow, starting with the introduction containing a thesis and what Student 30 described as a "hook" (Student 30.first-year.1). Seeing the format as a writing sequence presented fluency problems to them of the kind Rose (1980) described. For instance, Student 39 described taking "a lot of time for me to get started" on his writing assignments, seeing "just getting started" as his "main" writing obstacle in part because of the stress past instruction placed on opening sentences:

> I've always been told what the first few sentences are of your essay are what catches the reader most and makes them want to read it. And it's also the first impression. Like, if they have a bad first impression, they're just going to assume the rest of it is going to be bad, so it doesn't really help, so. Yeah, I usually just think about what would be the, you know, the best first kind of words to start it off. (Student 39.first-year.1)

Only three students (10%) at the start of the semester indicated they routinely started their texts elsewhere. By the end of the semester, only one student (5%) described the need to start at the beginning, and this was because her instructor had them submit draft sections of a paper for feedback sequentially, starting with the introduction. At semester's end, four students (18%) described feeling comfortable starting elsewhere, often finding it a strategy for overcoming the difficulties of getting started. For instance, Student 41 told me her process typically includes a few days of taking notes on her thoughts; when she would start writing she would "jump around," starting different paragraphs based on topics listed in her notes, and starting first with the paragraph topic she was "the most interested in" (Student 41.first-year.2), a strategy that leverages interest as a way to overcome all the other barriers to getting started. Student 48 described tending to write her introduction last "because sometimes that's just the way it comes to me" (Student 48.first-year.2). Student 54 claimed her current practice of writing her introduction last so that she can accurately summarize what she ends up writing, discovering her message along the way, is not a practice that she did in high school:

> Yeah, and that's not really what I did before coming to college. But now I realize that you don't really have a full idea maybe in the beginning, but as you're writing, your idea might, you know, change. And then you're like, okay, well then that should go in the intro. (Student 54.first-year.2)

In making this change in her process, Student 54 is clearly coming to see writing as epistemic, a means for her to discover what she wants to say and not merely the tool for her to say it.

These rather mature, expert writing practices (Flower et al., 1986; Flower & Hayes, 1980; Sommers, 1980), which seem so robust at the end of the first-year course, seem to recede in their descriptions of their writing processes in subsequent annual interviews. Substantial revision is never mentioned by so many participants again, with only two participants in each interview in the following two years discussing revising substantively in response to feedback they sought out or their own detection of issues in their draft. Descriptions of tending to start at the beginning of papers also picked up again during the third interview the year after the first-year course, with six participants (32%) describing this tendency.

However, descriptions of feeling tethered to starting to write at the beginning decreased in subsequent interviews with only one participant (8%) describing their process this way during the fourth (junior year) interview. At the same time, and unlike substantive revision, descriptions of feeling comfortable starting elsewhere increased, with five students (42%) naming this practice in the fourth interview during their junior year. Student 22, a transfer student who took a first-year composition course at another university, described in her junior year how her outlines progressively grow into drafts as she works on different parts of her argument, a process that she did not use in high school, where she experienced instruction she perceived as insisting she begin writing at the beginning of a text:

"In Every Part of Your Writing, You Should Be Inside of It" : 97

I didn't do it in high school. I don't know why. I guess because the teacher taught us . . . so—they were so religious about it has to—you have to start the paper like this, you start like this, and for me, I like to do my own—I like to approach it my own way, and I'm kind of stubborn like that. So I guess that's when my papers didn't turn out all that great in high school, but throughout college my papers were much, much better because I chose my own . . . way to do it. (Student 22.jr.1)

Feeling freed from this false and rigid rule with a seemingly long history—this was a rule Rose's (1980) participants found gave them writer's block—some participants seem to have carried their liberation with them from their first-year course into subsequent years of college, dramatically changing their approaches to invention and arrangement by infusing in them a sense of flexible playfulness. This change allowed them to follow their own interests, start with what they perceived to be easiest or hardest, and strike where they found their irons hottest rather than wait for the perfect first sentence.

Without the scaffolded structures provided by the first-year course, it appears most participants returned to their earlier writing processes that truncated revision to mere editing, and then only if time allowed. In his sophomore year, Student 39's description of his typical writing process included a passing reference to his awareness that "a lot of people" write rough drafts, but this is not part of his process. Instead, he researches, thinks, then writes, starting at the beginning and working to the end:

I usually get a rough idea of how I want to go about it. And then I'll, you know, read up on it, get some background information so I know how I can actually make an essay out of it. And then I'll get the documents and what I have to prove and stuff like that, and I'll, you know, get that all together. I don't actually write it down. I'll actually just, you know, write the essay as it goes, and then I'll just, you know, tweak it or whatever. I know a lot of people do rough copies. I've actually never done that. I just, you know, figure it out in my head and then just write it down. (Student 39.soph.3)

Other studies have found some initial positive impacts of a first-year writing course on students' writing processes and rhetorical knowledge having limited longitudinal influence, with students returning to older, well-worn practices and modes of thinking in their sophomore years (Haas, 1994; Wardle, 2007). If substantive revision was only begun because an instructor insisted upon it, it makes sense that students would stop the practice when it was no longer insisted upon. Given the intensity of the labor required for substantive revision, students had to be convinced of its benefits to continue it and be sufficiently invested in a text to undertake it, especially if they saw they could earn grades they desired without doing it. However, the loosening of a perceived rule (that one must begin writing a text at its beginning) is a change several students appear to have made and kept. They experienced the benefits of laying this false rule aside, finding greater fluency and overcoming a frustrating block to getting started. This change required little labor to implement and, in fact, made the labor of writing easier. It thus continued on with several participants, even if not explicitly cued in future writing contexts.

In each interview I asked participants what advice they would give to new college students just starting to write their first college paper; in later interviews I asked them to consider what they might say to their former selves in that situation. They most frequently gave suggestions about how to tackle the writing process, such as to seek help from your professor or TA during office hours or visit the writing center. Reflecting the change in the descriptions of their own processes discussed above, advice to not procrastinate saw a bit of an increase from the start (when seven, or 23%, of participants gave this advice) to the end of the first-year course semester (when nine, or 41%, of participants gave this advice). Interestingly, another type of advice that increased as the first-year course was concluding I coded as "attitude/mindset." This was advice encouraging new college writers to approach writing from an attitude or mindset that might be unfamiliar to them from their high school experiences and was encouraging, emotionally supportive, or motivational. Two participants (7%) gave such advice during the first interview, but this jumped up to six participants (27%) in the second interview at the end of the first-year course. Student 38 went from advising new college writers to take care with research, citation, and punctuation during our first interview to in the second interview encouraging them to "find something that you're passionate about" to write about (Student 38.first-year.2), echoing the advice the peer mentor gave Student 43, discussed at the start of this chapter. Student 30 went from advising new college writers to keep their writing tightly focused on one topic and to take care to "grip the audience" from the start (Student 30.first-year.1) to in the second interview encouraging them to not get discouraged if they face new challenges in the new setting of college:

> Don't get discouraged if you don't do so great on the first paper. Because in high school you could have been a great writer, and everything, and you still are a great writer, but it's a little bit different, different expectations. So

"In Every Part of Your Writing, You Should Be Inside of It" : 99

don't see that first grade and be bummed out, like you're not a good writer or anything. Because you probably are you just need to adapt to the new ways. (Student 30.first-year.2)

In this advice, Student 30 asks the new college writer to see writing as a cultural practice with different expectations and conventions in different communities, allowing new college writers to see themselves as newcomers to a community rather than interpret the gaffs that inevitably come with this as signs of inferior intelligence or ability.

The way Student 43 and Student 30 moved from giving advice I would describe as in line with "current traditional" ways of emphasizing text correctness and form to offering advice that stressed mindset, motivation, and personal interest illustrates another trend I saw in how the advice participants offered changed from the start to the end of the first-year course semester. More participants suggested during the first interview than during the second interview that new college writers like themselves should work to tightly focus the topic of their papers (from seven, or 23%, to one, or 5%), structure their papers (from five, or 16%, to one, or 5%), grab their readers' attention from the start (three, or 10%, to zero), and edit their papers (four, or 13%, to two, or 9%). In other words, Student 43 and Student 30 were not alone in moving away from current traditional advice likely emphasized in their high school experience at the conclusion of the first-year course, and those types of advice did not return during interviews in later years.

What Participants Appreciate About Their Own Writing

Another question I asked that I watched participants' responses to change after taking the first-year course was, "What do you like about your own writing? What do you think you are good at doing in your writing?" Participants gave a range of responses to these questions, which I developed 11 different codes to account for, including, "I don't like anything about my own writing." In fact, the number of responses thus coded dropped from the second interview on. During the first interview, five respondents (16%) indicated along with Student 34, "I don't like my writing right now" (34.first-year.1). This number decreased to two (10%) during the second interview. Responses that saw increases were ones I coded as "organization" and "style": The number of participants who described appreciating how they can organize their writing increased from three (10%) in the first interview to six (30%) in the second interview; the number of participants who described appreciating their style of writing increased from one (3%) in the first interview to three (11%) in the second interview. These comments suggest some possible growing attention to aspects of their writing they have increased control over in college, as they moved away from the five-paragraph form and from the prohibition of using the first-person pronoun and discovered other options for arrangement and style. Student 39 described these qualities in his writing that he likes as his efforts to ensure audience understanding: "I like to make sure that it's all, you know, one coherent thing. And, just that they can understand it, and that I was able to explain it to them, so that they can understand—so that, when they're done, they understand what I was trying to say" (Student 39.first-year.2).

Transfer From First-Year Course

The changes in attitudes and professed changes in writing-process practices after taking the first-year course suggest some evidence of transfer of learning from the first-year course to other contexts where this learning would be relevant. Recently Driscoll and Cui (2021) posited the useful concept of "visible transfer" for describing the kind of transfer that can be readily documented in an interview—transfer of knowledge of which the writer is consciously aware. Visible transfer differs from "invisible transfer," which Driscoll and Cui (2021) documented can indeed occur coming out of a first-year course, but the bearer of knowledge seems unaware that the transfer has occurred, perhaps having no recollection of where or when they learned something. Because a good deal of expert writing knowledge is tacit knowledge, which bearers do not recognize they possess but which powerfully guides many of their regular writing practices (Flower, 1989; Freedman, 1993; Wilder, 2012), it would make sense that interview methodology, which can only document what a participant is consciously aware of or can recollect, would be imperfect at documenting moments of transfer as writers gain greater expertise. Methods such as the discourse-based interview (Odell et al., 1983) and stimulated recall (Dipardo, 1994) have been developed to help interview participants communicate the tacit knowledge they possess. I used some portions of the full discourse-based interview methodology to help my participants uncover tacit knowledge. The writing samples they brought to each interview were pieces we looked at together and that I asked them questions about, such as how they wrote the sample and where they learned to do what they were most proud of in the sample. In this section I will discuss the visible transfer that participants described where their first-year course was the source of the knowledge they applied later in other contexts. I will also discuss what participants said were barriers to such transfer.

In total, my coding of interview transcripts documented 13 different participants describing 32 incidents of visible transfer where the initial learning occurred in the first-year course and was carried over and used, transformed, or adapted in a new, seemingly appropriate context. Some of these 32 incidents include participants describing over multiple years how they are still using information or mindsets they acquired in the first-year course in multiple new contexts. For instance, Student 30 described during the semester she took the first-year course how she had transferred the sense of feeling called on to express her own views, rather than remain neutral and objective as she had felt encouraged to in her high school writing, from her first-year course to a literature course she was taking concurrently. In her sophomore year, she referred again to this encouragement to express, develop, and argue her own views from the first-year course helping her to write a "legal research paper" on campus sexual-assault reporting. So, that one change in mindset and purpose for writing that Student 30 claims she acquired in the first-year course has successfully carried over for her into multiple contexts, and thus I counted these as separate incidents of transfer. As this suggests, some participants were the agents of multiple incidents of transfer, returning in subsequent years to tell me about how they continued to draw from something they learned in the first-year course again and again over the years. These participants could also narrate incidents of visible transfer stemming from different knowledge they also obtained in the first-year course. For instance, Student 30 also told me in her junior year about how she was using knowledge of APA and MLA citation styles she learned in the first-year course and how she still consults the Purdue OWL web resource that was introduced to her in that course, a form of visible transfer she had not mentioned in earlier interviews. Likewise, Student 37 told me of his concurrent transfer of the use of drafts from his first-year course to a sociology course he took the same semester, then in his sophomore year told me of his continued and active solicitation of the peer review he was introduced to in his first-year course in his current courses, and in his senior year told me of his continued use of the knowledge he acquired in the first-year course of how to navigate library databases. In this sense it appears that some participants were more prone than others to recognize transfer from the first-year course. These transfer-prone participants could have been influenced by an approach their individual first-year course instructor took, since these instructors had wide latitude in their approaches, or could have been primed for transfer by their disposition, such as the one Driscoll (2011) described as "explicitly connected," confident that what they did in that course would be of use to them later and thus inclined to seek opportunities to later use knowledge they acquired there.

As illustrated in the examples in the above paragraph, some of these incidents of transfer were of a participant's continued use of a resource or particular skill or knowledge of a particular convention, such as those associated with documenting sources. But most, I think, can better be described as transfer of a mindset, a new (for the student) way of thinking about writing. So, while continued, voluntary use of peer review is transfer of a particular practice, it signals an embrace of writing as a social and rhetorical act; a concern for eliciting a desired effect on a reader and a willingness to revise in light of a reader's concerns and suggestions. Continuing this practice voluntarily also suggests the participant more fully embraces seeing writing as a process, a significant development in the participant's understanding of writing from high school, where fixed form and timed testing were emphasized. Student 38 described in both her sophomore- and junior-year interviews feeling liberated from the five-paragraph form in her first-year course, a liberation sparked by an instructor's passing comment but that seems to have seismically changed writing for her. Here is how she described the instructor's comment in her sophomore interview:

> I remember, in that class, she said a little like tip thing. You know in high school, it's like you have the intro, and then two body paragraphs, and then the conclusion? But, I used to think that you had to do that. But she was like, "You can just make as many paragraphs in between your intro and conclusion that you need to make it coherent. You don't want them to be in only two paragraphs if you're proving so much stuff." So, I have quite a few paragraphs in between because I had so many points. I didn't want to have it be like three pages long of a paragraph. So, I split it up in between some stuff. (Student 38.soph.3)

In her junior year, Student 38 was still running with the freedom to break away from the five-paragraph form she felt granted by that first-year instructor's comment, a freedom that extended beyond form to also point-of-view as she felt authorized to express her own views in her writing:

> LAURA: Can you look back and point to any experiences that were particularly useful to you in getting to where you are now as a writer?

"In Every Part of Your Writing, You Should Be Inside of It" : 103

STUDENT 38: When I did the [first-year course]. That we had one paper, which was I think the first paper I had to write that was more so rejecting all the rules that you used to have on writing. It was—you would use "I" in it, and you would—it wasn't the four-paragraph paper, and it was about your experience that you had to write about. And so it was much more emotion and a lot more in-depth, like, details and you were a part of that paper, instead of you just writing this thing that you don't even care about. It's just a formality, you know, that you have to do. That influenced me, I guess, because it showed me that in every part of your writing, you should be inside of it, and, it should have a little bit of you in it no matter what kind of way that is, and you shouldn't be afraid to break loose of the restraints that you used to know and to explore a new kind of writing, I guess.

LAURA: That's nice. That's great. Yeah, you mentioned you no longer have that five-paragraph kind of model you always have to use anymore. Are there other restraints you feel like you've broken away from that might've been useful when you were younger but, you know, you don't have to do them anymore? Like, when you mentioned that one paper for [the first-year course], you used the first-person pronoun, I. Is that something that you still use in writing?

STUDENT 38: Yeah. I think it depends on what classes you're taking, but it's definitely been more present in my college than it ever was in high school. Because in high school, it was, like, you never do that and even sometimes in my high school classes, they didn't want us to say "our" or "we." And now, it is kind of you're supposed to because that's a whole—it's you as a whole and you as an individual, also. You the class as a whole is trying to make a point, but you as an individual are trying to make one point, so you can't make your own argument and paper without saying those words, you know? (Student 38.jr.4)

The transfer of a mindset, as Student 38 tells us, can have far-reaching effects, transforming her entire understanding of the purposes of writing—not to fill a form but to communicate an argument of her design. The effect of the instructor's comment loosened old, seemingly hard-set rules, just as Rose (1980) postulated such a comment could work on a writer, enabling her to write more complex arguments suitable in her advanced coursework.[2]

Student 53 in his junior year similarly looked back on his first-year course as a location for the origin of writing practices he continued to use years later:

LAURA: Is there anything else you find yourself still drawing on, informing your writing today from that class?

STUDENT 53: Definitely the collaborative aspect. That was something I was so uncomfortable with, and I was definitely just critical of myself as a writer coming into college and throughout high school. Because I think you just you read a book and you're just like I could never write a book. I could never write a poem like this, or I could never write an argumentative paper. It just seems so intimidating. But in [the first-year course] I think it was like our final project was a collaborative essay. I've never written a collaborative essay before where I have to write a paragraph that explains this specific idea or this specific argument. And then we have to—everyone writes so differently so we have to find a way to edit everything so that it kind of sounds like one voice again. And so that put me so far out of my comfort zone. [Chuckle] I can still laugh at how I acted and how funny we all were as freshmen trying to do that. So that I take away so much more because now all of my classes are collaborative, and I enjoy it. It's just so much more enjoyable. And I definitely take that away. (Student 53.jr.3)

Just as the first-year course gave Student 38 permission to use first person and to break away from a fixed paragraph form, Student 53 described how the first-year course helped him navigate a new and intimidating experience of collaboration that was "far out" of his "comfort zone" then but that he now embraces and continues to find value in. To embrace collaboration is to see value in the perspectives of others in building new knowledge, it is, again, to embrace a view of writing and knowledge building as social, a mindset far greater than a mere practice or skill.

Learning From Failure

Sometimes the change in mindset could be motivated from what could be seen as a negative experience, such as receiving a lower-than-expected grade. When I asked Student 33 about grades he received in the first-year course that he had expressed disappointment in, he described them as motivating him to undertake real change in his writing habits and mindset:

LAURA: Were your [first-year course] professor's expectations for your writing similar or different from your other professors? I'm kind of curious about the B minuses in [the first-year course] and then the As that you've gotten since. Does it seem like they were looking for something different or was it you that changed there and not the professor?

STUDENT 53: I feel like I changed. You know, I've gotten better at writing from there. I feel like it wasn't bad that I got a B minus. I guess that kind of gave me a message to, you know, do a lot better. (Student 33.soph.3)

In fact, at the end of the first-year course semester, the majority of participants identified writing they did for this course as their recent "failure" when I asked them to tell me about a recent experience with writing that did not feel successful to them. The 13 (60%) who identified a portion of their work in the first-year course as unsuccessful tended, like Student 33 looking back the following year, to describe the failure experience as a learning experience.[3] Also looking back in the following year, Student 42 put the lesson she learned in that course this way, "I thought I was a good writer and then I learned there was a lot that could always be improved" (Student 42.soph.3). Right at the end of their first-year course semester, these participants described an array of lessons learned through failure, from Student 40 learning he was required to revise, to Student 41 learning that Rogerian argument differed greatly from debate-style argumentation, to Student 44 learning that rhetorical analysis is less about what is said than how it is said, to Student 53 learning he writes better when he plans, to Student 39 learning his instructor would push him to explore all the implications of his claims. These were failures defined by the participants and not by instructors' grades—in fact, when participants chose to reveal grades to me they were seldom actual failing grades. And while these may turn out to be lasting lessons in some cases, I did not include them in the above tallies of transfer incidents unless I was shown concurrent or later evidence of the lesson applied in another seemingly appropriate context. As can be seen in Table 1.7 in Chapter 1, these participants' tendency to ascribe blame to themselves for their failed writing experiences was typical of participants describing failures occurring outside of the first-year course and by participants who did not take the first-year course. However, participants could also ascribe blame to instructors, whether of the first-year course or other courses, for things like providing too much or too little guidance. Disliking writing about personal experiences was named by more than one participant as a cause for their lack of success on an assignment in the first-year course that asked them to do so.

Hindrances to Transfer From First-Year Course

Not all participants narrated such eye-opening experiences in the first-year course that had a lasting, transformative impact upon them. Most incidents of visible transfer from the first-year course were described to me during the third interviews done during participants' sophomore year when 10 participants (53%) narrated transfer incidents. The junior year interviews saw six participants (46%) narrating transfer incidents originating from the first-year course, the senior year three (33%), and the post-graduation year one (20%). Thus, roughly half the participants of the sophomore- and junior-year interviews did *not* narrate incidents of visible transfer originating from the first-year course, even when asked directly about what they may still be using from their first-year course. Twelve participants explicitly told me they did not see transfer occurring from the first-year course, with three of these participants returning to tell me this again in subsequent annual interviews. In this section I take seriously the concerns these participants articulated about the lack of usefulness or connection they felt between the first-year course and subsequent writing experiences.

Some participants, like Dave in McCarthy's (1987) classic study of a student navigating writing across the curriculum, described their tendency to compartmentalize the knowledge they gained and used in a particular course, seeing it as inapplicable in another course. In the interview at the end of the first-year course, Student 44 described this tendency succinctly: "I kind of just approach each course separately" (Student 44.first-year.2). With that view firmly in place, Student 44 returned for interviews in subsequent years to assert again and again that he did not transfer writing practices or knowledge from the first-year course. For instance, in his sophomore year, when I asked him if he saw any connections between the first-year course and his current writing sample, a political science paper in which he wrote an argument supported with research, he said, "It feels different. I just can't think of any connections so I think it's a completely different type of writing" (Student 44.soph.3). Student 45, a student whose experience I discuss more fully in Chapter 5, revealed in response to this question that he didn't see any connections because he didn't consider the science writing he held in his hand to be writing: "I don't consider that writing, honestly" (Student 43.soph.3). He held fast to this view throughout college, even as his scientific writing grew in length and complexity and came to more closely resemble the rhetorical work of published scientific genres. This kind of compartmentalizing seemed to lead him to also not see connections between the writing he did in his first-year course and in other courses in the humanities, such as an African American history course for which he wrote in response to the film *Dead Presidents*. After insisting he saw no connections between what he described being asked to do in this paper, which included (as he read from the assignment sheet) having "a concise thesis" and being "well organized and properly cited" (Student 45.jr.4), I pushed further to ask if he really didn't recall being asked to write a thesis statement or conduct research in the first-year course. He seemed to realize in that moment that he had been asked to do these things during his first-year: "Uh, in the one where we had to go interview people. Yeah. There was a thesis there. . . . I honestly, I wasn't thinking about that at all" (Student 45.jr.4).

Another reason for a lack of visible transfer after the first-year course was the lack of explicit cuing in later contexts to apply knowledge or practices from the first-year course elsewhere. Student 37 told me during our second interview at the end of his first-year course that he did not produce a "very rough discovery draft" of the kind he used in his first-year course for the paper he wrote that same semester for a sociology course because the sociology course did not have peer review or instructor feedback built into its schedule (Student 37.first-year.2). He did not voluntarily seek out feedback and treated the first draft of his sociology paper as the final draft, one he only reread once for editing purposes. Without a draft requirement and feedback built into the course, Student 37 interpreted the writing in sociology as not a social process, it was "just me writing it, re-reading it" in contrast to the discussion "with our peers and stuff" that his first-year course used class meeting time to achieve (Student 37.first-year.2).

Another reason that participants cited for not transferring writing knowledge and practices from the first-year course was that they perceived the writing they did in other contexts to be too different for any guidance from the first-year course to apply. For instance, Student 41 explained that what he called "different writing formats" kept him from applying anything he learned in the first-year course to a philosophy paper he wrote during the same semester he took the first-year course (Student 41.first-year.2). He described the format of the philosophy paper this way:

> The beginning, you just had to talk about your thesis. And then you had to write about the claims that backed up the thesis. And then the conclusion was kind of a very short and cut and dry conclusion about it. (Student 41.first-year.2)

In contrast, he recalled in the first-year course using the APA style to write a paper with an "abstract, and then you wrote your literature review, and then the conclusion was longer and more intricate, I guess" (Student 41.first-year.2). Thus, indeed, Student 41 experienced writing two different genres with different audiences and purposes, but he seems to recall nothing from his first-year course that would prepare him for inevitably encountering new genres. Instead, he couldn't "really think of anything that" his first-year course "had to do with philosophy" (Student 41.first-year.2). Similarly, Student 58 claimed the writing she did in her first-year course and her criminal justice class were "completely different types of writing" with her criminal justice classes asking for "more research based on actual incidents and laws and things like that" while in the first-year course she found "it was more writing about yourself and like personal experiences" (Student 58.soph.3).

This perception that the writing done in the first-year course was predominately "personal" and thus unlike writing done in other disciplinary courses was shared by a number of participants. Students 44 and 57 brought this concern up in their explanations for why they did not attempt to transfer knowledge about writing from the first-year course to their other courses. Student 57 brought up this perception when explaining to me why the lengthy business capstone paper she brought as her writing sample during her junior-year interview was representative of her recent writing. She began by explaining her capstone paper was less "emotional" and "more technical, where you're analyzing something in a business manner and then giving your feedback in a professional way" (Student 57.jr.4). She said her earlier general education courses, most particularly her first-year writing course, were where she was asked to produce "emotional" writing, which involved "sharing your opinions and how you feel," in contrast to her business writing, which she saw as going to "translate into when I'm in the workplace" because it "is exactly the stuff I'm going to have to do" (Student 57.jr.4).

Such perceptions may explain the responses I received to the question I posed in each interview, in which I asked participants about the writing they anticipated being asked to do in the future, and would it be familiar to them and related to writing they had previously done or would it be new and unfamiliar? In both their first interview, when participants were just entering the first-year course and reflecting primarily on their high school experiences, and the second interview just as they completed the first-year course and were reflecting primarily on it, half of respondents said they expected to face unfamiliar genres in their near futures, with another 25% responding they were unsure if their future writing would be familiar to them or not. The proportion of respondents replying that they felt familiar with the genres they would write ahead increased incrementally each year thereafter, as participants began taking more courses in their majors. But worth noting is that participants felt the road ahead for their writing was just as mysterious after taking the first-year course as it was before. The participants who discussed what made them unlikely to transfer knowledge from the first-year course to writing in their other courses claim that the course gave them practice in some genres that they were not persuaded they would write again in the future. For instance, Student 44 told me she expected writing to feature prominently in her political science classes because she understands political science to be "a lot of opinion-based and theory" that members of this discipline write about to express to others (Student 44.first-year.2). However, she doesn't think the writing she did during her first-year course will in any way relate: "I don't think so. I think it's going to be totally new for me" (Student 44.first-year.2). As they exited the first-year course, only one of the participants majoring in a discipline in the humanities indicated she was familiar with the kinds of writing that lay ahead for her. All the STEM and business majors responded by either claiming they felt they likely did not have writing in their future courses or the writing ahead would be unfamiliar to them, and the social science majors were evenly split in seeing the writing ahead as familiar or foreign.

Conclusion

The first-year course had immediate and long-lasting impacts on many participants' experiences. They entered it under the weight of many preconceptions from high school ELA instruction, where, for many, writing was presented as a linear procedure to produce the five-paragraph form in an objective and neutral voice, and often in timed conditions. In the first-year course they found a small group of peers in close proximity to their instructor where they were called on to interact and participate in experiencing writing as a social and rhetorical activity. This experience affected the way many thought about writing and, even if only briefly, the way they practiced writing. The most notable changes the first-year course prompted in many of the participants that my interviews with them documented were:

- CHANGES IN PERCEPTION OF THE PURPOSE OF WRITING IN SCHOOL SETTINGS. Participants left high school seeing the primary purpose of writing in school as a means to earn a grade, an occasion for assessment. While participants continued to view a purpose of writing in college as an opportunity for instructors to test their knowledge of course content, participants left the first-year course much more inclined to describe the purpose of writing in college as an occasion to express (and often develop and support) their own ideas.

- CHANGES IN WRITING PROCESSES. During the first-year course semester, participants tended to engage in substantial revision, often in response to peer and instructor feedback on earlier drafts, in ways they said they never did in high school. While a few participants reported continuing to seek out instructor and peer feedback on drafts in later college years, most participants dropped the practice of substantial revision when it was no longer a course requirement or when feedback was not included in a course's instructional time. However, a lasting change to many participants' writing processes was a change away from seeing the organization of a text's final product as a blueprint for its writing process. In other words, many participants realized that they could begin the writing of an initial draft of a text at any point in the text and not necessarily with the text's first sentence. Sometimes a first-year course instructor's seemingly casual comment on this served as the prompt that helped participants treat writing as a looser, not rule-bound, heuristic process in which they (rather than an instructor) could control sequencing. This proved liberating and improved writing fluency for many participants, especially as older habits of producing fewer drafts or reverting to starting writing closer to deadlines returned for many participants.

- CHANGES IN MINDSET ABOUT WRITING. Changes in a set of attitudes toward writing seem, for a number of participants, to best character-ize the impact of the first-year course upon them, one they carried with them, or transferred, to new writing situations in the years following the first-year course. While it isn't possible to characterize one mindset for all participants, attitudes they describe the first-year course had a role in impacting include a growing tendency to see writing as:
  - knowledge building rather than mere reporting of knowledge already obtained
  - social and collaborative, with multiple steps of the writing process, from invention to revision, serving as occasions for interacting with the minds of others
  - rhetorical, with increased attention to insuring an audience receives and is persuaded by the writer's intended message
  - an opportunity to share and develop one's own views—views that have a place in academic writing and should not be effaced in report-ing what more established experts have written. One can use "I" in academic texts

- form following function, rather than the other way around. A writer has choices in arranging a text, choices with rhetorical impacts. Writing is not just a container or worksheet that needs to be filled
- difficult. The writing process takes time and concentration. Sometimes writers learn from writing experiences they feel they did not succeed in

Many readers will recognize in these shifts some of the threshold concepts articulated by writing scholars in Adler-Kassner and Wardle's (2015) collection *Naming What We Know*, most clearly that "writing is a social and rhetorical activity" and that "failure can be an important part of writing development," indicating that the approach to the first-year course taken at this university helped some of its students come to see writing in ways that align with portions of the knowledge base of writing studies. As shown in Chapters 1 and 2, some students at this university who did not take the first-year course came to embrace some of these views by other means, most notably by the rich writing opportunities offered by some of the academic major programs on this campus.

However, not every participant experienced such shifts in their views on writing, even later in the context of writing in their majors. Some participants surely evidenced what Driscoll (2011) termed a "disconnected" disposition, disinclined from the start to see future utility in what the first-year course had to offer. But others seemed more unpersuaded than uninclined to see that the first-year course had anything to offer them would apply to their futures. And if they could be open to persuasion, it may be the case that the first-year course could have done more to connect with them. This is a problem long recognized. Bergman and Zepernick (2007) diagnosed it as a problem of disciplinarity, where students associate the first-year course with the discipline of English and then don't see it as applicable to other disciplines. Even though the program that houses this first-year course is not affiliated with the English Department, and is physically located in another building, participants frequently described the first-year course as an English course and a continuation of their ELA instruction from high school. It is revealing that participants pursuing majors outside the humanities were most likely to feel unprepared for the writing they felt lay ahead for them.

The use of personal writing in the first-year course emerges here as a practice participants held sharply contrasting views on, emblematic of the challenges of trying to meet *all* students in a way that can help them in their writing futures. For some, the assignments that asked them to write about and reflect on their own lives were liberating, an illuminating and productive break from the five-paragraph form, timed-examination preparation, and an alien neutral "academic" voice. However, for others, these assignments were at worst experienced as highly uncomfortable and intrusive and at best experienced as providing practice in a kind of writing they were convinced the academy would never ask of them again. Thus, the personal writing assignments commonly assigned in this program's first-year course acted as an open door for some to see writing in a powerfully new light and for others as a closed barrier, perhaps encouraging some students to discount instruction in other genres or writing matters in the course. The power of the effect of such assignments on many participants means these types of assignments most certainly should not be abandoned. But the doubt in their future utility that led many participants to tell me they felt the course had not prepared them for their future writing deserves to be addressed, a topic I will turn to the concluding chapter.

4

"You Should Write to Know What You Don't Know"

Three Case Studies Tracing Affordances and Limits of the First-Year Course

The following case studies of three students who took the first-year course and participated in interviews throughout their college experience and beyond show us how the trends described in the previous two chapters play out in individual experiences, including how experiences in the first-year writing course can encourage or discourage transfer of learning. These case studies likewise demonstrate how individual experiences can defy the trends I've thus far reported in ways I am left struggling to account for in the literature of our field and my own imagination. I share these case studies because they are, in key ways, representative of the experiences of other participants and in other ways show us how each participant's experience is unique and cannot be accounted for in the trends my numeric tallies of codes show. In other words, they serve as a counter point to my analysis of wider trends, fleshing out tallies into fuller experiences and keeping this project honest for showing some of what its conclusions cannot explain.

Together these case studies illustrate the complex array of relationships students forge between the personal and the academic. In the first, Student 39's experience shows us the powerful positive impact of a first-year writing course in helping a student navigate new expectations for writing in college and in developing critical thinking skills that enrich and deepen

https://doi.org/10.7330/9781646426584.c004

his professional and personal communicative goals for years to come. But Student 39's experience also shows us a student's understanding of the limits of what he learned in his first-year writing course when he confronts different conventions and purposes for writing in disciplines outside the humanities. Student 39 and Student 48 add further illustrations to those experiences already documented (Baird & Dilger, 2018; Falconer, 2022; Haas, 1994; Lerner & Poe, 2014) that show us how hands-on, apprentice work in a lab can provide a rich education in the rhetoric of science.

Student 48 and Student 51 show us how a low grade in the first-year course can leave lasting stings that can cloud memories of the experience of the course and thwart opportunities for transfer. While Student 48 and Student 51 may have this unfortunate experience in common, they present us with polar opposite senses of the relationship between the personal and the academic. For Student 48, provided she is interested and invested, they are always intertwined, whether she's writing a personal narrative or writing to share her original laboratory research. For Student 51, they are always sharply split, with her academic writing receiving but little of herself and her self-sponsored writing withheld from the academy even when it could be appropriate.

These case studies also allow us a deeper glimpse into the ways race, class, and disability are always already shaping students' experiences with writing. One can see this in the support Student 39 received from other members of his family who attended college and in the ways the homogeneous political views of his predominately white home community controlled his early drafts of thesis statements in college. Student 48 framed her disability rhetorically as she worked to astonish her teachers and speech therapists by exceeding what she perceived to be their meager expectations for her. And Student 51's immigrant experience turned her mother's memories of her as a precocious child writer in Nigeria into something like a ghost taunting her, but not ultimately moving her, to join the voices of the emergent minority writers she admires and write in her American present.

The Development of Student 39's Critical Thinking and Understanding of Science as Rhetorical

What Student 39 shared with me about his experience with writing over the course of six interviews and five years reveals the powerful role a first-year writing course can play in not only helping students acclimate to college but also to embolden their critical thinking in the ways advocates for the course claim it can, serving students beyond the classroom and in their civic, political, social, and interpersonal lives. Further, Student 39's experience shows us his first-year course provided knowledge about writing that he successfully transferred to the writing he did in other courses in college, adding evidence to the growing number of studies documenting productive transfer from this particular class is possible (Donahue & Foster-Johnson, 2018; Driscoll & Cui, 2021; Johnson & Krase, 2012; Yancey et al., 2018, 2019). However, this is also a story of how Student 39 came to recognize the limits of the knowledge about writing the first-year course taught him. Relatedly, this story documents Student 39's growing awareness of the rhetorical nature of writing in the sciences, an awareness he achieved through a mixture of trial and error and apprenticeship, but which he wished, retrospectively, could be supplemented with the same kind of explicit attention and structured support he received in the first-year course for writing in the humanities.

Student 39 entered college intending to apply to medical school later but a little unsure what he wanted to major in. He took a variety of classes and discussed his options with members of his new community of friends in his dorm. In this he was a lot like other students who described the social life of the dorms as an important part of the college experience—a place where many, like Student 39, tested out ideas for papers as well as for life choices. He began as a declared biology major but considered public health and criminal justice before settling on biology with a minor in Italian. He consistently described himself as a capable writer who had received praise for his writing in his past schooling as far back as elementary school. His uncle, who had earned a PhD and coauthored a book, provided mentorship that helped Student 39 decide to pursue an MA in biology before applying to medical school, and his aunt, who earned a BA in English, was someone whom he repeatedly turned to for feedback on his writing, especially high-stakes pieces such as his application essays for college and graduate school. He may then have had exceptional familial support in navigating college that was unavailable to participants who were the first in their families to attend college.

However, for all this support, he entered college feeling unsure if his preparation would be adequate for what writing lay ahead for him in college. Because most of his high school writing instruction centered on literary analysis, he felt he had to think back to middle school and earlier to identify writing assignments he found useful or feedback on his writing he found helpful. He recalled using writing to explore issues beyond response to literature in these earlier years, such as "a family heritage project" in eighth grade

116 : "YOU SHOULD WRITE TO KNOW WHAT YOU DON'T KNOW"

that "was like eight pages" and for which he researched a great deal about his family's Italian culture and immigration experience (Student 39.first-year.1). Student 39 felt more masterful in genres like this project and his college admission essay that allowed him to write about himself or explore more deeply his own interests than he did in literary analysis. He complained about his memories of writing about literature in high school a good deal during our first interview. He said he "had a lot of trouble getting like a whole page" (Student 39.first-year.1) for those assignments, which he said were presented to him as a puzzle where there is one correct but hidden answer or, as he put it, "we had to explain the hidden significance, and like what the author was trying to hide within the text" (Student 39.first-year.1). While he "felt like there was never really any right answer just because it's an interpretation," his teachers "always said there was a right answer" (Student 39.first-year.1). In this context of prior writing instruction, Student 39 indicated he was not fond of peer review and collaborative writing projects. In his past experience, peer review's usefulness crumbled under the weight of peer pressure to be liked, which led to perfunctory and inflated responses on checklists provided by instructors. He felt attempts at collaboration were challenged by the difficulties of having a coherent or "solid, focused" voice represent divergent views (Student 39.first-year.1). In his views on peer review and collaboration, Student 39 expressed sentiments very similar to most other participants during our first interviews.

Near the end of his first-year course he reflected on his past preparation for writing in college and found that the focus on literary analysis did not prepare him for researching other topics, summarizing that research, and advancing his own argument on them. As he put it, "Actually, now that I think about it, all of high school was just, like, reading books and then writing your opinion about it. That really didn't help with this at all" (Student 39.first-year.2).[1] And while his interview transcripts do not provide evidence of his first-year course having an impact on his writing process (as he said at the end of that course, "I never did a draft"), he credits the course's discussions, peer review, and instructor feedback with expanding his knowledge of social issues, encouraging him to consider other perspectives and radically rethink what it means to support an opinion. The writing sample Student 39 brought to our second interview was his first paper for the first-year course, a personal narrative paper he wrote about the death of a family friend caused by a drunk driver for which he received a B+ and that he recognized drew on skills he had previously used to write his college application essay. But he described the final

"You Should Write to Know What You Don't Know" : 117

paper for this course as his recent unsuccessful experience and said he was generally not alone in having trouble moving from a high school understanding of *a research paper*, which he understood to report factual information from sources, to the understanding of *a researched argument* expected in his first-year course for this paper. Yet this assignment was also the one he described as the most useful recent assignment he experienced because he learned a great deal in the process of researching and writing it. For this assignment, Student 39 chose to write about how the media portray police, a topic near to him as he was considering criminal justice as a possible major, and he brought this paper up in response to a number of my questions. When explaining why this paper felt like a failure to him, he shared that in a conference his first-year course instructor helped him understand that his draft's claim that "the media shouldn't be allowed to say, you know, bad things about police" (Student 39.first-year.2) raised first-amendment issues he had to consider. Student 39 explained that he hadn't realized such issues were pertinent: "I didn't really understand that because, you know, I just went right from the assignment. It said find an argument, so I thought, okay, I don't really—it could be just any argument I want, and, you know, I didn't realize I had to actually take into consideration legal matters" (Student 39.first-year.2). Later, in response to my question about what he thought he would take with him from the first-year course, his response referenced "the difficulty" of this paper and

> how it was kind of like a wakeup call for college in, you know, what's kind of expected of you from now on. Because it really did help to explain, you know, what writings are going to be like in the future. It's not going to be just easy, where you can just say whatever. You need to back up everything. And, the more I kinda looked into that, the more I realized that just my opinion by itself won't be enough to justify what I'm trying to say. You really need to show arguments and research where they prove something, or disprove something. (Student 39.first-year.2)

Student 39 added that in researching for this paper he watched a video available online of the police killing of Eric Garner, an event he "didn't really know much about" at first and thought perhaps might have been justified police action (Student 39.first-year.2). But he told me his research changed his mind and changed his paper:

> I actually researched it, and I looked at the video, and I found that, you know, this guy was actually physically choked to death by a police officer. So, I had to write about how, if, you know, the police were actually at fault

in that. And I kind of changed my perspective of what I thought about that. (Student 39.first-year.2)

He brought up experiences in the course radically altering his perspectives again in response to my asking if he enjoyed his first-year class. He said that though it "was really tough at times" and he would "say to myself that I hated it," on the whole he enjoyed it and that the class

> actually helped me find, see different perspectives of kids. Because I grew up in, like, a very white town where it's literally like 98% white. And, the African American kids in my class helped to give me, like, an actual kind of perspective on, you know, how they've faced, you know, racial prejudice and stuff. (Student 39.first-year.2)

Suffice it to say, in the final days of this course, Student 39 credited it a great deal with altering his perspective on important social issues like racism, inviting him to not only rethink what it means to write an effective argument but rethink and question topics in ways counter to the perspectives espoused in his home community.

These significant developments in what I think it is fair to call Student 39's capacity for critical thinking, what so many proponents of such a course hope it can inculcate in students, are developments Student 39 went on to claim in later interviews he successfully transferred in writing for other courses. In his second year of college, he claimed what he learned in the first-year course about supporting his claims rather than merely asserting his opinions transferred to writing he did in a history course he took the semester after completing the first-year course and in a criminal justice course in his sophomore year. For his 20th-century History course he was asked to analyze the film version of George Orwell's *Animal Farm*, a paper he recalled receiving an A– on. He told me he was "so relieved when they told us about how we're going to be writing an analysis like this because that's kind of what we did in this writing class," referring to the first-year course (Student 39.soph.3). He explained, the "writing class helped me structure it better" and "it helped me get the thesis straight" and "it was good to have the knowledge with the citation pages too" (Student 39.soph.3). The history professor clearly signaled to students that supporting their claims with evidence would be key, or, as Student 39 recounted, "He said, 'Of all things, be sure that you back up all of your statements with facts. Incorporate everything from the book and outside and the film'" (Student 39.soph.3). The practice the first-year course gave him in this provided a familiarity Student 39 found very reassuring, "I felt pretty

"You Should Write to Know What You Don't Know" : 119

comfortable handing it in" (Student 39.soph.3). He shared this paper with me as his writing sample as well as described it to me as his most recent successful experience with writing. Student 39 explained that the second paper in his first-year course, a rhetorical analysis paper, specifically prepared him for this paper. He looked back on the rhetorical analysis paper as his most recent unsuccessful experience with writing, but one that taught him a great deal. He had read carefully the instructor feedback he got on his rhetorical analysis and recalled the guidance on writing an analysis when writing his history paper the next semester. As he put it, "I feel like if I'd just gone from high school writing to something like this [his history paper], I would have done a lot worse" (Student 39.soph.3).

Student 39 anticipated what he learned about analytic writing and argumentation in his first-year course would help him write a research paper for the criminal justice course he was taking when we spoke during his sophomore year. He understood that for this paper what was required was "backing up your opinion or view on a certain point" and in this he found it "like the rhetorical analysis we had to do in the writing class" (Student 39.soph.3). He had already confirmed this hunch with the course's graduate teaching assistant: "I even asked my teaching assistant if this is more of a rhetorical analysis, and she said that, yes, it is, because you're explaining your viewpoint while also providing facts to back it up" (Student 39.soph.3). While "rhetorical analysis" may not be the most apt genre description for this criminal justice paper, the need to support reasoned claims with evidence is clearly a practice the TA tried to signal to him he should carry over, and this is a practice Student 39 continued to credit the first-year course in helping him understand and carry out. During this sophomore-year interview, Student 39's advice for first-year students writing their first college paper was to understand "it's not anything like you did in high school" because "you can't just state your opinion and just keep going with it like in a high school essay where, you know, you could get away with that. In college, they really need you to . . . prove that and back it up" (Student 39.soph.3).

Interestingly, Student 39 brought up his view that critical thinking is essential in our final interview, the year after he graduated, in response to my last question asking if, knowing my interest in learning from college students about their experiences with writing, he had anything to add or anything to suggest to those who teach writing that hadn't already come up in our conversation. For some context, this conversation was carried out using online video conferencing because we met in the early first summer days of the COVID-19 pandemic, a time of intense political polarity on public health and racial justice (the police killing of George Floyd having occurred just a month before we spoke). Gesturing to these recent events, Student 39 wanted to share with me his views on the importance of digging deep into issues with analysis, supporting views with facts, and considering other perspectives. He said,

> The one thing that I think has really gotten under my skin since I've started college is everyone is a sort of critic, but no one really get—no one's—how do I explain this? So it's really like the political climate and everything. And everyone sees one single thing on social media. They read the headline of it, and then they tell someone else, "Oh, my God. You know, this, this, and that." But the question is, did you read it? Do you understand it? And then you can start having your opinions and stuff and so on. But I feel like a lot of people just read sort of what's on the surface, and they don't read into it. They don't think about it, or they don't look at—especially, they don't look at it from the other side. And I think that's, you know, it's unfortunate because regardless of whether you agree or disagree, you do have to remember, you know, you live and you work with people who see the world differently. So, you should look at it from the other side. (Student 39.post.6)

He said he wanted to share these views with me because he felt that

> kids don't really do that anymore. And I think it's from a lack of willingness to sort of dive into it deeper and really get the, read the nitty-gritty of it and be able to understand it in a way that you can have a better discussion of it. And I feel like especially now kids are sort of afraid to even take that step, because they don't—they want to avoid conflict altogether. But it doesn't have to be that way. So, I just wish kids would read a little bit more critically. . . . I feel like a lot of people just look at sort of the surface of it and don't look any further than that. (Student 39.post.6)

I see strong implicit connections between these comments calling for students to practice critical thinking and the comments he made in interviews during his first 2 years of college about what he learned and gained in his first-year course. That learning that got "under my skin since I've started college" (Student 39.post.6), stayed with him after college, and in turbulent times he saw the continued need for imparting it.

However, for all that Student 39 credited his first-year course with helping him argue in a nuanced and sophisticated manner in his history and criminal justice courses, in his sophomore year he also began to recognize some differences in disciplinary conventions for writing in these courses that his first-year course did not help him anticipate. During this interview when I asked if there was anything college writing instructors could do to improve their instruction, he said in his current criminal justice course "they want me to do, like, footnotes . . . and I have never done a footnote ever. Like, I've heard of, I know what footnotes are. I just really don't know how to incorporate that into an essay at all" (Student 39.soph.3). He said he asked the course TA "all these questions about footnotes, and I'm still really confused about that" (Student 39.soph.3). He pleaded that "it would help if we learned about every, I guess, method of writing, including footnotes and whatever else that we might be unfamiliar to" (Student 39.soph.3).

Student 39's recognition of disciplinary differences became more pronounced in his junior year. A subtle but significant shift in his discussion of writing occurred in his junior-year interview. While he had been taking chemistry and then biology labs since his first year of college, it wasn't until his junior year that he began to discuss the writing he did for them *as* writing in our interviews. That year the writing sample he brought to our interview was from his biology lab, and he described this writing as his recent successful writing experience. What seems to have influenced his coming to see his scientific writing *as* writing was his experience of some biology labs that took this writing very seriously. He described TAs giving students feedback on drafts of lab reports with the expectation that they would revise them. As was the case with other biology students I spoke with (such as Student 48 and Student 45), Student 39 experienced a variety of approaches to writing lab reports over his years of study, from labs that asked for reports that were quite literally worksheets to be filled in to labs like the one he was in junior year that placed a high priority on students learning the conventions of writing in biology, providing in-progress feedback, and promoting student autonomy by asking them to devise their own hypotheses and use and locate relevant secondary research to build a case for the exigence of their experiments (see Baird & Dilger, 2018, for a discussion of the competing approaches to teaching research in the natural sciences—verification vs. inquiry—that it appears these students experienced across different sections). Additionally, when we spoke, Student 39 was also enrolled in a biological anthropology course that provided a rigorous education in reading published scientific studies, teaching him how to summarize them and interpret their visual components.

This increased immersion in both reading and writing IMRAD (Introduction, Methods, Results and Discussion) formatted articles related to biology seems to have heightened Student 39's awareness and understanding of the

122 : "YOU SHOULD WRITE TO KNOW WHAT YOU DON'T KNOW"

significance of stylistic differences between writing in biology and the writing he did for his first-year course. When walking me through the writing sample from his biology lab, he explained to me that in this genre writers need to be very explicit and clear with readers: "You *tell* them, you want to be very clear cut" (Student 39.jr.4). He went on to explain that he recognized this was a stylistic difference from other types of academic writing:

> Where I know in some other essays, they want you to *not* actually explain it, but let the entire paragraphs explain what you want to talk about. But for this specifically, they say they want you very specifically to say this is the experiment you're carrying out. You expect to see this, and be very specific with it. And so there's no room for interpretation. (Student 39.jr.4)

This comment about what readers or teachers want in "some other essays" reminded me of feedback Student 39 had received on his personal narrative essay from his first-year course instructor. The instructor comments written on that essay that he shared as his writing sample in our second interview critiqued the essay for being "too explicit" next to claims he made in its conclusion, which explicitly pushed readers into "making the right decision and not getting in your car after drinking." In our discussion of this comment, I understood the instructor to likely be encouraging Student 39 to follow the adage "show, don't tell," advice Student 39 had followed elsewhere in his narrative and was praised for by his instructor, where he let the details of the story of a family friend's death at the hands of a drunk driver poignantly speak to the injustice of this act. Now Student 39 was recognizing that this adage does not apply to all genres, that explicitness was required in his scientific writing, and thus his decision not to transfer this guidance on writing to his biology labs was appropriate.

This recognition did not lead Student 39 to discount all he learned in the first-year course as such recognitions have led other students to do in this study and others (Bergmann & Zepernick, 2007; Jarratt et al., 2009). He continued to credit the course with greatly helping him in crafting and supporting claims and generally structuring his papers. He continued to draw insights on using transitions to enhance the coherence of his papers' arguments from his first-year course experience. But the recognition seems to have informed a recommendation he left me with at the end of the junior-year interview when I asked as I always did if he had anything further to share with me. This time he responded with the suggestion that his university consider WID-based first-year courses tied to students' majors. As he put it, he thought that in the first-year course they should take into consideration what each of the students—like what they're writing, what type of writing they might be doing in the future. . . . It'd be good to put students, like a group of students who are interested in a certain major or topic, into the same class. . . . Kinda, so like history majors in one class, and then science or whatever. . . . Students have different majors and different things that they want to do, and they're going to have to do different styles of writing for that major. But the thing is they're all being—well, not forced, but like they're all doing one certain style. (Student 39.jr.4)

I asked him what that "one certain style" was he was encouraged to use in his first-year course, and he identified it as "English writing," similar to the writing he did in English in high school. In this he was like Student 48 and others (Bergmann & Zepernick, 2007; Jarratt et al., 2009) who associated first-year composition with the discipline of English and thus questioned the applicability of the guidance it offered to writing in other disciplines, even as he recognized that what he wrote in his first-year course was considerably different from the literary analyses he wrote in high school English courses.

Student 39 still clearly saw value in what he learned in his first-year course and continued to insist on its value in his senior year when he explained that "anytime I write something now, I really do kind of reflect on what we learned in that class" and that what he learned about argument structure in that class is "always in the back of my head whenever I start to write stuff" (Student 39.sr.5).[2] But as he moved more fully into writing in the biological sciences, he craved focused, explicit, and guided attention to scientific writing like he had experienced for writing in the humanities in his first-year course. In his postgraduation interview he also called for a WID writing course, though now he wonders if it could perhaps supplement rather than replace the first-year course as he experienced it:

> I think I've mentioned this to you before, but I still stand by it. I think it would be really great to have, obviously, the general [first-year course] that everybody takes, but I also think it would be a good idea, as, maybe, a follow-up, you take one that's more relevant to your major or the field you want to go into. So you would have a [first-year course] relevant to maybe sociology or to business or science or along those lines so that this way you have sort of the groundwork from the first one, and then the second one you take maybe sort of sets you down the path, so that you're more familiar with writing that you might be doing in the future, or at least, how to read and dissect things that are relevant to your career path. I feel like today, that no matter what you do, you're going be writing to some degree. Any of the

majors at this school, you're going to have to write to someone somewhere along the line. So I think that'd be really cool to have a sort of follow-up class. (Student 39.post.6)

Student 39 explained that he longed for such a class that would focus on and explicitly unpack writing in the sciences because the trial-and-error approach he experienced, one where he felt it was assumed he already knew the conventions of writing in the sciences and one where he had to fail in early assignments in order to get feedback he could decipher and apply in later assignments, was stressful. As he put it,

> You don't know how to write lab reports or science papers until you get the ones you hand in back. And when you're a freshman and you're taking a college-level lab course for the first time, it's not pretty. Like, they mar—and, you know, they're not nice about it. They'll mark you down for whatever because that's the expectation they have for you, and they want to tell—let you know that for a college level, this is the type of lab reports and writing that they expect from you. So, and it's funny, there's sort of a learning curve with it where the first one or two labs you hand in it, they're marked up like crazy. And then when you review it, you understand better. Oh, okay, this is what I need to do. (Student 39.post.6)

Our final interview, when he reflected back on the difficulty of his first labs, was held during the first year of his MS program in biology, a degree he decided to pursue before applying to medical school because of his experience working for course credit in his genetics professor's lab. In fact, a project he began as an undergraduate in that lab was about to become the basis for his MS thesis. In this interview, Student 39 spoke of his scientific reading and writing with remarkable rhetorical sophistication, showing signs of the development of this rhetorical knowledge of scientific writing from previous interviews. For example, while as a junior, Student 39 was aware that his biology labs required a clearer, more direct style than the narrative writing he did in his first-year course, in our final interview he showed added awareness that this style wasn't only used to make readers' work easier but also as an ethos appeal:

> You have to be very clear with that because there's a big stigma with a lack of clarity, it becomes sort of untrustworthy in the sense that it's, like, what are you hiding, or what did you not include? Maybe something didn't work, and you don't want to show that. So you have to be very transparent and put it all in very plain text for everyone to see. (Student 39.post.6)

In this interview he demonstrated understanding of science as a communal and rhetorical enterprise, one where studies build upon each other but where the need for replication for sound science is in tension with the need for originality in order to be published, and publication is "everyone's goal" (Student 39.post.6). Indeed, he hoped to eventually publish his thesis and was proud to be listed as a middle author on a paper emerging from his professor's lab that was being sent out for peer review. He explained to me the significance of author name order on such publications ("it's not really a coauthor. It's more like I helped on his project") and like other scientists used the term "papers" to describe these publications ("I'm saying 'papers' just because that's what I always read now"; Student 39.post.6). He explained how previous papers are cited in the beginning of a new paper to both show the progress of science and exigence for the current project, using terms similar to those Swales (1990) did in his genre analysis of research article introductions:

> A big, big portion of the research is—before you even get to the lab stuff is background and knowing how you want to structure it. And a big part of that is reading what's already been published and sort of being able to pick parts of that that you think are relevant to what you want to do and sort of restructure that in a way that you write it down. You know, this is what I want to do, and based on someone who already did something similar, I'm going to follow a similar path but do this differently. And then you have to put that into writing and be able to explain that to someone else who doesn't really know much about it. So the purpose being you know the most about your own research more than anyone else because it's your own, but the idea is to be able to explain it to a very broad audience of people who have an idea—you know, may be familiar with it, but you have to sort of hold their hand and get them to follow the same steps that you took. (Student 39.post.6)

Clear influences supporting his increased rhetorical awareness of scientific writing apparent in the transcript of this final interview are his move to reading scientific articles for the purposes of his own primary research and his immersion in the culture of a working lab where he learned from listening to experienced scientists and graduate students speak about their writing and received mentorship from them. Student 39 himself recognized that he began to read differently when his reading was motivated by his own desire to contribute to this research:

> Every once in a while, I would read, if there was a really interesting one that was published about something relevant. I would read it, but I didn't

really appreciate it as a scientific paper as much as just, like an article. I still looked at it as just a plain text article, and not that there was any method to it. But once I was in my senior year of college and I started having to read scientific papers for my own project, then I understood better how to read in a way that I could get the information quickly and pick out relevant information for my own work. (Student 39.post.6)

In this description of targeted reading, Student 39 sounds somewhat like the expert scientists Charney (1993) observed reading who did not read linearly and used text features like abstracts and subheadings to more quickly and critically ferret out what they saw as the key information from a text. Student 39's observations of scientific writers in his genetics professor's lab seems to have greatly influenced his writing process. While in the first year of college he professed to never writing drafts, he now claimed, "There's not a single person I know that just writes something down, first try, has no one look at it, and then sends it out. I would imagine that's, like, a recipe for disaster" (Student 39.post.6). He now identified as a writer primarily because in observing his genetics professor, who had become a mentor, he observed how central writing was to his scientific work:

He writes the majority of his time. When he comes in, he's writing for grants and for papers to be reviewed and stuff. And, you know, that's his profession, and he has to get funding for his lab, so it's really important to him. And I think seeing the stress that he puts on writing sort of imprinted on me how important it is to be able to write well and to get other people to see things the way you see, or at least to give that idea to them so that they can understand it and ultimately, ideally you want them to agree with you and say, "Oh, you know, you're right, and I see it the same way you do." (Student 39.post.6)

Student 39 also revealed that in preparation for medical school he had "shadowed" some physicians and learned in doing so about their uses of writing. Observing doctors prepare audio-recorded patient notes for later transcription by someone else taught him that for these notes "you do have to know in your head how you would want it written down" (Student 39.post.6). The writing sample he shared during this interview was the statement he used to apply to medical schools, and in it he discussed the importance of successful communication in a physician's work, expressing his own desire to be a physician who communicates simply, clearly, informatively, and impactfully while "taking into consideration" his patients' "diverse backgrounds."

In this we may see some braiding together of what he learned about critical thinking and alternative perspectives in his first-year course and the discipline-specific styles of his biology major.

In Student 39's experience we can see the life-altering impact of his first-year course experience in his development as not only a student writer but as a person. Even after college, he extolled the course's importance to his development as a writer and critical thinker and saw the continued need for entering college students to have such an experience. The way the course expanded his perspective beyond that of his predominately white home community and changed his thinking about race is life altering and represents incontrovertibly, I would think, what all stakeholders hope a college education can provide. That he had this experience in a required, general education course is important to recognize, even as such insights could potentially be obtained in other courses. Student 39's interest in science and motivation to settle on a major after some consideration of options may have meant he never would have had this experience if it wasn't required. Indeed, before this course was instituted as a requirement, many students' writing-intensive courses may have been much like Student 39's biology labs, providing only discipline-specific writing guidance.[3] Equally important, Student 39's personality and beliefs about knowledge and schooling may have predisposed him to value the first-year course even if required (Driscoll & Wells, 2012), seeing it as connected to his reasons for attending college (Driscoll, 2011) and feeding his omnidirectional interest in connecting knowledge gained across disparate courses (Driscoll & Jin, 2018).

However, WID advocates and those who question the first-year course universal imperative can also find in his experience evidence for the limits of that course in helping him develop as a writer in his major, where the experiential education of a working lab with its social interactions, observations, and apprentice-style instruction transformed his understanding of scientific writing as being not only *writing* but a highly rhetorical enterprise. As he absorbed this experience, he deemed some of the adages of the first-year course as inappropriate in this context. Previous research (Baird & Dilger, 2018; Falconer, 2022; Haas, 1994; Lerner & Poe, 2014) has well documented the importance of the lab experience in developing in undergraduates a rhetorical scientific consciousness, so Student 39's experience can stand as one more illustrative example. Student 39's ability to recognize the affordances and limits of what his first-year course had to offer is not always seen in participants in this study or others (see Bergmann & Zepernick, 2007; Jarratt et al., 2009). His first-year writing course, his apprenticeship in a working lab, the feedback he received on his writing from any instructor willing to provide it, the mentorship his degreed aunt and uncle provided on his writing and on navigating academia, all these influences and more came to shape his sense of agency (Driscoll & Jin, 2018) to pick and choose where and when it was rhetorically appropriate to transfer learning—to keep alive and apply where appropriate the humanistic and civic lessons of his first-year course and the conventions and communal practices of the biological sciences, and to even recognize that he was making these choices.

Student 48: The Disciplinary and the Disciplining Are Personal

Over 5 years I got to know Student 48, a biology major and sociology minor, as an animated and dedicated student and writer. She dutifully came to all but her senior-year interview. I observed some of her beliefs and practices associated with writing that she brought into college carry with her throughout her college years and beyond and some of her beliefs and practices take dramatic turns. For all that remained consistent in her views on writing, our regular meetings also illustrate, I believe, the importance of longitudinal work in facilitating the rapport that takes time to build between researcher and participant. Our final interview, in the year after she graduated, shed entirely new light on aspects of previous interviews dating back all the way to her first year of college that would otherwise have remained opaque to me.

As so many other participants did, Student 48 proudly brought to our first interview her college entrance essay, a two-page essay that described hearing loss she experienced as a young child and her determination to overcome misperceptions and obstacles set up against her since then or, as she described this essay to me,

> I wear hearing aids, so it's about the way the hearing aids made me want to be more ambitious and achieve more in life, and, you know, it's more about my dreams and ambitions and definitely like a more personal essay. (Student 48.first-year.1)

In it, she describes regularly challenging her teachers' and speech therapists' sense of her limitations by earning academic recognitions, volunteering to help those with disabilities, and learning to play violin, guitar, clarinet, and piano. She described her desire to go to medical school so she could "treat every patient as a 'normal person' and share my principle that there are no limitations in life."

In our first interview she described this college entrance essay as her recent successful writing experience and one she enjoyed writing a good deal. She described working closely with a high school English teacher on her statement, reading her drafts at her teacher's desk and taking into consideration her teacher's feedback, a process she described as very different from her typical writing process because typically she preferred to write alone and did not seek out others' feedback. In this she was like so many of her peers who told me their college entrance essay, because of its perceived high stakes, was the first (and sometimes last) time they engaged deeply in a process of writing and revising drafts in response to feedback. Student 48 disliked the firm length limit set for the college entrance essay, but she liked the opportunity to write about her own experience, in contrast to the argument writing assignments she experienced more frequently in high school. Her less successful experience she described as her AP English exam because of the constraint of the time limit.

Constraints placed on her writing, like these length and time limits, recurred as something she bristled against in all our other interviews, as did her fondness for writing about her personal experience. In most interviews she projected a sense of knowing herself as a capable writer, though not one likely to seek out writing on her own. She often mentioned her custom of writing complaint letters to businesses and being rewarded for the effort with goods or services. She was proud of the efficacy and politeness of her email- and letter-writing practices, which she put to use in her sophomore year by undertaking a leadership role in her sorority's various philanthropic activities. More than once in the annual interviews, when I asked if she identified as a writer, she said she "probably could write a book" (Student 45.first-year.1) but was unlikely to do so if not motivated. Her favorite writing assignments gave her such a motivation to write and a chance to express herself or share her original research, without making all the decisions of form and rhetorical purpose for her—she repeatedly bristled against length minimums and limits and guidelines that she felt overly constrained her choices.

Two other constant refrains I heard each year I spoke with her were the utility she found in a technique a high school teacher shared with her for calculating how many subtopics to plan for when writing a paper and her sense of the lack of utility for her of peer review. In our first interview she was eager to share with me the planning technique she had learned in high school; in fact, it was the first thing she mentioned in response to my first question on writing advice she would give to a new college writer:

130 : "YOU SHOULD WRITE TO KNOW WHAT YOU DON'T KNOW"

> I would say to not be too superfluous about what they're writing, you know, kind of stick to the idea of what the topic is about. And in fact I wrote a paper for another class last semester and I told the professor an idea that I learned in high school. It's a technique of writing long papers. If you have a five-page paper, you have the intro and the conclusion, two paragraphs, now let's see you do two paragraphs per page, so—because around 6–8 sentences is about half the page, double-spaced, so you, well, you do five times two, that's ten, but then you take away for the intro and conclusion, so you have like eight body paragraphs to write, and then you kind of just write down eight ideas, and you don't have to do all of them because sometimes one paragraph might be longer than the other, but just to start out with eight ideas, and then see what you end up with. (Student 48.first-year.1)

Student 48 brought up this method for calculating the number of subtopics to plan to address again in all interviews through her sophomore year, each time presenting it as helping her not overwrite, which she claims is her tendency, and to make the potentially daunting task of a longer paper appear more manageable and thus helping her avoid anxiety and writers' block.

Her attitudes toward peer review seemed rather constant over all the years of the study, too. In our first interview she said she had experienced peer-review activities in high school, and she said that while routinely "a lot of people come to me" for feedback on their writing,

> I don't really rely on other people so whatever someone said, if they said like, oh, that sentence, I would look at it but in the end, if I was confident with it, I wouldn't take it out, I wouldn't change it. I trust myself with my writing. (Student 48.first-year.1)

After experiencing peer review in her first-year course, she again stressed "I kinda just trust myself with my writing. I don't really trust others" (Student 48.first-year.2). She repeated such comments, emphasizing that editing for grammar and spelling is a strength of hers (and limiting the usefulness of peer review to editing), in each interview through her junior year, when she stated rather definitively, "I don't feel like I ever need peer review" (Student 48.jr.4).

If her views on planning and peer review remained constant across 6 years, her views on collaboration changed rather dramatically. During our first interview, when I asked if she had ever done any collaborative writing, she told me about her experience with collaboration in writing a paper for a freshman seminar she took the prior semester, one that focused on "bio tech" and asked students to produce a collaborative research paper and poster. She also mentioned a "Socratic seminar" in her AP English class in high school. In both these instances of collaboration, she complained, collaborators did not equally commit to putting in the same "effort," which is why now "I'm not like a group work person" (Student 48.first-year.1). Then she smiled and shared that in these early days of the semester, her first-year instructor had indicated he shares her views on collaboration: "My professor for writing now, he doesn't—he hates group work too" (Student 48.first-year.1). About this, she was "kind of glad" and appeared relieved (Student 48.first-year.1). However, during our interview at the end of this semester, she indicated he had put them into groups to collaborate on devising a thesis for their analysis papers on the novel *A Brave New World*, a book she did not enjoy reading and an assignment she did not feel motivated by. In our next interview the following year, she looked back on that experience and explained more fully that he had put them into groups because a lot of students were "struggling" with the analysis paper, but her feelings about collaborative writing remained the same:

> I don't really like group work to be honest . . . I hate writing group work. I just don't like it. If I could kind of abolish it altogether I would. I just do not like it because I have my own ideas, other people have their ideas, and then ideas clash, and then the paper's not good. (Student 48.soph.3)

However, in our fourth interview, during her junior year, her views on collaborative writing changed a great deal. A course in her minor, sociology, required groups to produce a zine together, collaborating on text, visuals, and arrangement. She named this assignment as her recent successful experience in writing. Her group of four students centered their zine on "trans families." Their group included a transgender individual whose contributions Student 48 greatly valued: "It was really awesome to get like his insight into it and actually have some actual hardcore like proof or evidence of what goes on" (Student 48.jr.4). I asked her if this meant she had changed her views on collaborative writing, and she said while she still got annoyed when all group members didn't contribute equally and would choose individual or small groups over large ones, she recognized that this one group member "offered double information than what any one of us could've done, you know? And so, it's pretty cool" (Student 49.jr.4).

Another dramatic change in her writing practice that our interviews documented was in Student 48's use of writing outside of what was required for academic assignments. Throughout college, Student 48 indicated that email communication—which she was proud of her efforts on for her philanthropic work in her sorority and her professional-sounding complaint letters to businesses—was her only significant use of writing outside of what schoolwork required of her. However, in our final interview conducted after she had graduated, when she had settled into work as a lab technician for a neurological institute and was applying to nursing schools, she revealed she had begun keeping a journal. She said she was inspired by a show she had watched and suspected her current regular work schedule meant she found regular free time to devote to it. She found it to be "like you're talking to no one, but you're talking to someone" (Student 48.post.5) and helped her process her experiences in the same way talking to a friend did for her.

Student 48's changing relationship to aspects of writing seem influenced by many experiences and contexts, most notably experiences related to her major and minor. Writing in her sociology minor was extremely important and influential, and she appreciated it most when assignments met her criteria for academic writing she cared about: she wrote of her own experience and had some latitude in how she designed both the experiment and the paper. During her sophomore year she described such a sociology assignment, the one she brought as a writing sample and described as her recent successful writing experience: a paper she wrote for a sociology course in which she was asked to document and reflect on the experience of violating a social norm (she chose to share tables with strangers in the campus library). This example begins to make clear that what Student 48 means by writing about her own experience includes academic experiences, such as experiments in sociology and in biology. In her junior year, she told me about writing she did for work associated with a professor's lab (not a lab course but a lab she did extracurricular work for starting in her freshman year) that she found "interesting because it's based on information that I've done research on" (Student 48.jr.4). For this writing she claimed to be drawing from, or transferring, writing knowledge associated with arrangement, style, and visual communication from her freshman seminar on "bio tech" (which first introduced her to this lab), the main difference is that now she presented primary research she had a hand in conducting rather than reporting only secondary research conducted by others.

Her reference to this writing presenting primary research as "personal" and highly motivated stood in sharp contrast to a comment she made in the midst of her first year of college: "Writing, for science, I don't really think exists. I've never heard of a professor saying, 'Write something for this class,' especially, I think, just because the classes are too big" (Student 48.first-year.2).

"You Should Write to Know What You Don't Know" : 133

Like other biology majors I interviewed, her lab reports moved from fillable worksheets to longer, more professional papers over the course of 4 years. Her ongoing work in the professor's lab was also highly influential in her evolving understanding of writing. While she spoke negatively about the pedagogical practice of peer review every time I saw her, in her junior year she also spoke positively of getting feedback from the PI of this lab and her lab partner on an outline for a paper presenting her work in this lab that she was preparing. Understanding that Student 48 braided together her sense of the personal with "hands-on" (Student 43.soph.3) research, it makes sense that she began keeping a personal journal during her first year of full-time employment in a lab. She wanted to tell friends about what she was experiencing in the lab and in other parts of her life, and when friends were not available, she turned to the journal to document and share.

As has been documented with other students (Haas, 1994; Lerner & Poe, 2014), Student 48's work in a lab contributed to her rhetorical education as she came to see writing in the scientific community as *authored*. In her junior year, when discussing working in the lab, she mentioned distinguishing between first- and second-tier scholarly journals and had a clear awareness of a scientific review article as a genre separate from a research paper. She spoke with the graduate students in this lab about their work publishing papers and was excited she might be listed as a second author on a paper presenting research she contributed to. The line from her positive experience writing a personal narrative at the start of her first-year course to her writing up original research in the context of the lab looks in retrospect like a straight one. About her personal narrative, she had said:

> I mean, my first paper was a successful one, and it was interesting just because I've never really written a narrative before, so it's almost like you're telling a story, so I had to say it from the third person. Well, actually, from the first person 'cause I got to say "I" and, you know, "me." (Student 48.first-year.2)

And, 3 years later, about her scientific paper emerging out of her lab work, she said in comparison to her freshman seminar paper:

> This one's going be my information. So, I'm definitely going to have more of a say on—like, I won't have to use as many references because it's going to be my actual information that I've done the research on. It'll definitely be longer. I'll have my own charts and pictures and whatnot. So, it's definitely more on a *personal* level rather than the other one was kinda like, "Well, this person

said this, and that person said this," and . . . I'm definitely going to be using some secondary resources, . . . but, again, this'll be a more *personal* paper. I can use "I" more frequently, and just like less references that I'll have to put in there. It won't be as reference heavy. (Student 48.jr.4, emphasis added)

For Student 48, telling the story of her life and the story of her work on the lab are alike in that she gets to acknowledge herself as the author of the knowledge. Like Rachel, the psychology student in Herrington and Curtis's (2000) longitudinal study, the personal and the disciplinary are tightly intertwined for Student 48, and presumably many other students, too, putting into question a tendency in writing studies to see personal writing as sharply distinct from disciplinary or "academic" writing.

Yet despite Student 48's positive recollections of the personal narrative assignment during the semester she wrote it, Student 48's assessment of her experience in the first-year course took a notably sharp negative turn during her sophomore year. This turn puzzled me for years. At the end of the first-year course, she described her experience as largely positive with the one complaint that she did not care for *Brave New World* and thus struggled with the assignment to analyze it. At that time, because she forgot to bring it with her to our interview, she promised to send me her personal narrative, which she had described with such clear pride. However, I did not hear from her again for 3 months, when she sent me instead the research paper titled "Environmental Risk Factors for Breast Cancer in BRCA 1 and BRCA 2 Carriers" that she wrote at the end of her freshman seminar the previous semester. This was also a paper she was clearly proud of and had referenced in our first interview and again in later interviews. But she offered no explanation for why she decided not to send the paper she originally intended to from her first-year course. In our next interview in her sophomore year, she was much more negative in her assessment of the utility of the first-year course, including the personal narrative assignment, which she says looking back on was the only assignment she enjoyed but whose guidelines she found annoying and made it "like I don't even want to write it anymore because I can't even write what I want to write. I have to write it based on what he wants" (Student 48.soph.3). She had expressed satisfaction with writing the narrative her way during the first interview, so this truly puzzled me.

An explanation I came to that I found somewhat satisfactory is that perhaps she was upset with the grade she received for her personal narrative or for the course and had only learned of the grade in the time between our second interview and the third. In the second interview she told me she didn't know what grade she received on it because she had "never checked," but she was confident "from what he said, it was a good paper," one she was proud of "thinking outside the box" in (Student 48.first-year.2). At the time I told her I was surprised that near the end of the semester she still had not inquired about the grade of her first paper. She explained, "I like to check everything at the end" (Student 48.first-year.2) because checking throughout a course gave her anxiety. The turn from appreciating the freedom of this assignment to complaining about its instructor guidelines made me suspect she had learned in the interim that the grade she received was accompanied by strictures highlighting guidelines she had not met, and this colored her recollections of what she originally presented as a positive, empowering experience. Her attitude when asked to recollect the first-year course in our fourth interview, during her junior year, was similar. Though all my questions focused on writing, she did not refer to the first-year course in answering them unless prompted. When pressed, she said the course was not one she was drawing from in her writing today because rather than "genuinely learning how to write anything" (Student 48.jr.4), she saw the course focused on her interpretation, and this is something she had come to be convinced is not something that can be assessed objectively. Her recollections of the course were of being confused with the goal of assignments and disliking the group work; as she put it, "definitely not my groove here" (Student 48.jr.4).

However, our final interview, held the year after she graduated, shed an entirely different light on her feelings about the first-year course. During that interview, she revealed that she felt she had been accused of plagiarism by her first-year instructor on one of his assignments. She brought this up midway through the interview as soon as I brought up the topic of early college writing in my annual question asking her what advice she would give to a beginning college writer. Her advice was to "write what you want to write and don't follow the standard" (Student 48.post.5). She connected this advice to what "I think I've told you in the past," her disagreement with professors setting "standards" such as paper length and other matters of form, but she also said she gave this advice because "there are a lot of professors that want you to follow their standard explicitly, and then you might get penalized for it" (Student 48.post.5). After explaining to me how important it was to her that her decision to follow the IMRAD structure in the writing sample she shared this year was her choice rather than an instructor "mandate," she then made a causal connection between such mandates and accusations of plagiarism:

136 : "YOU SHOULD WRITE TO KNOW WHAT YOU DON'T KNOW"

"I think . . . when we have these mandates . . . we see a lot of cases of plagiarism" (Student 48.post.5). She explained that while there are certainly "a lot of cases" of "direct plagiarism where a student will just copy and paste" (Student 48.post.5), there are also other instances where an instructor believes plagiarism has occurred when in fact the instructor's assignment design so constricted student choices that some appearance of plagiarism—of student texts looking so similar as to appear to be plagiarized—is inevitable. And being accused of this type of appearance of plagiarism is something she experienced. Or as she put it:

> STUDENT 48: I know I personally experienced it where I would write something that I did not copy from anyone. I didn't ask anyone for their ideas, and someone else will have a very similar paper, and the teacher would say, "Well, you know, what is this?" And it's like, "Well, you asked us the same question. You asked us to have this—to follow the same guidelines. You're bound to run into two or more of very similar papers."
>
> LAURA: Yeah, that makes sense. So that happened to you? Did the instructor accuse you of copying or somehow some academic dishonesty?
>
> STUDENT 48: Yeah, I mean, not to a point where he was threatening to go to, you know, the dean but, uh, he definitely point— . . . It was in freshman year. It was the [first-year writing] class. He pointed it out. And it was a few of us and one of the people involved was a person that, you know, it was my best friend, and we always sat together in class. So obviously, they can look at. But you know, rest assured, neither one of us ever on the side talked about the paper or asked each other for ideas. And I think that needs to change. I think English teachers need to expect that if they're going to ask the same question to 50 students and they're going to require the same mandates, then they're going to get a lot of the same things. (Student 48.post.5)

She indicated the assignment was the analysis of *Brave New World*, the assignment that during the first-year course she had explained to me had given lots of students difficulty—difficulty the instructor responded to by placing students into groups to devise a thesis together that they would share but write individual papers supporting. At the end of our interview, when I always invited participants to tell me what I should have asked about or what they still wished to say about their experience with writing in college, Student 48 returned to this experience, indicating that she hoped sharing it with me might lead to instructional practices allowing for more student freedom of choice in paper design and fewer acquisitions of plagiarism of the kind she experienced.

"You Should Write to Know What You Don't Know" : 137

Her sharing this experience forced me to reevaluate the ways she had talked about the first-year course in previous interviews and to see a new reason for her souring on its usefulness in our third interview. Prior to the third interview, plagiarism came up only once, during our first interview when she explained how in writing her freshman seminar paper she assiduously cited her sources to avoid accusations of it. She made no mention of plagiarism at all during our interview near the end of her first-year course. But during our interview during her sophomore year, when chaffing against writing assignment specifications on page counts, she said she feels

> that's when students start to plagiarize because then they're just trying to get anything and anything possible that they can get their hands on. I think that's not great because we don't want students to plagiarize, but then what choice do they have when it comes to having to just fill in the blank? (Student 48.soph.3)

Whereas earlier I had suspected she learned of a lower-than-desired grade in the first-year course between our second and third interviews, I now suspected she had (perhaps additionally) had the experience of the insinuation of plagiarism between those two interviews and as a result had changed her earlier view of the course as being inspiring and useful if sometimes annoying and unclear in its utility to her future.

The insinuation of plagiarism, even if not penalized or taken further, left a lasting sting—it was really the only thing about the course she spoke of with any vividness during our final interview. I am left wondering if she waited over 4 years to tell me out of embarrassment. I can now see in our third interview she strongly hinted at a possible accusation of plagiarism, but I didn't hear it until our final interview, when she was more explicit about it. Her words were ambiguous enough that I also do not know if she did technically plagiarize or if she had a valid point about a collaborative group asked to work together to pursue the same thesis and work within the same constraints may produce strikingly similar results. But I am left thinking of the weight of that insinuation that she carried for years and wanted to make sure I heard in our final interview in the hopes of inspiring change. I am left hoping that in this she may be right—that we need to understand the long-term painful, discouraging impacts of such insinuations, that, as instructors, our emotions around this issue may run strong (Robillard, 2007), but we can aim to make assignment guidelines have meaning rather than arbitrariness for our students and treat patchwriting and collusion as opportunities for teaching (Howard, 1995),

138 : "YOU SHOULD WRITE TO KNOW WHAT YOU DON'T KNOW"

not policing (Zwagerman, 2008). Student 48 let me know from our first meeting that she was not one to let roadblocks instructors set before her deter her; I am not so sure all her peers could be as strong.

Student 51: Dividing (and Not Doing) Personal Writing and Academic Writing

I still have many questions about Student 51's views and beliefs about writing after coding and reflecting upon our interview transcripts, so much so that I feel I have to write this case study to explore them further. I hope that sharing the experiences she shared with me can enlist others in helping to make sense of the ways academic writing disappointed someone who so strongly identified as a writer. Unlike Student 48, Student 51 erected strong walls between academic writing and personal writing. Her views on writing seemed to change very little over her college years. She wrote quite a lot for school but opted to keep her engagement in these writing projects minimal. Self-sponsored writing she did for creative pleasure ever retreated in her review mirror but remained a steadfast signpost for her identity.

Student 51 shared aspects of her biography that returned like touchstones over our five interviews. She was born in Nigeria. Her family moved to the US when she was 9 years old. Her mother frequently conjured memories of her from her early childhood in Nigeria, a time that became hard for Student 51 to recollect. In her mother's memories, Student 51 was a precocious writer—talented and interested in writing from an early age. Her mother told her that in their Nigerian living room neighbors would find "pencils and papers everywhere" (Student 51.soph.3) because of her interest in writing, whereas she thought her interest in writing didn't begin until they moved to America. Her mother correcting her memory affirmed for her that "writing has always been part of me. That's just how I express myself, before education" (Student 51.soph.3). Student 51 vividly recalled, after moving to the US, sitting in a church located a block from her family's house in the Bronx and writing stories that she shared with her friends and family. She described this as the only time in her life when she involved others in her writing process, sharing drafts and seeking feedback. When we first met, she shared this memory in response to my question of if she involved others in her writing process:

> No, I mean not like in terms of writing essays. Just in terms of like when I was younger and church was boring, and I would write little stories and then I would show my friends and they would be like, "Oh my gosh, you need

to keep on writing it," and then I just get bored and I'd just write another one the next Sunday. (Student 51.first-year.1)

Each year she shared an anecdote that signaled she sensed her family held a great deal of pride in her writing ability. For instance, she recalled when she was 12, her older brother, "the smartest person I know" and also someone she knew to be "very honest" (Student 51.soph.3), read something she wrote and praised her strongly for it. She said this text was something she wrote when she was "feeling so sad," and that it was "personal writing" but also fictionalized: "It wasn't of me. It was . . . a character I created" (Student 51.soph.3). She shared the piece with him because it "came from my heart" and she thought highly of its quality. She can no longer locate this piece, and its loss saddened her, but her emotions around recollecting it made her think "maybe I can really do something with writing" (Student 51.soph.3). These memories of writing creatively when she was younger tended to come up each time I asked if she identified as a writer, as did her family's pride in her writing ability.

Her family identified her as a strong writer and repeatedly turned to her for support with their own writing. Her older brother turned to her for help with his college application essay, and each time we met she shared with me how she had been helping her mother with her writing for nursing school. These memories contributed to Student 51's strong sense that writing is a part of her identity, both in the past and possibly in the future. During our first interview she explained, "I always get something out of every writing experience because when you write you're literally thinking, and you're writing, you're learning more things" (Student 51.first-year.1). In her junior year, when I asked her if she saw herself as a writer, she answered by again explaining that writing is intertwined with her ways of learning; to understand something, she writes about it. In the way that others are "visual learners," she is a "writing learner . . . I write to learn it" (Student 51.jr.4).

From our first meeting in her second semester of college onward she described herself as a self-sufficient writer—she never asked instructors or peers for feedback on her writing, in part because she felt her interest and passion for writing prior to her schooling had shaped her into a complete writer, someone who already knew how to write, or at least knew more than her peers. In fact, in our first interview she described as an unsuccessful experience her experience writing her college admissions essay because her high school English teacher played too great a role in shaping it, and, as a result, "it was just cliché. I wish I took more responsibility in actually writing it. I think it would have been better" (Student 51.first-year.1). Like many other participants, she indicated she did her best writing when she was interested in the topic assigned. In our first interview, when asked what she would recommend universities do to improve students' writing, she said instructors should get to know their students and their interests because "writing is supposed to be something fun, and it's also supposed to be a way to understand the world around you" and students will be more likely to have such an experience if they care what they are writing about (Student 51.first-year.1).

However, after our first interview, when she said she still wrote creatively in her free time, Student 51 said in every interview she was not writing outside of her schoolwork anymore. Even in our first interview she suggested she was falling away from the practice, she "can't bring myself to write" the stories in her mind because the perfectionism she places on her writing makes the challenge seem insurmountable, and the demands of writing in college leave her with little time or energy for it (Student 51.first-year.1). One way her perfectionism was revealed was in response to my question in each interview asking her to define good writing. She regularly named the works of popular, published literary authors as exemplars of good writing, and described writing that is "beautiful" and has an "impactful voice" (Student 52.first-year.1), thus setting a high standard she felt she did not (yet) meet. But a longing to write came up every year. In her sophomore year, she declared "I intend on writing a book" but was "scared" the "competitive" nature of book publishing might hurt her stories that feel to her "kind of like family," and this fear was "part of the reason why I don't write it" (Student 51.soph.3). She recognized the perfectionism that was blocking her writing paradoxically prevented her from improving as a writer: "I think I have the potential to be a great writer, like, a really great writer, but I'm not honing my skills, so I would say I'm an average writer" (Student 51.jr.4). Even in her final year of college she felt inspired by her recent favorite shows *Atlanta* and *Insecure* and her sense that "right now society, as it should be, is thirsty to see a perspective from minority people" to try to turn "a story in my head right now that I've had since high school" into a script (Student 51.sr.5).

This passion for writing she expressed as entwined with her home identity and sense of self stand in marked contrast to her discussion of her academic writing from which she stridently separated her sense of self. What she told me near the end of her first-year course seems to hold true throughout her entire college experience: "I try to disconnect myself from my writing because writing can be very personal and you don't really want it to be personal like

"You Should Write to Know What You Don't Know" : 141

when you're doing academic stuff" (Student 51.first-year.2). Her disconnection did not mean she didn't do much academic writing—on the contrary, most years Student 51 talked about doing a good deal of academic writing. Nor did she shy away from difficult topics in her school writing; the writing samples she shared contained papers that tackled sophisticated academic topics, such as her first-year philosophy paper on Thomas Hobbes and her junior-year political theory paper on Plato. Her sophomore year, when she took mainly courses to prepare her for a possible business major, stood out for how little writing she did. But by her junior year she had settled on a political science major and was back to doing a lot of writing. Yet in our final interview the disconnection she earlier identified seemed just as pronounced, if not more so: "I don't care about any of these papers I submit academically. As long as they get a good grade, it's fine" (Student 51.sr.5).

This lack of care didn't mean she didn't consider her readers. She said her tendency was to try to select an angle on any topic she wrote about that her teacher-readers would find interesting or a stance against the grain: "I'm trying to be like not like every other student just because, you know, it can get boring to say what it is expected of you to say" (Student 51.first-year.2). She did this in part to alleviate her own boredom but also to alleviate her readers' boredom, though, to my surprise, the same semester she took the first-year course she confessed "I don't think the professors read" (Student 51.first-year.2) her papers, but rather the TAs do. (Her first-year course did not have a TA, so this comment suggested to me that when I asked her about her writing for school that semester, she started off mainly thinking of the writing she did for her history, philosophy, and political science classes until my questions specifically prompted her to reflect on her first-year course.)

Her lack of engagement with academic writing seemed to manifest itself most noticeably in her tendency to start writing assignments shortly before they were due. This tendency was with her in her earliest days of college; in our first interview she described her recent successful writing experience as a success because she managed to earn a B+ in her comparative politics class despite the fact that she "waited till the last minute" to write an important paper for it, managing to "crunch it out" and get to class on "three hours of sleep" (Student 51.first-year.1). And it persisted to the end of college when she described writing her 15-page paper for her internship in a state assemblyman's office in 2 days, even though she was aware of the assignment from the start of the semester. In interviews at the end of the first-year course and in her junior year, she even recommended procrastination when I asked what advice she would give to students beginning their first college paper, explaining that this method provides "intense focus" but can be "draining" (Student 51.jr.4).

One strategy she developed for managing the stress of writing under a tight timeline was combing assignment descriptions for clues for content and arrangement. For instance, in her sophomore-year interview, when describing her typical writing process, she shared that she particularly likes when her instructors share in advance their rubrics, especially those that "will tell you what they're looking for" (Student 51.soph.3). She would interpret the rubrics' statements of objectives as a map to sequence her essay:

> Sometimes in the rubrics it tells you the chronological order of how the essay's supposed to be . . . so then you know how many paragraphs you're supposed to put into certain parts just because it's worth more. And so you know how to structure your essay just by looking at the rubric. (Student 51.soph.3)

What made her 15-page paper for her legislative internship on gun control legislation "easy" and her procrastination on it "not so bad" was the "question prompts to answer" that appeared on the assignment sheet (Student 51.sr.5). She said she is a "big fan" of such prompts because they do the work of organizing her ideas and paper for her. Indeed, the subheadings she used in this paper were each connected to a prompting question on the assignment sheet. In this preference for and reliance upon assignment prompts, Student 51 was not alone—each year between one quarter and one half of participants indicated they relied heavily on assignment guidelines and particularly appreciated guidelines that provided outlines or steps for them to follow, sometimes revealing that they used this guidance to bypass process steps in research or writing that it seemed the assignment intended them to accomplish. These behaviors are like those Nelson's (1990) research with student process logs uncovered: students relying upon and even demanding from instructors detailed clarification on writing assignments as a way to bypass process steps such as conducting ethnographic observations (notably, students who performed the intended process steps in Nelson's study sometimes found that the overly detailed guidelines hindered them).

With its curriculum intentionally designed to encourage students to bridge their personal interests with academic inquiry, the first-year course Student 51 took in her second semester would seem to have been an opportunity for her to stitch together her desire to use writing as a personal and creative outlet with her academic work. However, it appears Student 51 refused the invitation to cross this bridge and was actively repelled by her perception of her instructor's insistence that students personally reveal themselves in their writing. When we first met, she had only been to the first two meetings of the class and was optimistic about it. She told me her instructor said

> writing should make you have more questions than what you started off with. So it's like you should write to know what you don't know. And I feel like that's very interesting. I think we're going have to be very analytical with our writing and stuff, so I think it's going be cool. (Student 51.first-year.1)

However, when we spoke at the end of the semester, she told me she didn't think her writing improved as a result of taking the first-year course, she received no useful feedback or advice on writing, and she greatly disliked the "scaffolding" her instructor emphasized, finding activities such as developing "strands" of "binary oppositions" on a topic to "formulate a claim" to be "tedious" and got in the way of her writing process, which she was unwilling to change (Student 51.first-year.2). Some of her confusion about the strategies her instructor was trying to impart may stem from the fact that Student 51 gave up on doing the reading from a course textbook that presented the strategies because she felt the instructor covered the same material in class. The following year, she again stressed that she did not find the strategy instruction in the first-year course helpful, and she did not think it improved her writing. She suspected writers discover the strategies that work for them on their own and that trying to bypass that discovery with strategy instruction isn't effective.

Student 51 indicated she did appreciate the first assignment of her first-year course, an "inquiry into ourselves": "I liked that one because we had to write from a different perspective, and I feel as though I got to understand myself" (Student 51.first-year.2). However, she "tried to not go too personal" or revealing, in part because she didn't want "to be depressing in my writing," even though she sensed her instructor "wanted us to talk about personal stuff, like sob stories," but also in part because of her intention to keep the personal and the academic far apart in her writing (Student 51.first-year.2). But she thought she would carry with her from the course this assignment's asking her to write from another's perspective because it was useful in "expanding the scope" of her thinking (Student 51.first-year.2). Yet in our next interview, during her sophomore year, she indicated she did not enjoy writing in her first-year course and didn't appreciate being "forced" to explore and write about personal and "sad" experiences (Student 51.soph.3). She said she thought her first-year instructor "wanted to get us to look at the universe a little bit different than when we came into the class," and while this goal may have been accomplished with other students in the class, it was "not for me" (Student 15.soph.3).

I searched the transcripts of our interviews for possible reasons Student 51 offered for why, beyond her stated desire to keep the personal and the academic separate in her writing, she so discounted the instruction she experienced in the first-year course (I found it telling that, unlike most other participants who took the first-year course, Student 51 never shared a paper from this course as one of her writing samples). I found two. The first she mentioned during the interview near the end of her first-year course. When I asked her what she saw as the purpose of writing in her college classes, she made a sharp distinction between the purpose in her first-year course and her other "academic" courses that she illustrated with an example from her history class on Vietnam. In the first-year course, Student 51 was encouraged to use an

> argument style where . . . it shouldn't be really, like, harsh. You shouldn't be trying to strike the person down, while in the Vietnam class, the professor was like, "Writing should be about, you know, it's like an argument. It's like you have to strike the persons down." . . . He was so into it. . . . And then she's like, "No, you have to, you know, understand the person's viewpoints and then figure out ways that it can interact." And he's like, "It's either you win or you lose." (Student 51.first-year.2)

In this he said/she said drama, Student 51 recognized a sharp difference between the Rogerian argumentation style emphasized in her first-year course and a more combative stance encouraged by her history professor. Given that the history professor's argumentation preference appears to have been similar to the preferences of her philosophy and political science professors, Student 51 may have discounted the instruction offered in her first-year course because she saw it as contradicting and therefore not helping her in writing in other disciplines. Perhaps tellingly, she brought the paper from her history class on Vietnam as her sample of recent and representative writing to this interview, explaining that she liked how she took a stance that questioned a conventional interpretation of a historical actor.

She revealed a second possible reason during her junior-year interview when she looked back upon her first-year course experience and claimed to not recall anything except receiving a "bad grade" for the final paper of the semester:

"*You Should Write to Know What You Don't Know*" : 145

STUDENT 51: I was doing well in everything and then this paper, I think, got, like, a 70 or something like that which is the lowest grade I've gotten on a paper in this school, and I was, like, "I didn't even think it was that bad." I think my thoughts were all over the place. That was probably why. Maybe she didn't appreciate the art of that.

LAURA: That was somewhat intentional, then, on your part? You meant to sort of cover a lot of ground?

STUDENT 51: Yeah, because the way the assignment was set up, it was supposed to be, like, your personal—it was supposed to be a personal thing. It wasn't an academic paper in the sense where it was really structured so that's why, but it's fine.

LAURA: Were you trying to do something maybe a little experimental or risky and it just didn't work, or—

STUDENT 51: No. I was just trying to be myself and write a paper and write how I felt.

LAURA: Yeah. Well, I'm sorry. That's too bad that didn't—

STUDENT 51: No, it's fine. I don't care anymore. (Student 51.jr.4)

Like Student 48, a first-year course instructor's evaluation of a written performance appears to have left a lasting sting, a clear memory, even with protests to the contrary about no longer caring.

The bridge her first-year course offered was not the only such offer to support bringing together her academic and personal writing Student 51 appears to have rejected during her college years. During her sophomore year interview, she explained she was writing very little for school as she focused on taking business courses and no longer pursuing self-sponsored writing even as she felt some regret in turning her back on it: "I think I mentioned this before, but that's the problem that I do have with writing. I think it's a reflection of myself, so I think I have a bad habit of, like, I would really, really be invested in something and then I'll just fall off of it" (Student 51.soph.3). The writing sample she brought to this interview was unusual because it was not written in response to a course assignment, by far the most common type of text participants would bring when asked to bring a recent and representative sample of their writing. She explained that the two-page, four-paragraph text she shared in which she mused on the power and limitations of the human mind was written over the summer in response to encouragement from her college counselor to "just write something quick . . . write something for 20 minutes" (Student 51.soph.3). I asked why her counselor asked her to do this, and she

146 : "YOU SHOULD WRITE TO KNOW WHAT YOU DON'T KNOW"

said it was "because I also told her about my writing and the fact that I don't write a lot, or whatever" (Student 51.soph.3). During this same interview, shortly after Student 51 shared this interaction with her college counselor and shared that her intention to write a book felt blocked by her fear that literary writing is highly competitive, I think I found myself moved by motivations similar to her college counselor to depart from my prepared questions and ask if she had ever considered taking a creative writing class while in college. Her response was, "No, definitely not" (Student 51.soph.3). When I asked her why, she responded:

> STUDENT 51: I don't know. I think that the writing class was kind of like a bad experience.
>
> LAURA: The [first-year course] was?
>
> STUDENT 51: Yeah. And if it's anything like that, I definitely wouldn't want to do that. (Student 51.soph.3)

Our two further interviews over the next 2 years show no indication that she reconsidered and took a creative writing course or that she continued the free-writing practice her college counselor encouraged.

Our final interview, held days before she graduated, found her reflecting on her college writing. She was adamant that a theories of globalization class in which they read and wrote about the works of theorists such as Marx and Rousseau that she took the previous semester stood out as an "exception" to her college writing experience and was a class "I really love because I feel like the professor actually cared about what we had to say. He actually cared about our perspective" (Student 51.sr.5). This experience felt "different" to her "because it's like he wanted us to have a voice while we wrote. And I feel like I really cared about that paper because I did have a voice, and I was arguing for something I cared about, and I was just learning and connecting everything together" (Student 51.sr.5). I pressed her on how distinct this really was from her other courses in which she wrote arguments and the courses she took in her first year of college, such as the required first-year course, but she insisted that "this globalization class was probably the only class—the only real—the only class I felt in this way, where I could express myself in the writing" (Student 51.sr.5). It differed from the first-year course because in that course she "just wasn't really that interested in what I was writing about. . . . I think we were supposed to write about something sad or something" (Student 51.sr.5).

After graduation, Student 51 had plans to teach English in Japan and then apply for law school. Both these plans she presented as compromises with her

"You Should Write to Know What You Don't Know" : 147

parents. They approved her going to Japan so long as she had plans to teach, though her real purpose there was to pursue her growing interest in fashion, an interest she nurtured at least since her junior year, when she became the director of member relations for a business student organization devoted to fashion. She still cherished stories she began inventing in high school about the fascinating characters she would observe on the train in her Bronx home and was "excited" to try to return to that writing but also still "scared" because "I just feel like if I write it, it finalizes things. And I think that that's what writing does for me, which is a good thing because it helps me get things done. But then it's like I don't—sometimes I don't think I want the story to be finalized, and I feel like writing about it might finalize it" (Student 51.sr.5). It seemed over the years her creative outlet shifted from writing to fashion, though a nostalgia for writing remained: "That was always something besides the fashion and everything else. I always wanted to tell stories" (Student 51.sr.5).

Unlike the nostalgia expressed by participants in the Wayfinding Project for expressive writing in college (J. Alexander et al., 2020a), Student 51's nostalgia was for expressive writing before higher education, before school even. And unlike the students profiled by Chiseri-Strater (1991) and Roozen (2009b) who maintained high walls between their personal and academic writing during college, Student 51 abandoned her personal writing during college. Student 51 succeeded in college writing by the definition of those who define success as receiving passing grades with minimal expenditure of time. She wrote a great deal about difficult subject matters, but year after year she expressed dissatisfaction in it. Given her perpetual resistance to bringing the personal to her academic writing, I am left unsure what could have helped her have more satisfied feelings of coming to voice like she did in her globalization theory course.

Student 51 remains something of an enigma to me. And in this regard, she reminds me of the enigmatic Francois from Herrington and Curtis's (2000) *Persons in Process* who "seemed to resist giving information" by which his instructors "might gain access to his 'subjective world' and his own sense of identity" (p. 350). This similarity to Francois suggests to me the likelihood of a gulf of culturally embodied knowledge separating white researchers from Black student participants, pinning the conundrum back on researcher ignorance rather than participant mystery. Like the high-performing Black students Kareem (2018) interviewed at a predominately white institution, Student 51 did not name race as a factor influencing her experiences with writing, though, like Kareem, I wonder if its influence may be present nonetheless. Keels (2019) described how many of the Black women in her sociological study of Black and Latinx students' experiences transitioning to college on predominately white campuses undertook a "strategic disengagement" from their campuses' student cultures in response to the microaggressions they endured there. As Keels (2019) put it, the young Black women discussed in her case studies

> entered college with a strong sense of the central role that campus life would play in their present and futures selves. They were completely open to embracing campus life. Early in their first year, however, they and many of the other Black women interviewed found it necessary, in order to persist in their education, to strategically separate their academic identity, or how they understand themselves as students, from their institutional identity, or how they understand themselves as students at that institution. (Chapter 4, para. 2)

Did Student 51—for similar reasons, but reasons she either did not choose to share with me or was not conscious of—author a similar strategic disengagement between her identity as a student and a writer?

Many such questions for me remain, some of which challenge what I see as the key findings of this study. Did the bad grade in Student 51's first-year course that she didn't reveal to me until 2 years later spread a cloud over her experiences with writing in college, one that left her somewhat defensive, like Student 48? Did she perceive the person she revealed in its pages as rejected by her first-year writing instructor? Did Student 51's romanticizing of her childhood writing experiences and strong core identification as an expert writer actually interfere with her writing experiences in college, leaving her distrustful of peer review and uninclined to consider instructor feedback or engage in processes of revision? (For the importance of new college writers seeing themselves as novices, see Reiff & Bawarshi, 2011; Sommers & Saltz, 2004.) If this is the case, then Student 51's strong identity as a writer yet lack of engagement in using early writing process steps for invention stands in contrast to claims I make in Chapter 3 about a possible relationship between identifying as a writer and a willingness to tackle these steps. Or is my interpretation of her persistent procrastination as a lack of engagement incorrect and a sign of my own biases? I share this case study because for every trend in data I report elsewhere, there is a Student 51 that does not fit it.

Concluding Remarks: Identity and Transfer

All three of the participants discussed in these case studies told me again and again over the years of the study that they identified as writers. Student 39's capacious disposition toward the new knowledge and experiences college afforded him helped him take from his first-year writing course practices and attitudes toward critical thinking and cross-cultural communication that he intended to carry with him into medical school and beyond. He developed a strong identification as a budding scientist that helped him identify the limits of the rhetorical education he received in his first-year course and then work to transcend those limits and continue his education in rhetoric and writing while immersed in the disciplinary context of scientific lab work. As the work of Falconer (2022) suggests, his identity as a white man with supportive family members who successfully navigated college before him undoubtedly helped him achieve these gains.

Seemingly incongruously, Student 48's and Student 51's identification as writers appears in some ways to have held them back from transferring knowledge about writing from their first-year writing course in the ways Student 39 did, though the research (Reiff & Bawarshi, 2011; Sommers & Saltz, 2004) on the ways initially accepting a novice identity may support transfer may help explain this seeming incongruity. Student 48, as a person who "wear[s] hearing aids," and Student 51, as a Black Nigerian immigrant, share marginalized identities along with their shared identification as "complete" writers who have figured out writing processes that work for them and that their first-year writing course cannot touch. Or rather, if it did affect them, the first-year writing course seems in hindsight to have only done so negatively, wounding their pride as writers with what they perceived as negative evaluation and suspicion of their abilities. That they entered the course as proud writers suggests the sting of this negative evaluation may have hurt all the more. Drawing from her qualitative research of Latina student writers, Regidor (2023) recently theorized the concept of "literacy trauma," which may be inflicted in writing classrooms, may be recurring and long-lasting, and may disproportionately affect "students who have historically been at the margins of higher education" (p. 11). Such experiences, I think, complicate for writing instructors the message from the literature suggesting students benefit from early novice identifications and learning from failures, including the findings I share in Chapter 3. How do we inform our practice with these findings if what they teach us is that our actions as respondents to student writing can just as likely discourage transfer of writing knowledge and practices, and even do real harm, as they can motivate and support transfer?

Student 39's relative privilege in comparison to Students 48 and 51 likely explains some of the reason why his case study is a story of more and more success, of more and more transfer of writing knowledge, and of more and more doors opening for him (though certainly not without struggle). It did not go unnoticed by me that Student 39 and Student 48 both began college with aspirations of attending medical school but only Student 39 ended college on the road to accomplishing that goal. Student 48 experienced setbacks along the way, briefly considering abandoning the goal of medical school because "my GPA just definitely won't let me in" (Student 48.soph.3) and instead pursuing a career in law enforcement like her father, "a retired cop" (Student 48.soph.3), though eventually settling into a plan to attend nursing school. Her work from her first year of college on in a professor's lab shaped her identity as a scientist and knowledge of scientific genres and writing practices as firmly as did Student 39's extracurricular lab experience, but only Student 39 went on to a graduate program in science and medical school. I think what I am trying to say here is that identity very much matters for a writer's "success," but our identities are micro-multifaceted and work in ways that simultaneously support and inhibit the likelihood that we will embrace and transfer knowledge about writing. Such awareness humbly suggests to me some of the limits of conclusions about the importance of identifying as a writer that I offer elsewhere in this book.

While all three of the participants described in these case studies strongly identified as writers, rejecting the identity of a writer is one of the common threads that connects the experiences of the participants I turn to discuss in the next chapter.

5

"Being Able to Write Things Quickly, Easily"

Low-Self-Efficacy Student Writers' Theories of Writing

> A good writer doesn't make that many mistakes, and gets their ideas on paper, like, one time. (Student 31.first-year.2)

Many longitudinal studies of college writers acknowledge that their findings may not be representative of the wider population of college writers because their findings likely reflect volunteer bias. Their participants, willing to return year after year for interviews and share written work, likely have a greater interest in writing or greater pride in their writing than their peers who did not take up the call to volunteer for such a project. Additionally, as discussed in Chapter 1, most of the larger longitudinal studies have been conducted at exclusive institutions where students tend to come from financially and educationally privileged backgrounds and experiences that help heighten their sense of self-efficacy as writers. For instance, Carroll (2002) remarks that for her study of writing at Pepperdine

> many of our study students, coming from economically advantaged or selective private and public schools, said they thought they were good writers in high school, that they actually liked to write, and several pointed to outstanding high school teachers who had helped them become better writers. In fact, in a survey of the 1994 entering class, 66% rated themselves as above-average writers. (p. 51)

https://doi.org/10.7330/9781646426584.c005

As a result, such studies often conclude as J. Alexander et al. (2020a) do with a call for studies that include writers who have negative emotional reactions to writing (p. 588).

The present study does not escape concern related to volunteer biases. While all participants were initially identified using random-selection methods, only those who took the additional step to respond to an email solicitation to participate in a study of their experiences with writing in college are represented in this study. While my participants may have been vocal about not experiencing the same quality of prior preparation or access to supportive resources as participants in longitudinal studies of writing at institutions of greater privilege (see Chapter 1), the majority of participants indicated they identified as what they called a "decent" writer, able to succeed at high school and college writing tasks by earning passing grades on them. However, a minority of participants stridently denied having an interest in writing or pride in their writing. Indeed, this minority of participants, year after year, described how uncomfortable writing made them and how embarrassed they felt about their writing processes and products. This chapter focuses on what we may learn from this subset of writers in this study. They deserve this close scrutiny because students holding these views about their writing seldom volunteer to participate in longitudinal studies of college writers. While they may represent minority views among my volunteering participants, they likely shed light on the experiences with and attitudes toward writing of a broader majority population of students at institutions with resources similar to my study site.

Eight participants consistently answered two interview questions the same way, in some cases year after year for 5 years. I regularly asked about two-thirds of the way into the interviews whether the participant identified as a "writer" and if they felt they could "write well." Many participants demurred at the label "writer" as part of their identity, seeing the label as an honorific title or a profession to which they had not, or not yet, earned entry (for instance, some would offer examples of published and highly successful novelists, whether Stephen King or Toni Morrison, when explaining they were not writers while these figures were). Some pointed to peers they viewed as particularly talented in or passionate about writing as writers even if writing was not (yet) their careers. However, even if not identifying as a "writer" out of humility, most participants claimed to be "good" or "decent" writers, recognizing they had found ways to manage the process to be productive or to achieve the goal of earning high or passing grades. I allowed participants to define for themselves their sense of success and quality of writing, so while they may have differed on what they considered good writing or a good grade (with, for instance, a B being disappointing to some and worth celebrating to others), the majority of participants self-identified as capable writers. But the eight participants who are the focus of this chapter consistently answered both questions negatively, firmly eschewing "writer" as part of their identity and claiming to be bad at writing in the twin senses of their writing processes and their written products being flawed.[1] As discussed in Chapter 2, participants who took the first-year course were more likely to answer affirmatively my question, "Is being a writer a part of who you are?" than participants who had not taken the first-year course. But the eight students who consistently answered negatively this question *and* the question about whether they can write well were almost evenly divided between those who had taken the first-year course and those who had not.[2] Three of these eight participants had not taken the first-year writing course.[3] The other five took the first-year writing course during their first year of college.[4]

I cannot fully attest as to why these participants chose to participate in the study nor why all but one chose to return for additional interviews. Like many similar studies, I offered compensation for their participation, and some told me the Amazon gift cards I offered helped them purchase textbooks each year. In the final round of interviews of the study I asked students how they felt about their participation in this study and what, if any, effect it may have had on them. The two students who participated over 5 years of this study in this group gave interesting responses. Student 58 indicated that participating forced her to remember and learn from her past writing experiences: "I think it just forced me to try and [laughter] remember things that I either liked or didn't like and why, I guess" (Student 58.sr.5). She gave the example of the interviews prompting her to recall times she procrastinated, reminding her not to do that again:

> If it was a significantly positive or negative experience, it could be beneficial [to remember]. Like, if I was, like, "Oh, last time I did that paper, I did it at—till 5:00 in the morning. [Laughter] I don't want to do that ever again." (Student 58.sr.5)

She indicated that such reflection on her experiences with writing is not something she would have done on her own: "Because I tend to just do it and then never think about it again. . . . Because I just like to submit what I have to submit and never think about it again" (Student 58.sr.5). When I asked her why that is her tendency, she indicated it was because "I don't like writing" (Student 58.sr.5). When pushed to discuss why, she said that writing takes a great deal of effort; her thoughts fly faster than she can write them and as a result "I feel like, if I'm writing, I can't get my thoughts out" (Student 58.sr.5). She is confident others enjoy the process of expressing themselves in writing, a feeling that is foreign to her. Previous longitudinal studies have noted the positive effects on participants of the regular reflection on writing this research methodology asked of them, leading them to advocate for weaving ongoing reflection on writing into the curriculum (Jarratt et al., 2009). Student 58 here indicates that such reflection can be especially valuable when asked of students who might rather run from it. She came to recognize reflection's value and return for it year after year.

Student 45 gave a very different response when asked if his participation in this study had any effect on him. He told me, "I always thought about the purpose of why you're doing this" (Student 45.sr.5). He went on to explain that while he doesn't think his participation had an effect on his writing, he did appreciate that my research signaled that someone cared about students and their experiences, that improving things for students like him might be a goal for researchers like me: "I don't think it had an impact on my writing, but the fact that someone's doing research on this made me aware—made me more aware that they're trying—I don't know—just to improve things for college students" (Student 45.sr.5). This appreciation for a feeling of care about his experience of a large institution seems in part of have kept him returning each year. It may also indicate his dissatisfaction with his experience with writing in college, a feeling he signaled during interviews in other ways as well over the years, such as his repeatedly shared impression that he generally wrote more and was asked to write more research-based papers in high school than in college.

In this chapter I aim to shed light on a key second commonality among these students that distinguished them from my larger pool of participants that became clear to me only after my coding and analysis work with interview transcripts: a shared definition of "good writing" as writing that is produced easily and quickly.[5] In contrast, ease and rapid production were named as qualities of good writing by only four participants who identified as strong or decent writers—only 8% of my 49 other participants—and these participants offered this definition only one time each, offering other definitions in other interviews.[6] I came to realize that this conception of writing not only distinguished in my study those who did not consider themselves capable writers from those who did but also carried real and negative consequences for these student writers and may, at least in part, indicate that one's conception of writing caries a causal connection to one's abilities, perceived and real, as a writer.

In every interview, right after I asked each participant if they saw themself as a good or capable writer, I asked them to define what "good writing" or what being a "good writer" meant to them. Their responses sometimes treated qualities of written products, such as clarity or concision, sometimes dispositions of the writer, such as confident or passionate, and sometimes aspects of the writing process, such as taking a great deal of time on the writing. In total I developed 19 different codes to capture the many qualities of good writing that participants described in all of the interviews. But only one of these came to mark a sharp difference between the responses of those who identified as good or "decent" writers and those who did not: a conception of good writing as writing produced quickly by good writers whose goodness is in part displayed by the effortlessness of their writing process.

Defining Good Writing as Quick and Easy

Those who defined good writing as writing produced with ease, quickly, tended to posit good writing as something very much out of their grasp but enviably obtainable by good writers. For instance, in her first interview, Student 6 offered this definition of good writing:

> It's a culmination of things. How it's being able to write something quickly. I mean obviously people have deadlines, so being able to write things quickly, easily, making it sound good, and getting your point across with good grammar and good spelling. (Student 6.jr.1)

Her inclusion of successfully getting the writer's point across with near perfect mechanics of grammar and spelling highlights another aspect of these definitions: their belief in an enviably perfect product that can be produced without much frustration or even effort. For instance, Student 31 emphasized in her first and second interviews that a good writer only needs one draft:

> I feel that writers are . . . people who can write about anything at any time, at anywhere, they'll get their ideas out there, no questions asked. Like, my friend, . . . she was a writer. . . . She was those types of people who had really complex ideas. She was a poet as well. And she was the type of person who could have complex ideas and get A's on every paper and she never did any second drafts. She just got it out there, got that A, and kept it moving. (Student 31.first-year.1)

At the end of the semester in which she took the first-year course, Student 31 returned to this idea of perfection achieved in only one draft in her definition of a good writer, as you can see in the quotation prefacing this chapter. In these definitions the low-self-efficacy writers posited the existence of enviable untroubled writers, often implying a contrast to themselves, as Student 58 does here: "I guess a good writer is someone who can be passionate about their writing in a way and someone who doesn't really have as much trouble organizing their thoughts" (Student 58.soph.3).

Student 45's adherence to a definition of good writing as quick and easy was remarkably steadfast. With the exception of his fourth interview during his junior year, Student 45 defined "good writing" as being produced rapidly with ease each time we met. Table 5.1 presents all of his answers to this question over the years. When I asked Student 45 each time to tell me about a successful experience he had with writing recently, more than once he pointed to a writing task he was able to complete quickly. For instance, in our second interview he responded to this question by telling me about a misunderstanding about deadlines that forced him to produce a major paper draft for his first-year writing course in only 2 days, saying, "I guess that would be successful" (Student 45.first-year.2). Similarly, in his junior year to tell me about how he felt he was improving as a writer he told me about a writing four-page paper that he used to have to "take a whole weekend off just to focus on," but that "this one, I did like in a couple hours. . . . So, I feel like I'm getting better with being able to, you know, grind it out a lot faster than I used to do" (Student 45.jr.4).

If I Sometimes Succeed at Writing, It's Because I Am Sometimes Lucky

Because this understanding of good writing as something produced quickly and easily did not match their regular experiences of writing, these students thus tended to attribute fatalistically their successes in writing to luck and good fortune. In a later interview, Student 58 explained that her good grades in writing should be attributed to her being lucky, since her troubles with writing do not match her definition of a good writer: "I can definitely get a better grade on a paper than I will on a test, but it'll never be because I actually think the writing is well. It's just—I don't know. I just get lucky, I guess" (Student 58.sr.5). This conviction that their success comes through luck led them to discount efforts they take to be rhetorically successful with their writing as signs they are not good writers. For example, Student 33 discounted

"Being Able to Write Things Quickly, Easily" : 157

TABLE 5.1. Student 45's response to the question "How would you define good writing?" or "What does it mean to be a good writer?" during each interview.

Interview	Student 45's definition of "good writing" or "good writer"
1. Start of spring semester and first-year writing course, 2016	Someone who can just . . . write maybe like a short essay but in a short amount of time with . . . good rhetorical strategies that would help prove their point, I guess.
2. End of spring semester and first-year writing course, 2016	I don't know. I think I need more time. Like, it takes me longer to write something good, compared to a good writer. So it would take me longer to do something. Yeah.
3. Fall sophomore year, 2016	I've said this before. I feel like someone who could like [snaps fingers] just [snaps fingers] write a large amount, like maybe like a seven-page paper, in like one day, less than a day.
4. Fall junior year, 2017	I feel like good writing, if you look at like poets or authors they have like a deep meaning behind their writing. I feel like that's good writing, but like for science, you know, it's just copy and paste, basically, translating the numbers into words. But writing, I don't know how to explain it, but if you read like a story—if you can write a good story, I feel like you're a good writer.
5. Spring senior year, 2019	STUDENT 45: Uh, no. The only reason I'll do good on these is just because they're telling us what they want. But, otherwise, I'll have a hard time, even when I'm talking, too, getting the message across—like, saying what I want to say. You know? LAURA: So, then, being a good writer means that that could come more easily to you, you think, to get your message across? STUDENT 45: Pro—yeah, I think—yeah. Yeah. LAURA: Not struggle at it? STUDENT 45: Yeah. Yeah, exactly.
6. Spring post-graduation, 2020	Someone who, I think I said this before. Someone who can just, on the spot, can express themselves. Like for me, it's always hard to find the right words to use. . . . So, someone who can just quickly, you know, prepare something that's very well written.

his repeated practice of seeking out individualized feedback from his professors and his close attunement to provided assignment guidelines and instead attributed whatever successes he had in written assignments to being lucky:

And then I went to her—because honestly, I feel like I'm not that good at writing essays. But, I guess I get lucky sometimes, and like last semester and spring, I had this criminology class and we had to write a lot of essays. And it was an eight-page final essay. And I was worried. I thought I was going to do really bad. But he—it turned out that he really liked it. Yeah, so I guess I got lucky with that, yeah. But yeah, she provided a guideline and then I went to her, and she explained in detail what she wants. (Student 33.soph.3)

Driscoll and Wells (2012) discuss how a disposition inclined to attribute success or failure in writing to factors beyond the writer's control, such as luck, is typical of low-self-efficacy writers. In Baird and Dilger's (2017) longitudinal research of students' internship experiences, student writers' embrace of a disposition of "ease," or desire to "make writing easy" (p. 706), led them to shy away from "the difficult work of transfer, including the negotiation of prior knowledge and even [their] own identity as a writer" (p. 705). Their sense that writing should be easy was disruptive of their success as writers in ways that had real consequences on their lives, leading them not to persist with difficult or unfamiliar genres and rhetorical situations posed by new jobs or internship applications and ultimately in at least two cases leading their participants to quit a new job and have applications for internships be rejected (p. 705–706). Such conceptions of writing were not serving these students, reinforcing their low self-efficacy with unrealistic expectations for perfection attained quickly.

Consequences of an Untroubled Theory of Good Writing as Quick and Easy

When these students understand their occasional success in writing as the product of luck because their writing did not come quickly and easily, and thus must not be actually "good writing," their definition of good writing remains undisturbed, even reinforced. As you can see in Table 5.1, Student 45 maintained this understanding of good writing throughout his college career and beyond. A biology major also pursuing a minor in neuroscience with plans to next attend medical school, Student 45's views on and feelings about writing remained steadfast through his experience in his first-year writing course, the writing he did for several general education courses, and the many lab reports he produced each year.

Student 45 generally seemed to lack strategies for managing the frustrating and difficult elements of writing, and what strategies he did gain he gained very slowly. For example, as can be seen in Table 5.2, his response to my

TABLE 5.2. Student 45's response to the question "When you get stuck when working on a writing assignment or experience writer's block, how do you overcome it?"

Interview	Strategy for resolving writer's block
1. Start of spring semester and first-year writing course, 2016	I usually—I just stay there. Like, think. Sometimes it takes me the whole day. I don't stop, I'll just stand in front of my computer and think.
2. End of spring semester and first-year writing course, 2016	If I got stuck, I usually just stared at my screen [laughter] until I could pass through it. . . . I'd just sit there and wait.
3. Fall sophomore year, 2016	I'll sit down and figure it out.
4. Fall junior year, 2017	I'll look back to—well, for this class, I look back to the example—or the guideline. Or, if I really can't get it, I go to the office hours and ask.
5. Spring senior year, 2019	The TA's the last resort thing. I usually just look at it for a while [laughter] and think about it. And then I'll ask a lab partner if they know how to do it. If not, all right, let's just go to the TA, and see if they can help us out.

question about how he generally deals with writer's block was essentially the same for our first three interviews. Rather than employ strategies for invention or seeking support, his "solution" is to stick with the frustration by sitting before his computer screen for hours. Only in his junior year does he indicate that he has gained some practical strategies for resolving writer's block, such as reviewing the assignment guidelines and seeking out the help of an instructor.

Not only did Student 45 not see himself as a writer, he did not see the writing he was regularly called on to produce as writing. As suggested by the definition he offered for good writing in his junior year (see Table 5.1), it became clear that Student 45 did not consider the bulk of the writing he did for his science classes as writing. While Student 45 explained to me that he considered nonfiction writing on scientific matters for a popular audience by writers like Malcolm Gladwell as writing, the writing he did for his science classes was merely "translating the numbers into words" and not generative of deeper meaning (Student 45.jr.4). During his sophomore year, when I asked him if there was anything he learned in his first-year writing class that he was using when writing his weekly lab reports, he said he didn't see the purpose in making such a connection because unlike the genres he produced in this first-year writing course, his lab reports do not count as writing: "I don't consider that writing, honestly" (Student 45.soph.3). In this he was like 40% of the students in the first-year writing course in Driscoll's (2011) study of student attitudes toward the likelihood of transfer of knowledge from this course to other contexts. Driscoll (2011) concluded that this perception that writing for courses in the sciences is "not writing" may thwart the transfer of potentially useful knowledge from first-year writing:

> If students do not see the disciplinary writing they are doing in courses outside of FYC as "writing," they will probably have difficulty in transferring useful writing knowledge and in developing more complex rhetorical skills in disciplinary courses because they are not able to use, adapt, or build upon previous knowledge. (p. 18)

The experience of Student 45 supports Driscoll's claim here. Because Student 45, who mainly wrote lab reports over his college years, did not see these reports as *writing*, the idea of transferring knowledge from his first-year writing course to his writing of them did not occur to him as worthwhile or possible, even as he had me to prod him to consider this as a possibility, year after year, and even as his writing for his labs grew in complexity, length, and genre sophistication. During his senior year, this view compelled him to bring two writing samples to his interview. He "dug up" a short, less than a page, letter written to explain "ethical relativism" to a friend from a philosophy course because "that class was the only class where I was actually writing" (Student 45.sr.5). And he brought a 14-page lab report following the IMRAD structure with headings and subheadings and including an abstract; several tables, diagrams, and images; and a reference page listing ten sources, including some scientific papers as well as his course lab handbook and textbook. He commented that this lab report is "probably the longest thing I've done in college" and that producing it was a "drag" but ultimately "a good experience" (Student 45.sr.5). But he almost didn't bring this sample in and made sure to bring the philosophy assignment, which he felt more confident counted as writing. And he was clear about this counting being in his eyes, not his projection of what he thought I assumed writing to be: When explaining to me yet again that he did not consider himself to be a writer, he pointed to the 14-page lab report he brought and said, "I don't consider that writing" (Student 4.sr.5).[7]

If the writing he did for his numerous biology classes was not writing as presented in his first-year writing class, then of course he would not think to transfer learning from that class to his science writing. Student 45 exited the first-year course unsure of its purpose and thus unlikely to seek to draw from it in future scenarios: "I don't really know the purpose. It's just—I don't know. I think we just wrote because that was the class. We had to write. Yeah. It was a writing class, so you write [laughter]" (Student 45.first-year.2). In his senior year he continued to be unsure if his first-year writing class was of any use to him. My analysis of the transcripts of our six interviews pinpoints three opportunities for the transfer of writing knowledge that could have greatly benefitted Student 45 but which he did not take and for which his conception of writing was a contributing impediment.

In high school, Student 45 took the AP English Language and Composition course (what he called "AP Lang") that he credited with helping him succeed in some of his first writing assignments in college, such as an art history paper that he completed the semester before he took his first-year writing course. He credited that class with teaching him "about rhetorical strategies" (Student 45.first-year.1), a phrase he used again to describe what a good writer uses (see Table 5.1). When I asked him to specify what he meant by this, he said, "Like using like appeals to ethos, logos, pathos, and, . . . repetition, stuff like that" (Student 45.first-year.1). In addition to the three classical rhetorical appeals and issues of style, he described the course as also introducing to him the concept of audience and exigency, concepts he found new, compelling, and helpful. He described prior writing assignments in high school, like comparison and contrast papers, as "kind of pointless writing, I think. . . . I wish more English classes made you think about what you're writing and how people are going to read it" (Student 45.first-year.1). In his sophomore year he described a successful experience with writing by harkening back to the art history paper he wrote in his first semester, a paper that he said was "about something that I wasn't really interested about" but that he "managed to" make "it seem like I cared" (Student 45.soph.3). While cynical, he seemed to be crediting his success in this assignment to his attention to audience and ethos that his AP Lang class taught him about. But by junior year he seemed unable to specify what "rhetorical strategies" he learned in AP Lang, claiming he was able to identify them when he saw them in texts but "can't remember anything specific" now (Student 45.jr.4). Unable to name them his junior year, he never mentioned again these "rhetorical strategies." In his first year of college, it seemed he placed value in and felt marginally capable to using the rhetorical strategies his AP Lang course introduced him to, aligning him with the dispositions of value and self-efficacy Driscoll and Wells (2012) identify as determining a student's sensitivity toward and willingness to engage in transfer. But the seeming lack of reference to these rhetorical strategies in his college courses, combined with his insistence that much of the writing he did in his classes for his major did not count as writing, appears to have led him to drop his attention to rhetorical matters in his writing and revert instead to seeing school assignments as "pointless writing" (Student 45.first-year.1). Anson et al. (2020) postulate that this lack of continued use of concepts like *audience* in later courses may leave students unable to develop their new writing knowledge (p. 314). Student 45 did not speak of rhetorical aspects of writing again until the year after he graduated when his work in a lab as a technician helped him "realize how important that, you know, writing is to these Ph.D. students. It's like one of the most important things to them, the publications and stuff" (Student 45.post.6).

Another instance of thwarted transfer occurred when genre knowledge imparted in his composition course was not connected to genre work he did in other courses. His first-year writing instructor took care to include hands-on work in genres outside of the humanities, an approach hailed by many composition researchers as a way to support transfer of knowledge from first-year composition to other contexts (Beaufort, 2007; Wolfe et al., 2014). His section of first-year writing required him to write an ethnography, a research and writing experience that he was initially extremely proud of but that he later seems to wipe from his memory. During our second interview in the final weeks of this first-year writing course, he spoke about the search for secondary sources and the "actual fieldwork" (Student 45.first-year.2) he did for this paper with enthusiasm. His description of his arrangement of this paper would seem to match the arrangement of many academic ethnographies, where in "the beginning of my paper I would use research papers, to like get stats" and "then, after that, I would go into my actual fieldwork. So, I would use my fieldwork to back up the papers" (Student 45.first-year.2). Given the freedom to choose any group to study, he chose to study the Muslim Student Association on his campus because "I'm part of the MSA" (Student 45.first-year.2). When asked what he would likely remember most from his first-year course experience, he named "doing the research paper, like, going to do the fieldwork" (Student 45.first-year.2) for his MSA ethnography. While he expressed doubt that as a biology major he would ever write an ethnography again, he did again name this assignment as one he could see himself drawing from and using what he learned from doing it in the future "if I ever do, like, an ethnography. . . . it was kind of fun to write, honestly. . . . I mean, it was a good learning experience" (Student 45.first-year.2). While he brought his personal narrative essay from his first-year class as his writing sample for this interview, it was clear he would have brought his MSA ethnography if that paper were fully finished when we spoke.

Indeed, in our third interview during the first semester of his sophomore year, he brought the MSA ethnography from his first-year class as his writing sample. Titled "The Importance of the MSA for the American-Muslim College Student," the paper was six double-spaced pages with an additional works cited list containing 10 entries of scholarly journal articles, books and sections of books, a dissertation, and a personal interview. He appeared proud of the paper, explaining that "it was the first time I wrote something like that" and "it was actually pretty fun to write" (Student 45.soph.3). When I asked him if he had experienced any writing assignments lately that he felt were useful to him, he responded by naming his MSA ethnography as useful for "others to read," a comment in which I heard echoes of the value he placed in learning about motivating audiences in his AP Lang course:

> STUDENT 45: Well, this was like a research paper that I wrote last year, so—I don't know, maybe it wouldn't be useful for me, but maybe for others to read.
>
> LAURA: Oh, okay. Why is that?
>
> STUDENT 45: Well, especially for MSA members, which is like Muslim Student Association, it could help people on the [executive] board have a better understanding of Muslim students on campus. (Student 45.soph.3)

When asked this year what he would most likely carry with him into the future from his first-year writing course, he again named the experience of writing this ethnography: "Probably the biggest thing that I learned is how to do ethnography-based writing, so going out, doing observations, researching, and then turning that into a paper" (Student 45.soph.3).

However, the following year, his junior year, he seemed to recall very little about this assignment. In this interview he expressed concern that he recalled being required to do far more research in high school than he had in college. This prompted me to ask if his MSA ethnography from 2 years ago was the last research paper he had written. His memory of factual details about this paper, such as its length and his use of research databases to locate scholarly articles, was distorted, and while he had used the term "research" to describe this paper in prior interviews, he no longer considered that an accurate description of this assignment as he could recall it: "I wouldn't even call that a research paper. . . . I think that was like three, four pages long" (Student 45.jr.4). Later when asked what he recollected from his first-year writing course, he recollected writing the personal narrative assignment and a video and PowerPoint he contributed to producing with a group on comparing commuting to campus versus living in a dorm, but he did not mention the ethnography assignment: "I think the only writing we did in that class was a narrative and one other thing, which I don't remember" (Student 45.jr.4). At this point I again brought up his MSA ethnography, asking if this was the assignment he could not remember. This seemed to trigger his memory, but only partially—the well documented six-page paper seems to be forgotten: "Uh, that was—we had to go like observe a group, I think, interview some people from it. But I don't remember exactly what we were supposed to do" (Student 45.jr.4). His perception of the novelty and possible future import of the assignment had also worn away:

> I mean, what we did in that class wasn't anything new. Like, I wrote narrative in high school before. I mean, the only thing I did do new is go on interview—but I don't see myself ever doing that again. (Student 45.jr.4)

For his writing sample this year, he brought in a three-page analysis of the film *Dead Presidents* he wrote for an African American history course. This paper cited three sources, all websites one would not require a scholarly database to locate. Yet, oddly, when I asked him if he used anything he learned in his first-year course when writing this film analysis, he said that in his first-year course "I don't think we did, actually, any assignments where had a look online for research," whereas for the paper he brought in "I did some research online for it" (Student 45.jr.4). The ethnography with several scholarly journal articles he brought me the year before, which he wrote in his first-year course, seemed to have been pretty firmly stashed "under the bed."

His memory of the assignment stayed there during his senior year, too; he did not recall the MSA ethnography he wrote at all, even when I prompted him about it.[8] While a genre quite different from his lab reports, this social science genre did encourage him to use research to write a literature review and to think about collecting and presenting data, genre features much more like his writing for his biology classes than the personal narrative he wrote for his first-year course. But this similarity does not seem to have helped him transfer, integrate, or repurpose knowledge and experience from writing the ethnography to his writing for biology. Instead, the MSA ethnography is seen as "the only time I had to do something like that, I think" (Student 45.sr.5), and largely forgotten. Again, the firm distinction he placed between the writing he did for English and humanities classes and the "non-writing" he did for his science classes seems to have encouraged him to forget, and not transfer, this experience of writing in a scientific genre in a writing course that presented a borderland location for exploring humanistic and scientific writing.[9]

Lastly, our interviews indicate that the personal narrative he wrote for the first-year course held potential for useful transfer in his later writing, but this potential was also missed. In his sophomore year, Student 45 began talking about his need to write a personal statement for his medical school applications—a topic that came up in every subsequent annual interview concluding with our final, post-graduation interview for which he shared his personal statement as his writing sample. This early and repeated attention to the personal statement struck me as signaling his anxiety about it. In his sophomore year, he told me that he had read the medical school application and seen the requirement for a personal statement, but "it didn't really give any information. So I have no idea what they're expecting" but that he was planning to attend an informational session offered at the university that he hoped would "teach us how to do that" (Student 45.soph.3). When I later asked if he felt prepared for the kinds of writing that he is doing now, he responded:

> I wish we did more writing that was specifically for like applying for stuff, you know. So like a personal statement. Maybe something in class that could have helped us tell—not like just tell any story, but tell a story worthy of sharing with someone that's trying to hire you. (Student 45.soph.3)

I asked where in the curriculum he thought it would be good to include such instruction, and he suggested the required first-year writing course. I asked if they had done anything like a personal statement in his section, and he replied, "Well, we did a narrative, but it wasn't really something that I would submit to, you know, for an application. . . . Because the narrative that I wrote, I talked about going on a trip with my family. That's not something that you would—I mean, that was just me. It wouldn't be something that I would have as a personal statement" (Student 45.soph.3). While he recognized that his personal narrative for the first-year course and a personal statement both call for story telling about the self, he saw them as too distinct for his experience with one to help him in composing the other.

I had seen the personal narrative he wrote for his first-year writing course because he brought it in as his writing sample during our interview conducted near the end of that course. In describing the personal narrative assignment, he said: "She said, 'Show, not tell.' So we had to do a lot of that. And she said

I didn't really do that well with doing that" (Student 45.first-year.2). When I asked him for his recommendations for improving the first-year course, he wished they did more research writing like he did in high school because "I don't really see how this—the narrative would help me" (Student 45.first-year.2). When I asked if he experienced any writing assignments he found personally useful, he responded by saying, "not the first one" (Student 45.first-year.2) while gesturing to this personal narrative. This was another assignment he was ready to stash in the box under his bed.

His first-year essay includes a fair amount of descriptive writing that succeeds at showing rather than telling. The point of the essay was to show that his preconceptions of his parent's homeland are as flawed as his extended relatives' preconceptions about his home in the US. He did this by describing his anticipatory thoughts that circled in his mind on the long flight there about his parents' homeland in the Middle East on the basis of movies and TV shows—thoughts of sand, camels, and turbans. The contrast to the vibrant, modern, and lush world he landed in was striking, and he described the clothing and scenery in vivid detail. He also provided details of the questions his cousins rushed to ask him about the US to show how they, too, had media-informed and incorrect impressions. The essay made its argument about preconceptions being off through these descriptive details. In contrast, the personal statement he gave me, which I understood to be a revision in light of the feedback the admissions officer gave him, revealed far more about the aspects of the medical school that interest him than it did about him. He told the medical school about itself, its qualities that attracted him. But in these 467 words, readers learn only that he is the kind of person who finds the programs and service components of the medical school attractive. The are no anecdotes that *show* he would be a good fit, only statements that assert he is a good fit. It would seem his first-year course supported him in using "showing, not telling" to accomplish a rhetorical goal in his personal narrative. The tough feedback he received from the admissions officer had not been as helpful in supporting his using this technique of implicit argumentation. He convinced himself that the personal narrative assignment from first-year writing was irrelevant to this and all future contexts and thus he did not draw from the skills practiced in it to show his capacity for cultural enlightenment to now show his positive character traits for a medical career path. Firmly placed in the box under his bed, he did not return to retrieve the knowledge when he could use it.

Evidence of Revising Definitions of Good Writing

The students Rose (1980) studied who suffered debilitating writer's block were often helped simply by Rose dispelling a myth about writing to which they clung. My analysis of interview transcripts locates evidence of three of the low-self-efficacy participants revising their understanding of good writing as produced quickly and easily, often in response to a trusted respondent to their writing performing the kind of veil lifting that Rose describes. Student 31's experience of being coached to revise her definition of good writing is emblematic of these shifts among these three participants in all ways but one: For Student 31 the revision began in her sophomore year of college, giving her plenty of time to still put into practice and refine her evolving understanding of writing. The other two students I spoke with who similarly revised their theories of writing did not do so until their final year of college. Prior to making that shift my transcripts document years of anxiety around and avoidance of writing, then anger that they didn't change their views of writing earlier.

The story of Student 31's ongoing transformation from a blocked and frustrated writer to one with strategies for managing writing's complexity is the story of the powerful voice of mentors intervening when she's ready to hear them. The transformation was accompanied and possibly enabled by two other shifts in views: coming to see that writing in college is different from writing in high school and coming to see that writing can be taught (and learned). When I first met Student 31, a sense that a good writer makes no mistakes was inhibiting her writing (her words on good writers producing perfect first drafts shared with me during her first year of college preface this chapter). Student 31 entered college as a biology major, but by the end of her first semester she made the decision to switch to English as her major (the role her lack of access to a prohibitively expensive course resource needed to support her writing in her lab coursework played in this decision is discussed in Chapter 1). Though she had not yet taken any English classes, she explained to me she recalled feeling more at home in her high school English courses and her required first-year writing course than she did in her first college biology courses. However, her grades in her first-year writing course were not as high as she hoped; she sounded disappointed to me when she sheepishly explained that a paper she wrote for that class received a B–. She described how her perfectionist expectations for her writing trapped her in recurrent, crippling procrastination.

In our first interview, just as she began college and her first-year writing course, Student 31 told me about her tendency to start writing assignments

168 : "BEING ABLE TO WRITE THINGS QUICKLY, EASILY"

the night or two before they were due, a process that sometimes led to successful grades in high school but left her unsatisfied. When I asked her what she would like to change about her approach to writing, she described a quest for perfection that left her blocked, emotionally drained, and exhausted:

> To not second guess myself a lot. Like, there have been times when I've cried, like, this isn't good enough. This isn't good enough. And I would just sit there for hours, trying to think of the perfect thesis that I can argue and support with facts. And that's probably the reason why I don't get it done. (Student 31.first-year.1)

She told me she had supportive voices in her life during these moments of crisis, but her perfectionist inner voice tended to resist them:

> My mother's always there to telling me to relax, it's just one paper. And then, my English teacher in high school, . . . he would just say, "Stop second guessing yourself, you're a good writer, you have good ideas. Just get them out there." And I'd just be like, "But—but it's not good enough." (Student 31.first-year.1)

During our second interview, at the end of her first-year writing course semester, Student 31 gave similar answers; she recognized her perfectionism led her to procrastinate, but she had not changed this practice. This may be because Student 31 saw no cause to do so at the time. She saw the writing she did that semester as very similar to what she did in high school, where she tended to succeed despite the stress her procrastination caused her:

> LAURA: Has reading and writing differed for you in college, as opposed to your experiences in high school? Are there any differences that you've noticed?
>
> STUDENT 31: Nope. It was the same, annotating, analyzing, stuff that I was doing in, like, 10th, 11th, and 12th grade.
>
> LAURA: Okay. Is writing changing for you in college, in terms of its level of difficulty? Does it seem easier, harder than it has been in the past?
>
> STUDENT 31: It, um—it seems the same. (Student 31.first-year.2)

Yet despite these claims, Student 31 described not performing as well, in terms of the grades she received on her writing for her required first-year course. She claimed to not be very engaged in the topics she was asked to write about that semester, but her old procrastination habits seem to have been identified by her writing instructor as contributing to her poor

"Being Able to Write Things Quickly, Easily" : 169

performance on these assignments. She had told me in her first interview that one thing she liked about her writing was how conversational it sounded, how it sounded like her talking. But the feedback she received on her writing in her first-year writing course continually described this style as posing problems for readers.[10] When telling me about the second paper for her first-year writing course, she connected a grade she was disappointed in to this style and to procrastination stress:

> The unique voice that I told you about, you could see a lot of it in that particular paper. I didn't get the best grade on it. I got an 81, but I felt that it was representative of me, because that was me, like, five o'clock in the morning. The words are just flying, but I made sure it made sense. (Student 31.first-year.2)

When I asked if she felt comfortable disagreeing with this instructor, she told me of how she ought to learn from this instructor's assessment rather than disagree with it:

> She's very approachable. So, if you disagreed on something, you'd be able to, like—she's the type of person that would hear you out, but I haven't felt the need to disagree because she knows what she's doing. Like I said, I didn't put my all into the writing. So I was like, okay, what she's saying I should probably take to heart because, you know, you did pull this out in one night, so there's obviously some work that needs to be done [laughter]. (Student 31.first-year.2)

But this was the same interview in which she defined good writing as something produced quickly and perfectly in one draft. The feedback she described most appreciating from her first-year writing instructor was about improving her style to sound less conversational and more "academic" (she was considering changing a word she used to describe Snow White in one of her papers from "stupid" to "idiotic" on the basis of this advice). Aside from modifying her style, she did not leave the first-year writing course intending to modify her writing process. Instead, she was adamant that instruction is ineffectual at causing such a change:

> LAURA: If you were to give the university some advice about what we could do to help students become better writers, what would you suggest we do? Is there a class, an assignment, an experience, any changes to your experience this semester or that you'd recommend?
>
> STUDENT 31: I don't think you could really tell or teach anyone how to be a good writer. It kind of just—for me, it kind of just happens. Like, you can

tell—you can teach them how to structure and how to use good grammar, but, in the end, what they write and how they write is what they write and how they write. (Student 31.first-year.2)

Like Grace in Knutson's (2019) case study of a low-self-efficacy writer, Student 31 initially believes writing cannot be taught (p. 200) and that good writing "just happens" (p. 206). Knutson (2019) describes how such a theorization of writing contributes to difficulties adapting to college writing for Grace. But also like Grace, Student 31 found a curricular home that supported her in questioning her initial theorization.

Her views changed dramatically in our next interview during the first semester of her sophomore year. Whereas the year prior her writing situation seemed to her the same as it was in high school, the writing she experienced her sophomore year felt markedly different to her. It seems she experienced receiving even lower grades than she did in her first-year writing course and took this as a sign of increased expectations in the sophomore year:

Actually, I believe that my [first-year writing] professor, since she was grading freshman papers, like there was only so much that she could expect. But now that I am a sophomore, it's like you've got to step your game up. You can't still write like you're in high school, even though you're in college. (Student 31.soph.3)

As a result of increased expectations and increased writing workload as an English major, Student 31 had a realization that she can no longer leave her writing "to the last minute":

LAURA: So, how does the writing that you're doing these days compare to what you remember doing last year and, and even in high school? Is it similar or is it different?

STUDENT 31: I tried doing the old way, and I ended up extremely stressed out.

LAURA: So, what was the old way?

STUDENT 31: The old way was to procrastinate and then like just bust something out and then get a pretty decent grade. But now I realize that I can't do it. It's not like I have just one English class and I can just put it off to the last minute. Like now I have three or soon to be four English classes at once. So, I actually have to plan my time out so that I don't fail any of my classes. And also to make sure that my writing makes sense, because even though I was good in English in high school and during my freshman year, college writing is actually a whole lot different than

"Being Able to Write Things Quickly, Easily" : 171

> high school writing. And some of the stuff that I used to do or used to say doesn't really cut it now. (Student 31.soph.3)

During this interview she reflected a great deal on her procrastination tendencies—tendencies she now sought to change. In announcing her intention to "start going to the writing center so I can get feedback," she explained she had never been before because her perfectionism led her to want to hide imperfect writing from others:

> I tend to write as like a solitary person, and since I'm a perfectionist, it's like I'm also my own worst critic. So it just becomes a really complicated thing where I don't want someone to see my paper, because I'm just like, "It's completely imperfect." But at the same time, when I read it, I can't really find anything wrong with it. So it's like a mixture of ego and anxiety at the same time. . . . But I'm trying to get over that this year, because I'm really just trying to grow as a person and also a writer. (Student 31.soph.3)

Her dissatisfaction with her procrastination had only increased, and she recognized that the emotional stress it caused her impacted her negatively, motivating her to try to change.

In describing her typical writing process during this interview, she began to narrate a predicament of two papers due on the same day that led her to reach out to her professors and initiate dialogues that turned out to be transformative:

> Normally, it's weird because I have an idea as soon as I get the paper. I'm actually really excited to write, but I'm also a perfectionist, which leads to procrastination. So I'm just like, "I want everything to be perfect. I'm going to do all my research. I'm going to take all these books at the library. Everything's going to be perfect." And then a couple of nights before the paper's due, I'm just like, "I made a terrible mistake." And it's like even as I'm writing the paper, I have ideas. So not only am I trying to get the idea down on paper, but I'm also trying to edit it to make sure that it makes sense at the same time. And it's a really, really stressful process. Especially since earlier this semester, I had two papers due on the same day, and I procrastinated both of them. (Student 31.soph.3)

The two papers due on the same day were the crisis point that prompted her interactions with two English professors, both of whom helped her navigate the immediate crisis (with extensions) and then stepped back to offer her specific writing process strategies and encouragement to modify her typical writing process with them. She narrated both interactions with dialogue,

172 : "BEING ABLE TO WRITE THINGS QUICKLY, EASILY"

suggesting she really listened to these professors and took their guidance to heart. Here Student 31 narrated how the professor of her writing-intensive English course prescribed for her a specific way to "combat" her perfectionism and procrastination through the practice of freewriting:

> I've found a way to at least combat it. And I'm trying—and I'm going to do it on the next paper I receive. Because I talked to my professor about it when I got my first paper back. And he asked what my writing process was, and I told him that my writing process is just to sit in front of the computer a couple nights before the paper's due and then just write. And then he's like, "See? That's what you don't do." Because—[he] always says that the first—that the very, very first rough draft is the worst draft that you could possibly produce. You're not supposed to hand that in. So he's just like, "So next time you start to write, what you do is you have like a notepad or a notebook next to you. And then you start writing, but if you see something that could actually possibly be an argument, you jot it down, but then continue to write. Because the writing is how you get your thoughts out, but the actual gold nugget of information may just be one sentence in that whole entire summary that you're writing. So type that out if that works for you, but also skim through it, cut a lot of stuff out, and then just focus on that one critical piece of writing that could make or break your paper." (Student 31.soph.3)

She seems to have really heard this professor give her permission to—in fact, dictate that she—produce imperfect first drafts and that she use writing epistemically to discover the things she wants to say rather than merely record already located claims. In another private conference, her other English professor that semester showed her how her "conversational" writing style led her to produce really long sentences; ones that "took up almost four lines" (Student 31.soph.3) and made difficult work for a reader, an explanation that motivated her to want to try to modify this style and gave her something to look for—sentence length—as she edited.

In addition to this procedural knowledge, Student 31 also really heard her English professor's guidance on genre knowledge specific to literary studies.[11] Student 31 explained that her writing-intensive English course helped her better understand that the target stasis issue in literary analysis is definitional (interpretive) rather than evaluative or existence (summary) (Wilder, 2012):

> So, coming into my sophomore year, I thought I knew what a thesis statement was, but after being in [the writing-intensive introductory English course], I realize that there is a difference between something—an

evaluative statement and an interpretive statement. A thesis statement is supposed to be interpretive, but what I normally do is evaluate. . . . And I also used to summarize a lot, which admittedly got me in just a tiny bit of trouble last year, but I guess since I was a freshman, they kind of just let it slide. But now it doesn't really work. (Student 31.soph.3)

It would seem, contra what she claimed only a year ago, that these professors are able to teach her writing, specifically procedural (how to brainstorm, how to edit) and genre (how literary analysis differs from other essay forms) knowledge.

Of course, these new intentions to visit the writing center, to use free writing, and to edit for style were more aspirations when I spoke with her than engrained practices. Because she did not participate in further interviews, I do not know if she followed through with these changes (her decision not to participate further could very well be a sign she did not want to be reminded of broken resolutions). But what I think is worth noting here is that her definition of writing was changing with the help of these professors' mentorship. The frustratingly unattainable goal of the perfect first draft was being replaced with an embrace of imperfection and procedural steps from freewriting to editing with a reader in mind. She registered this shift as rather significant seismic activity herself. This time when I asked her if she identified as a writer, the question perplexed her:

LAURA: Do you see yourself as a writer? Is that a part of who you are?

STUDENT 31: I, I don't know anymore.

LAURA: Okay.

STUDENT 31: God's honest truth, I don't know anymore.

LAURA: Did you feel like you used to know and you don't anymore?

STUDENT 31: Yeah.

LAURA: Something has changed in that regard?

STUDENT 31: I felt like I used to know. Like I used to be like, "Yeah, I can read and I can write," and now I'm just like, "I can read kind of and I can write maybe, if I try really hard."

LAURA: Yeah. So, things are being thrown into more uncertainty for you than you used to feel. That's interesting. Why do you think that is?

STUDENT 31: Well, it's because I've been making a lot of changes to myself, like emotionally. So, it's like my mindset is kind of changing along with my emotional state. Because beforehand, I was just like, "Yeah, writing.

Writing is easy. I can do this in a night flat. It's gonna be lit. All I need is a can of Monster." And now I'm just like, "No, [Student 31]. You need sleep and to get up for your class on time in the morning instead of walking to the library at 8:30 in the morning hating yourself for procrastinating. You can't keep doing this." (Student 31.soph.3)

Here you can hear her shifting from a definition of good writing that is easy and quick to one that sees it as the outcome of a process that takes time, that isn't easy. Student 31 is coming to associate her old definition with unhealthy practices and emotional disturbance and her new one with regular effort and support. Boice (1997) found such moderation can benefit both the mental health and the productivity of academic writers, while occasional "binge writing" correlated with increased measures for depression and decreased productivity. The potential impacts—for her physical and mental health, for her identity within her major, for her academic success—of the change in her definition of writing that Student 31 was on the cusp of making when I last spoke with her cannot be understated.

Lack of Impact of First-Year Writing Course

It is noteworthy, and troubling, how little an impact the first-year writing course seemed to have on the small group of low-self-efficacy student writers discussed in this chapter. Student 45, like other students in this group, in later college years forgot central projects from this first-year writing course that held potential relevance for the genres he would later write. Just a year after completing the first-year writing course, Student 31 claimed not to recall receiving any advice on her writing in that course. Student 31 associated the course with her high school experience of writing, and it took her sophomore writing-intensive courses in her new English major for her to find the motivation and guidance to change ineffective and unhealthy writing processes. And Student 58, who only began to question her definition of good writing as produced quickly and easily in her senior year after struggling for years with many writing projects for her criminology major, claimed in her senior year that she "can't remember too much" (Student 58.sr.5) from the first-year writing course and in the year after graduation claimed "honestly, . . . I don't even remember who the professor was" (Student 58.post.6).

Year after year, starting at the end of her first-year writing course semester, Student 58 would tell me, "We didn't really write" (Student 58.first-year.2) or "We didn't do much writing" (Student 58.jr.4) in the first-year writing course. Instead, she explained to me, they prepared "audio diaries," an assignment that with each passing year she described to me with greater and greater resentment. While at the end of the semester in which she had this assignment she told me she saw "no relevance to it" (Student 58.first-year.2), she did acknowledge a goal for the class: "I feel like that class specifically had a different goal than like any other class. It was more like to get you to learn like how to look at things differently, I guess. Like to see things for more than what they appear" (Student 58.first-year.2). But by her senior year she described deeply disliking the audio diary assignment because she felt it required her to disclose personal details and learn personal details about her classmates that she preferred be kept private or only shared voluntarily:

> STUDENT 58: I hated it in that class. I did not want to—it was interesting to hear other people's, but to actually have to do it myself and put myself out there, it was very annoying because I didn't want to share intimate details of my own life with my class. . . . We had to because if it wasn't something that had an emotional backing, we couldn't do it.
>
> LAURA: I see.
>
> STUDENT 58: Like, it had to be something personal to you or something like that.
>
> LAURA: Right, and you would rather keep that private—
>
> STUDENT 58: Yeah.
>
> LAURA: than share that with the class?
>
> STUDENT 58: Yeah, I didn't want to do it, but I didn't have a choice. (Student 58.sr.5)

She emphasized with repetition that she felt coerced to share and to learn intimate details about her life and the lives of her classmates. I asked her in her senior year to reflect back on the goal of learning "to look at things differently" that she had described during her first year to see how she could reconcile that seemingly positive goal with the negative views of the class that came to dominate her descriptions of it when looking back. Her response again emphasized the uncomfortable disclosure of personal information, suggesting that during her first year she may have been using softer language as a euphemism to hide her feelings about the class or that her views on the class changed over time when she looked back on it:

> LAURA: Years ago—I was looking over my old notes—you talked about maybe the class encouraging you to try to think more deeply about

things or have a different point of view. Do you think that is something that was useful to you as a college student?

STUDENT 58: Well, in the class we had to listen to other people's audio diaries. That's what it was. So, we learned way too intimate details about people's lives.

LAURA: I see.

STUDENT 58: So, I probably meant it in that sense, whereas, there was—I can't remember the exact details, but, there was one person who, he was, like, not like a TA, but he helped her in the class because he had taken it before.[12]

LAURA: Mm-hmm. Yeah.

STUDENT 58: And we had to watch his—and I don't remember what it was, but it was super depressing and sad, like something that happened to him. I think he had a parent pass away. And we were just listening to that. We didn't even know him, really. So, I guess in that sense, yeah.

LAURA: Yeah. Suddenly you know intimate information about someone you don't really know well.

STUDENT 58: Mm-hmm.

LAURA: Yeah. Yeah. So, in that sense, you thought more deeply about people, I guess.

STUDENT 58: In general, yeah. (Student 58.sr.5)

While the first-year writing course seemed simply not to have made much of an impact on Student 31 or Student 45, it left a negative impact on Student 58. Student 58 discounted the work with freewriting and audio diaries they did in her first-year writing course as not writing[13] and not relevant to her and more than bristled at the perception that she and her classmates were asked to reveal personal information. About the freewriting to music that she recalled being asked to do at the start of every class, she said, "I used to just sit there and write, 'I don't wanna be doing [laughter] this.' Just so she would see me typing something" (Student 58.sr.5). In this way, she may have the dispositions Driscoll (2011) described as *disconnected* and Driscoll and Jin (2018) described as *unidirectional*, or not seeing or seeking out connections between her first-year writing course and other areas of her academic and personal life. But it also may be the case that her section of the course did little to make clear for her what the connections could possibly be. Instead, every year we spoke, when I asked her for suggestions for how the university could help students like her become better writers, she suggested a course "solely made

"Being Able to Write Things Quickly, Easily" : 177

to help people become better writers" (Student 58.first-year.2), a class that would "strictly teach how to become a better writer" (Student 58.soph.3).[14] In our final interview after graduation she claimed to have finally encountered such a class during her final semester, too late to help her with the many criminal justice papers she wrote over the course of her studies for which she felt repeated trial and error were her only guides:

> I know the only class that really worked to provide feedback with writing was literally the last class I took my senior year of college. So, it was kind of pointless in a sense because it's like he was trying to teach us how to become better writers. But, if I would've taken a class that taught me that in the beginning, maybe it would've helped. (Student 58.post.6)

Conclusion

Chapter 2 shows us that a significant potential effect of the first-year writing course at this institution may be the development of a sense of self that includes being a writer as part of one's identity, but that effect did not manifest in the four writers discussed in this chapter who took this course (Students 31, 33, 45, and 58). While there are undoubtedly a complex array of reasons, from their particular dispositions to the particular approaches taken in different sections of the course, the evidence from my interviews strongly suggests that these students' conception of "good writing," which they carried into the course with them, was a significant impediment to their seeing themselves as good writers, to transferring learning about writing to other contexts where it could be useful, and to being curious about exploring and experimenting with their writing processes in ways that could help them develop a repertoire of sustainable and efficacious writing heuristics and strategies.

The low-self-efficacy writers discussed in this chapter repeatedly and firmly defined "good writing" as writing that is produced quickly and easily. Because their own experiences with writing felt difficult and took time, or were rushed yet trying due to avoidance procrastination, these writers interpreted these experiences as evidence they were not good writers rather than calling into question their definitions of good writing. It is thus conceivable that questioning and revising their definition of good writing could have wide-ranging implications for their sense of themselves as writers and their writing processes. Their definition of good writing as being quick and easy is a far cry from the complex list of thirty-five threshold concepts of writing studies articulated in Adler-Kassner and Wardle's (2015) *Naming What*

We Know. In his description of the threshold concept "writing is not natural," Dryer (2015) claimed that "it's useful to remember that writing is not natural because writers tend to judge their writing processes too harshly—comparing them to the ease with which they usually speak" (p. 29). Expecting writing to come quickly, easily, and naturally did indeed seem to be at the root of difficulties these writers recurrently narrated in our interviews.[15]

Letting go of this expectation and coming to see writing as messier, slower, and a process of discovery appeared to have been transformative for Student 31. For Student 31, the role of mentors and explicit instruction in writing process and genre strategies were pivotal in helping her come to question this definition. While this instruction for her was found outside her first-year writing course, these students' experiences nonetheless suggest pathways for developing this kind of impact in a first-year course. While the pep talks Student 31 received from high school mentors and her first-year writing instructor that tried to convince her she was a good writer did not succeed in changing her definition of writing or alter her ineffectual and unhealthy writing processes, specific strategy instruction that showed her clear steps for invention and editing did have this impact.

As Student 31 came to see, efficacious writing can be taught. But the seemingly negligible impact of their first-year writing course on these students' sense of themselves as writers and their definitions of good writing should push us to reexamine this course. The students in this chapter teach us that the mere practicing of writing with the hope that the experience carries over to future contexts and supportive, cheerleading feedback are not enough to prod their likely entrenched (Anson, 2015) views of writing in different directions. In the concluding chapter of this book I argue for directions the first-year course could take to persuade students like those discussed in this chapter to set aside their entrenched, unhelpful views on writing and pick up realistic and helpful views supported by decades of writing research. Central to these recommendations is one worth mentioning here because of its call to directly address the flawed and unreflective understandings of writing that students like those discussed in this chapter clung to for years even in the face of evidence that it was not serving them and may have had negative consequences (for instance, might Student 45's unrevealing personal statement, which drew very little from the relevant writing he did in his first-year course, have dissuaded some medical schools from accepting him?). The findings presented in this chapter support the preliminary findings of Smith et al.'s (2021) longitudinal study of writers at Northeastern University, which found that "theories of writing can disable as well as enable transfer and integration" and "that even some of our best and most successful students can harbor disabling theories of writing" (pp. 18–19).

Aiming directly at addressing students' definitions of writing in the first-year course would seem to be a potentially highly impactful goal of the course. The case studies presented here can be read as providing evidence to support recent proposals for the first-year course that aim to develop students' theories of writing. Yancey et al. (2014, 2018, 2019) have developed a curriculum for supporting students in authoring a rich, rhetorically informed theory of writing in a first-year writing course. Such a theory, or "conceptual framework of writing" (Yancey et al., 2018, p. 43), is essentially an extended definition of what writing is and how it works, or an answer to my annual question, "What do you understand good writing to be?" In this approach, students read about and explore key concepts, such as *audience* and *discourse community*, as they work to build a conceptual framework of writing. Similarly, Downs and Wardle's (2007) "writing about writing" or "introduction to writing studies" approach to first-year writing exposes students to scholarship in rhetoric and composition that can inform students about the messy complexity of writing processes and provide evidence to support seeing writing as epistemic. This direct reflection on writing, informed by the knowledge writing studies scholarship has built, could similarly assist students in building a more complex theory of writing than the one they entered the course with. More recent approaches that draw from the threshold concepts of writing studies crowd-sourced in Adler-Kassner and Wardle's (2015) *Naming What We Know* also make developing students' understandings of writing as rhetorical, process-based, and messy even for experts the center of instruction in the first-year course.

Conclusion

The research presented in these pages affirms again that a longitudinal perspective on student writing crucially expands and contextualizes what studies that provide knowledge of but one snapshot in time can tell us about how writers learn, develop, and respond to instruction. Student 48, whose experience I narrated in a case study in Chapter 4, stands for me as emblematic of this affirmation. Her decision to withhold describing her experience with a plagiarism accusation in her first-year writing course until an interview conducted the year after she graduated from college can teach us a great deal about how a longitudinal approach can foster a relationship based on trust between participants and researcher, but also how this trust may be impinged upon by institutional constraints invisible to the researcher. (For instance, did she wait to share this experience until after graduation for fear that sharing it earlier could impact the completion of her degree program? Did she feel compelled to share the story when she did to support students behind her who did not yet have the protection of their degrees in hand?) Her revelation encouraged me to reevaluate all our previous interactions, putting them in a new light and providing explanations for interactions that had been mysterious to me before. Had I been able to continue conversations with her and others—I am thinking especially of Student 51 as one for whom similarly demystifying

https://doi.org/10.7330/9781646426584.c006

revelations would be most welcome (see case study in chapter 4)—I could be drawn to revising many more of the conclusions I come to in these pages.

Beyond recognizing that a longer longitudinal study might provide opportunities for hindsight and reflection from vantage points further down the road in their lives and careers, I must acknowledge important further limitations to this research. Perhaps the most glaring limitation to me and my readers is my omission of the perspectives of the college writing instructors who worked with my participants, both the first-year course instructors and instructors in the disciplines who assigned writing. Having previously conducted writing studies research that aimed to account for the perspectives of all participants in a scene of disciplinary writing instruction (Wilder, 2012), I am highly aware that participants' perception of the same scene of writing instruction can vary dramatically. My participants' instructors might offer very different explanations of the successes and failures with writing that my participants narrated and very different accounts of what transpired in their classrooms. I must acknowledge and draw my readers' attention to this limitation. No single empirical study gives us full accounting of the object of study. Collectively, however, like puzzle pieces, the larger body of empirical research in writing studies helps provide a fuller image of this object. Mine should be read together with studies that do provide instructor perspectives, like those by Chiseri-Strater (1991), Beaufort (2007), Nelms and Dively (2007), and Thaiss and Zawacki (2006).

Publicly Funded Institutions Need More Support to Support Student Writers

That said, we desperately need studies of the experiences of first-year writing instructors and instructors attempting to teach writing across the curriculum at institutions with minimal resources allocated for this work, such as the institution studied here. My research exposed great disparities between the amount of writing and the quality of writing instruction that students experienced at my research site and that students experienced at institutions of greater privilege and resources that have served as the sites of most other longitudinal studies of college writing. The quality and quantity of writing instruction varied a great deal depending upon students' majors at my research site, seemingly much more so than at more prestigious institutions. In particular, students pursuing majors with some of the highest enrollment at this institution, such as psychology and business, seemed to experience notably fewer and less richly interactive writing experiences than students pursuing these majors at better funded institutions just a few interstate exits away. Realizing the interconnection of writing and learning, several of my participants were deeply angered and offended when they became aware of this disparity. My participants recognized that large class sizes and low expectations, including the expectation that they only take one or two courses designated as focused on writing, were among the institutional barriers that kept instructors from asking more of them, and supporting them more fully, as writers. Likewise, many of my participants experienced economic hardships and conflicts juggling work, family, and school that interfered with their ability to experience the interconnection of writing and learning even when instructors aimed to support it. One participant was moved to change her major because a course resource to support her writing in her first major was prohibitively expensive (Student 31, discussed in Chapters 1 and 5), and many more found there were too few hours in a week for them to attend classes, clock in hours at multiple jobs, and treat writing as a process of inventive discovery, feedback, reconsideration, and revision. It is my hope that this study helps us better understand students' experiences of these constraints at institutions like my study site. But we also need studies to help us better understand these constraints from instructors' perspectives; how issues like class size, writing-intensive course designations, the reliance on non-tenure-line labor, tenure or contract-renewal requirements, students' prior preparation, and more affect instructors' ability and willingness to enact the WAC best practices we have known for decades.

What my research exposes about disparities in foundational educational experiences between public and private and between financially precarious and well-endowed institutions should be a cause for alarm. While broad access to higher education is touted as a public good with the potential to level differences between the haves and the have-nots, my research exposes deep and damaging discrepancies in the kind of education offered at publicly funded universities reaching first-generation, financially unstable, and diverse students.[1] Some of my participants pursuing majors in the humanities, public health, and criminal justice experienced richly interactive occasions for writing repeatedly over their 4 years of college. Some of my participants who showed exceptional promise in the sciences were invited to work in their professors' labs and learned there as apprentices about the rhetorical functions and processes of writing in these fields.[2] But many more of my participants cannot be said to have experienced the opportunities to examine their own thinking that challenging writing assignments present or to have learned the genre and writing-process knowledge essential to advancement in the professions their majors represent in the increasingly more sophisticated and interactive ways experienced by their peers attending Harvard, Stanford, Pepperdine, or the University of Michigan. Instead, my participants were asked to regularly fill in bubbles on Scantron exam answer sheets, a memorization and regurgitation task familiar to them since high school. This is not access to equal educational opportunities. And this is not a problem individual instructors can rectify entirely on their own or that more WAC workshops (though needed) could adequately address. This is a deep structural inequity, one that only substantially greater funding for public higher education can address. And because most recently any new funding at my research site has been allocated almost entirely for new academic programs directly tied to narrow career tracks, I feel it is necessary to clarify that it is not only a matter of more funding but also an institutional reprioritization of how that funding is distributed. My research clarifies the desperate need to fund *existing* programs, particularly those that support pedagogical contexts that allow students to write to learn across all majors and in general education courses. Otherwise, the disparities in educations offered by most public institutions and institutions of prestige will only continue to widen, with the value and meaning of degrees offered by these institutions likewise diverging.

Key Findings Pertaining to and Recommendations for First-Year Writing

In these conditions the addition of a small, required first-year writing course can be seen as a step in the right direction, and indeed a great many of my participants who had not been required to take such a course recommended the university add this requirement. My research documents the benefits of a required first-year writing course and can be read as a rebuttal of the first-year course abolitionists who have questioned its value. My comparative and longitudinal study shows how the first-year writing course positively affected many students' identifications as writers, enriched their writing processes, and heightened their awareness, if not also increased the likelihood, of their transferring appropriate knowledge of writing from one educational context to another. For many, the course loosened the strict and arhetorical rules of writing their high school ELA instruction had previously drilled in them to meet the narrow and shortsighted goal of passing standardized writing assessments. By contrast, the first-year writing course fostered a mindset that allowed students to use writing as a tool for exploration and invention.

184 : CONCLUSION

Some students, like Student 39 (see case study in Chapter 4), credit the course with genuinely expanding their critical thinking capacities and appreciation of racial and cultural differences. For others it increased their appreciation of collaboration and fostered a social epistemic approach to writing. These are not insignificant developments in a writer's path. Indeed, participants in my study who took the first-year course were much more likely to identify as efficacious writers, an identification with real consequences for their willingness to persevere through difficult writing projects and trust that some of the challenges they encounter in the process of writing are not, in fact, signs they are not good writers but signs they *are* writers—writers who recognize that writing entails countless conscious decisions along the way, and that therefore good writing often isn't produced quickly or easily. These findings buttress the findings of others like Sitler (2020) who showed that students labeled as "basic writers" were helped to identify and behave as writers with the support of a variety of teaching practices in a first-year writing course.

But not all participants who took the first-year course experienced these outcomes, and some participants who did not take the course came to these outcomes by different means, in other courses or contexts and at other times in their college experience. As previous studies have found, some participants, showing a nascent if potentially misguided rhetorical consciousness, perceived the first-year writing course as being too far removed disciplinarily from their intended majors and career paths to be applicable and useful to them. This perception led them to discount and thus not transfer knowledge about writing to other settings. The use of "personal writing" in the course was a prominent reason why participants felt the course did not apply to their other college courses that required writing. Simply put, they did not see similar assignments in their disciplinary courses. Sometimes they couldn't see the connections even when they were there: Student 45 could not even see the personal statement for medical school he worried over for years as related to the writing about his own experience that he did in the first-year course (see Chapter 5).

RECONSIDER THE USE OF PERSONAL WRITING

In fact, the use of "personal writing" in the first-year course emerged as an issue around which my participants held strongly discordant views. A number of participants reported that this type of writing felt liberating for them when they encountered it in their first-year course. It helped them see writing as something bigger and full of more choices with potential rhetorical effects than the five-paragraph themes they had previously been confined to work within. As such, these assignments helped them to embrace "writer" as part of their identity, to use writing epistemically, and to seek out ways to transfer to other appropriate contexts what they learned about writing in their first-year course. In other words, for some participants, such "personal writing" assignments played a central role in the course having the significant, beneficial effects this study documents.

However, for other participants, writing assignments that asked them to share and explore their own experiences were perceived as, at best, benignly irrelevant to their development of writing skills and knowledge useful elsewhere in college or their careers and, at worst, uncomfortable and highly invasive of their privacy and even inflicting "literacy trauma" (Regidor, 2023). Either perception led some participants to tend to compartmentalize the course as a "one-off" experience they could box and place forever under their beds (Driscoll & Jin, 2018). When this happened, "personal writing" assignments actively thwarted the course's goal to support students as writers in their future endeavors.

Previous studies point to this fraught perception of personal writing among students. On the one hand, case studies by Herrington and Curtis (2000), Sommers and Saltz (2004), Beaufort (2007), and Rounsaville (2017) show us student writers who worked to infuse nearly all their writing assignments across their years of college with a sense of themselves. For such students, forging these connections and making their writing personal, even when not explicitly called on to do so, was essential to their development as writers, their persistence in college, and their gaining of disciplinary expertise. Because forging personal connections did not always mean writing personal narratives or even using the first-person pronoun, not always would these students' writing appear as "personal writing" to an unknowing reader. But these case studies allow us to see how these students' selection of topics for college papers in the disciplines were often connected to deeply personal issues and questions, and that these connections motivated them to treat writing as an engaged process of inquiry. We have reason to believe these case studies represent widely shared experiences: Over one-third of the student respondents to the large-scale survey project by Eodice et al. (2016, 2019) indicated that they found a college writing assignment meaningful when they were able to make a personal connection to it. Further, composition scholars have argued for the importance of personal writing on the grounds of its potential for promoting racial, ethnic, and gender inclusivity.

Hinojosa and de León-Zepeda (2019) argue from a Chicana feminist perspective for the importance of an *"autohistoria-teoría* assignment as a vehicle for students, especially Latinx students, to engage a historical consciousness, to make inquiries about their bodies situated in places" (p. 91) and to help students claim a space for their home identities in academic writing. Likewise, Kareem (2019) censures the exclusion from first-year writing curricula of discursive practices for "narrativizing personal experiences" commonly used for rhetorical effect within many communities of color and by writing scholars from these communities in their scholarship, such as "narrative sequencing" and "testifying" (p. 285).

On the other hand, personal writing does not appear to have the same positive educational effects for all students. Consider students such as Terri from Carroll's (2002) longitudinal study at Pepperdine (pp. 70–71), who, as a minority student experiencing financial hardships, has much in common with many of my study's participants. Teri, like several of my participants, vowed never again to draw from her personal experiences in her academic writing after uncomfortable experiences doing so in her first-year writing course and two introductory English courses. I think we have to take seriously the concerns of students like Terri and the participants in my study who shared similar experiences and reluctances to write about themselves. We cannot assume that a personal narrative assignment will be seen by all as an invitation to connect private selves with the public work of the academy. And yet, because such assignments are so powerfully motivating and groundbreaking for other students, I am loath to recommend we abandon them either.

So, what should we do? My findings on students' reactions to these assignments lead me to recommend that we offer students the choice to write about their experiences or to take another tack that still fulfills an assignment's goals. Other researchers (Eodice et al., 2016; Jarratt et al., 2009; Kareem, 2018; Regidor, 2023; Wardle, 2007) have concluded that some level of student choice in writing assignment topics and even genres notably increases student engagement. My findings support this recommendation in general (more on this below), but I see this recommendation as a particularly apt way to respond to the personal writing assignment dilemma presented by my participants. Many students may leap at the opportunity to reflect on and share their own experiences in writing. Others will be comforted to know they need not *have* to share personal details they would rather keep private because there is another viable option to the assignment that also fulfills the assignment goals, whether those be developing skills in reflection or narration or other objectives entirely.

That said, I—and I am sure many other writing instructors—want to ensure that all our students experience academic writing as welcoming to students' whole identities and wish to provide opportunities to connect academic inquiry with personal motivations. I do think Student 45 would have benefited from seeing the personal statement he wrote to apply to medical schools as related to the personal narrative he successfully wrote for his first-year course. I often find myself having to persuade students that the first-person pronoun "I" is allowed in academic writing in many disciplines and genres, not solely in personal narratives but in moments of textual metadiscourse when academic writers distinguish their own claims from those of sources they cite (Fife, 2018; Thonney, 2016). One personal narrative assignment that those students who are reluctant to share their personal experience may see as justified in the course is the personal literacy narrative, an assignment that asks students to reflect on their past experiences with writing. Such personal literacy reflection is not dissimilar from the interviews conducted in each year of this study, interviews that many participants who found "personal writing" distasteful returned for each year. That type of focused, personal reflection on writing we know from years of study (Yancey, 1998, 2016) supports students' development as writers.

However, the common practice of placing a personal literacy narrative at the start of the course and expecting it to serve as a bridge from students' familiar discourses to other more traditional academic genres later in the semester has been widely critiqued as inadequate to the task (Hall & Minnix, 2012). Bawarshi (2003, pp. 128–129), K. P. Alexander (2011), and Bryson (2012) have discussed how a myth of literacy at all times fostering upward mobility is powerfully woven into this genre, compelling students to conform stories from their life to this myth. Corkery (2005) describes the potential for the personal literacy narrative assignment to build student writers' confidence but also to alienate them if students see their home oral cultures in conflict with their sense of academic literacy; a concern that Regidor's (2023) recent research underscored by pointing out that literacy instruction itself may be a site of trauma, especially for minority and marginalized students. In light of these concerns, Corkery and many other writing scholars have issued calls to revise the traditional personal literacy narrative assignment, in many cases making it the center of the first-year course rather than the ineffectual bridge it had been (Lindquist & Halbritter, 2019; Mack, 2023).[3] Rather than completing a personal literacy narrative and moving on, these revisions include making it a first step in a semester-long inquiry about writing and discourse in

188 : CONCLUSION

approaches to the first-year writing course variously labeled "writing about writing" and "teaching for transfer" (Beaufort, 2007; Hall & Minnix, 2012; Hendrickson & Garcia de Mueller, 2016; Kerr, 2020; Wardle, 2007).

TEACH TO DEVELOP STUDENTS' THEORIES OF WRITING

The personal literacy narrative is an excellent entrance to a writing course that takes writing as its subject matter as well as its practice (Blaauw-Hara, 2014; Downs & Robertson, 2015; Downs & Wardle, 2007; Yancey et al., 2014). The results of my discussions with students who did not identify as capable writers presented in Chapter 5 have convinced me that this approach to a first-year writing course may be the most efficacious way to support such students. My work with these students revealed that their definitions, or theories, of writing may be what held them back from developing as writers. Defining "good writing" as something produced quickly and easily, they backed away from the practice of writing and identification of writer when their experience of writing was that it took a lot of time and was difficult. They clung to a definition of writing for years that was not serving them and that may have had consequences on their futures.

I longed to show Student 45 and the other participants who defined writing as he did the many studies that show that writers who are successful by a variety of standards devote a great deal of time to writing and find writing a sometimes painful struggle, such as Rymer's (1988) study of how highly published scientists write. I wanted to do so to attempt to persuade these students that their experience of frustration with writing is not atypical and perhaps even a sign they are doing it right, and thus persuade them not to give up prematurely in their efforts. A first-year course following Downs and Wardle's (2007) suggestions to approach the course as "intro to writing studies" could assign such research and help students relate to it, informing students about the messy complexity of writing processes and providing evidence to support seeing writing as epistemic. Even more helpful may be the approach advocated by Yancey et al. (2014) because it takes as central the development of students' theories of writing informed by writing studies research and theory. Such a theory, or "conceptual framework of writing" (Yancey et al., 2018, p. 43), is essentially an extended definition of what writing is and how it works, or an answer to my annual question of "what do you understand good writing to be?" In this approach, students read about and explore key concepts, such as *audience* and *discourse community*, as they work to build a conceptual framework of writing. In the course of this study, I came to believe that a more accurate, forgiving, and workable theory of writing could be of tremendous value across the range of my participants. Such an approach would have obvious benefits for low-self-efficacy writers, emphasizing that their experience with the challenges of writing is typical and a potential sign of growth. But it might also benefit many others who discounted the writing they did in their science classes as "not writing" or who were suspicious that what the first-year course had to offer them did not apply to the writing they did in other disciplines. Students enter first-year writing with theories of writing; we should be curious to learn these theories and discern where we may help students develop them.

TEACH GENRE AWARENESS

I was disconcerted by the number of students who felt on completing the first-year writing course at this institution that the road ahead for them in terms of the genres and types of writing they would encounter was unclear. My findings may help first-year course instructors see that even at an institution where WAC may not be terribly robust, students immediately went on to write in a great diversity of genres after the first-year course, and that visual and numeric elements, such as charts, graphs, movie stills, and photographs played a role in many of these genres. A first-year course more firmly rooted in writing studies may encourage instructors to have students read and write in genres beyond the standard thesis-first "paper." Because the intellectual background and training of most of the program's writing instructors lies in the humanities, familiarizing themselves with genre conventions prominent in academia but outside the humanities may help them support their students' writing journeys. Wardle (2009) asks instructors to see the "mutt" quality of many first-year writing assignments place them nowhere other than in a school landscape for writing with nowhere else to transfer genre knowledge gained in writing them. Banks (2016) goes further in asking us to "retire" the dominant first-year, thesis-forward essay in favor of genres and media that connect to Black youth culture and decolonize the first-year writing course. I make the suggestion for instructors to become familiar with genres beyond their comfort zone not because a one-semester first-year course possibly could or should introduce all the genres its graduates may go on to encounter in college and beyond but because if these instructors are to make a persuasive counterargument to those students who discount the writing they do each semester as "not writing," they need themselves to be convinced it is writing, too. This is important because to help students embrace "writer" as

190 : CONCLUSION

part of their identity, they and their writing instructors need to see the role writing plays in their academic futures and career paths.

While some participants were asked to write in genres like ethnography and audio diaries for their first-year writing course, simply composing in these genres did not seem to support their development of a rhetorical genre knowledge that could assist them when they encountered new genres (or help them critically and rhetorically understand the affordances and constraints of the genres they wrote in). For this, some work across different genres and some critical and rhetorical comparison of them is likely necessary, such as the comparative genre analysis assignments suggested by Wolfe et al. (2014). My findings support Wolfe et al.'s (2014) recommendation that some attention in this work to genres that use the IMRAD structure may help students like those in my study and Driscoll's (2011) whose perception that scientific writing did not count as writing led them to disregard their first-year writing course instruction as irrelevant to their later writing. They also support Wolfe's (2010) call to include critical attention to the rhetorical work of numbers, statistics, and the visual rhetoric of their presentation in public and academic discourse. Writing studies research has included all these features in its publications, facilitating working these goals into a "writing about writing" approach.

Promoting genre awareness need not foster uncritical acceptance of a particular discourse community's dominant practices either. Devitt (2004) and Bawarshi (2003) argue for fostering critical genre awareness and analysis in the first-year course precisely because this space outside of the discourse community of a student's chosen major or profession may offer the best vantage point for comparison and ideological critique of the affordances and constraints of genres.

TEACH PROCEDURAL KNOWLEDGE

The potential exists for a course devoted to developing students' theories of writing to become esoteric and not rooted in their lived experience of writing. The course should thus never lose its grounding in the lived experience of writing in community and with mentorship. My research documents a number of beneficial and long-lasting changes students made to their writing processes that were influenced by their interactions with writing instructors and peers. Though scholars like Beaufort (2007) and Russell (1995) describe how useful writing knowledge is so often learned most effectively in the context of a specific discourse community, writing process knowledge and rhetorical knowledge may be forms of writing knowledge for which heuristic precepts that are broadly applicable to many contexts for writers may be explicitly taught outside of a specific discourse community context or in a writing studies community context (such as using writing in epistemic invention or thinking about one's audience; Carter, 1990; Wolfe et al., 2014). The first-year course could be a place where resistant students might be persuaded by the research on writing that their theory of writing as quick and easy ought to be questioned as well as a place to practice some of the procedural strategies more expert writers employ in all their recursive, time-consuming messiness and effort.

My findings include stories of students receiving just-in-time, specific strategy instruction pertaining to their writing processes and genre knowledge. When students really heard and applied such sage guidance on writing from a trusted mentor, it led them to make real and lasting changes such as breaking away from a naïve belief that the writing process can never begin anywhere other than at the beginning of a text, a belief that created stressful and unproductive writing blocks. These findings lead me not only to recommend that such procedural instruction should have a role in the first-year course but also to recognize that such "tips on writing" may not be believed if students do not trust the source, and many of the participants in this study and others (Bergmann & Zepernick, 2007; Driscoll, 2011; Reiff & Bawarshi, 2011) did not trust first-year writing as a source for useful, transferrable knowledge on writing in their future contexts. I have found that undergraduates, with some support, can become capable, critical readers of writing studies research, especially because it often documents student experiences very like their own. This research can provide them the evidence to support taking the risks and investing the time and effort to make changes to their writing processes and genre knowledge. This research may thus bolster the ethos of first-year writing instructors in the eyes of their students so that the procedural and genre knowledge they wish to impart will be seen as credible and taken up. Just as we ask students to support their claims, an "intro to writing studies" approach to the first-year course encourages us to offer evidence in support of our guidance on writing processes.

One of the most important pieces of advice a first-year writing instructor could attempt to persuasively yet not dispiritedly impart is that writing can at times be very difficult and frustrating. The creation of new knowledge and the rhetorical work of expression, especially when the stakes are high or when the writer is deeply engaged or when the genre is unfamiliar, is difficult for even the most experienced writers, with process accounts documenting their emotional lows but also their exuberant highs as writing puzzles are solved (see, for example, Boice, 1997; Rymer, 1988). Falconer (2019, 2022, 2023) has documented several incidents of the profound impact a trusted mentor's words can have on minority, first-generation college students pursuing degrees in science when mentors take the time to explain that academic writing is difficult but doable and that lack of awareness of a genre's conventions is not a sign of intellectual inferiority but rather a sign of a discourse community newcomer in need of a map and a local guide. Her research has also documented the profoundly negative impact of mentorship that withholds such guidance and instead misinterprets a student's lack of understanding the white, middle-class rituals of "transactional gratitude" and "show[ing] initiative" in academia as disinterest (Falconer, 2022, pp. 57–60; see also Gonsalves, 2002). The consequence of such misunderstanding, rooted in the white privilege historically enmeshed in academic hierarchies, and the subsequent withholding of a discourse community's genre knowledge, has led one too many students to feel as Anne did in Falconer's (2019) ethnographic study:

> "People who are my color are not really that smart. We might be smart, but we tend to be stupid, as well. I don't know if you know what I'm getting at."
> What she was "getting at" was that she (and, she perceived, many other Black people) lacked the cultural capital to "do" school and science the way traditional (typically, White and male) students do. (p. 25)

As Falconer (2019) explained, what Anne really lacked were "the resources to decode a new discourse," an understanding of her "agency" in the spaces where scientists work, and the genre knowledge possessed by scientists (p. 25). When Anne worked with a mentor willing to play the role of discourse community guide, Anne went on to win a national award that marked her immense progress in mastering (and even innovating) the key disciplinary genre of the scientific poster (Falconer, 2019, p. 33). Falconer's (2023) work documents the transformational impact on many students of mentors "simply telling students that they will not get it perfect the first time and that revisions should be expected" (pp. 278–279). Such mentorship may be something a first-year writing instructor can at least begin to provide for students, though earning all students' trust will require effort and rethinking of approach.

Writing research on how individuals remix and layer knowledge gained from experiences with different discourse communities (Nordquist, 2017; Prior, 2018; Roozen, 2009a, 2009b, 2010; Rounsaville, 2014, 2017; Smith et al., 2021) suggests a possible role for the first-year course as a site of exploration of and reflection on the remixing and repurposing of literacy skills that students of the course have already experienced. The reflective research methods of such studies could be repurposed as prompts for personal literacy narratives in the first-year course to foster a reflective awareness of the assemblage of practices and influences one integrates over the course of one's literate life.

TEACH TOWARD CULTURAL INCLUSION AND SUSTAINABILITY

At institutions like my research site, and really at all but perhaps the most culturally homogeneous colleges, the remix of students' language practices will likely include variants of English historically and prejudicially marked as inappropriate for academic or "formal" writing, such as Black English, Spanglish, and Global Englishes. Approaches to first-year writing that are culturally inclusive and culturally sustaining seek to validate and include these variants, which rather than signifying informality all have a range of registers from informal to formal. To come to believe "I am a writer" in a first-year course, a student likely must see themselves in the discourse of the course and the wider academy and contexts where they wish to go on to write. Young et al. (2014) and Baker-Bell (2020) demonstrate how writing instruction that steers all students toward a mythical Standard English, asking minority speakers of other variants to code switch, can lead to marked decreases in minority students' self-esteem, while writing pedagogies that not only make room for but celebrate the variants of English and allow for code meshing lead to minority students' increased self-esteem. As my participants repeatedly informed me, to embrace "writer" as a part of one's identity takes a great deal of self-esteem. Whether because the term is used as an honorific for a highly respected profession in our society or because the myth of literacy presumes upward mobility, to be a writer is to be a somebody who counts. To increase the benefits of the first-year writing course that my research documents, more first-year writing instructors need to be educated in the linguistic and rhetorical richness and history of variants of English such as Black English (Baker-Bell, 2020; Banks, 2011; Carey, 2016; Gilyard, 1991; Perryman-Clark, 2013; Young et al., 2014) and Spanglish (Hinojosa & de León-Zepeda, 2019; Newman & García, 2019; Sánchez et al., 2019).[4] I make this recommendation as a writing scholar and teacher who has only recently learned, and continues to learn, a great deal about how these rich linguistic and rhetorical traditions can be valued and tapped in college writing instruction. Not only will writing classrooms informed by such knowledge likely enable more students to embrace "writer" as a part of their identity, they will likely better support an environment of trust needed for the mentorship instructors offer on writing's procedural knowledge to be believed and embraced.[5]

Indeed, pedagogies supporting students' language inquiry and critical language awareness (Baker-Bell, 2020; Gere et al., 2021; Perryman-Clark, 2013) would seem to be a more than sensible extension of pedagogies supporting genre inquiry and critical genre awareness (Bawarshi, 2003; Devitt, 2004) and writing as a topic of disciplined inquiry (Downs & Robertson, 2015; Downs & Wardle, 2007; Yancey et al., 2014). Arguments for making genre awareness and writing about writing foci of the first-year writing course have long carried a core critical component, asking us to explore the rhetorical *and* the ideological work of genres and discourse communities, the ways they enable *and* constrain writers. But the pedagogies informed by this approach have often not made race and linguistic diversity central concerns (Brown, 2020). As Gere et al. (2021) explain,

> Critical language awareness enables instructors and their students to investigate and understand both how discourse operates and, in the words of Keith Gilyard, "how the dominant discourse serves to regulate and reproduce patterns of privilege" (*True* 142). This includes exploration of language change, historical processes of standardization, distinctions between descriptive and prescriptive grammars, and an awareness that terms like "conventions" are grounded in standard language ideologies. (385)

First-year writing instruction can no longer assume that issues related to linguistic diversity are the province of experts in second-language instruction. Our students are already multilingual, whether international students (S. K. Rose & Weiser, 2017) or not (Ortmeier-Hooper & Ruecker, 2017). Martins and Van Horn (2017) describe how one writing program fused a "writing about writing" approach to first-year writing, including using a personal literacy narrative, with translingual awareness (Horner & Tetreault, 2017) in ways that supported multilingual and international students' deeper self-reflection and engagement with one another.

Findings Relevant to and Recommendations for WAC/WID

Because we want students to engage meaningfully in writing as a process, we have to find ways to make our writing assignments meaningful to them. My findings can supplement the work of others (Eodice et al., 2016; Jarratt et al., 2009; Wardle, 2007) to help us learn what makes writing assignments

TABLE 6.1. Participant responses to question "What advice would you give instructors who assign writing?"

Participant recommendations to instructors who assign writing	Number of times recommendation offered over course of study
Provide clearer expectations and feedback	30
Present fewer restrictions or requirements	27
Explain how to write in a genre or its citation style	13
Require draft-process steps	12
Be available, approachable	10
Teach a variety of genres	10
Recognize students as learners	9
Teach grammar	8
Require more writing	8
Include peer review	8
Recognize your tasks or authority can be intimidating	6
Conference with students about their writing	6
Devise assignments relevant to students' interests or careers	5
Share past examples of student writing	5
Offer a course that focuses on writing in your specific discipline	4
Teach how to research	4
Build on students' familiar interests	4
Provide feedback	4
Assign more creative writing	4
Give writing assignments early in the semester	3
Don't teach to a test	3
Encourage more collaboration	3
Allow rewrites	2
Encourage students to use your office hours	2
Don't grade all writing	2
Hold more discussion	1
No busy work	1
Provide some class time to do assignments	1
Hold higher standards	1

196 : CONCLUSION

meaningful to students. Many participants perceived earning a high or passing grade as the sole purpose of their college writing, a perception that motivated them to only invest enough time and effort to achieve that goal and no more. But others reported investing a great deal of engagement in the process of writing for their courses. Near the end of each interview, I asked what advice participants would offer to college instructors across the disciplines who assign writing, and their advice nearly always stressed ways instructors could support their students' becoming more invested in the process of writing. Table 6.1 presents the codes I assigned to their responses and the number of times they offered these responses over the course of the entire 5-year study. Their suggestions are ones I would by and large endorse myself, even as I recognize the top two most frequent recommendations can be read as paradoxical. Their request for clearer expectations at times echoed the students in Nelson's (1990) study who actively sought shortcuts around the process of discovery and learning that an instructor intended students to experience (though my participants often sought such shortcuts out of frustration and desperation in the face of many competing demands on their time). The plea for fewer restrictions can be seen as a desire to take more ownership over their writing, making choices on things like length and genre rather than having these choices made for them, in order to more fully experience their writing as a process of discovery and learning.

OFFER THE BLANK PAGE, TEACH INVENTION

How can we as instructors provide clearer expectations while not having that clarity serve as shortcuts or restrictions? This tightrope is one we would be wise to consider as we walk it. My findings, along with those of Eodice et al. (2016), Herrington and Curtis (2000), and Kareem (2018), can help illuminate how some key elements of student choice in scaffolded assignments can be crucial to at least prepare a possible ground for genuine student interest and engagement to blossom. While instructors may feel they are making tasks easier for students by not overwhelming them with choices or guiding them to topics and thesis statements they believe will be more successful, again and again students in this study described how their ability to design a question or develop a topic of inquiry within the parameters of an assignment encouraged them to engage and invest their emotions (to care or even be passionate) and their resources (their limited time, their attention).

Understandably, many may see asking instructors to allow greater degrees of choice in students' selection of writing topics as only compounding the problem participants identified of not providing clear expectations. But the benefits in increasing student engagement cannot be denied. My response is we need to teach what in rhetorical theory is called *invention*. We need to provide students the experience of truly beginning with the blank page or screen and considering how to best fill it, but rather than leave them on their own in these most important first stages of the writing process, we need to offer support and strategies for finding what to write, strategies they can take with them to the next opportunity for writing. Despite the resurgence in rhetorical approaches to writing instruction since the mid-20th century—a resurgence that emphasized explicit strategy instruction in invention—we still tend to focus our work with students on parts of the writing process other than the beginning. Aristotle devoted many more pages of his *Rhetoric* to invention strategies useful in all kinds of situations and for many kinds of audiences than he did to arrangement, style, memory, or delivery. Yet students regularly experience being given a writing assignment prompt and told to return for instruction once they have figured out how they will respond to it in a draft. When we teach writing, we tend to teach revision, which is of course important and encourages the practices of expert writers. But we need to teach the methods of invention that practitioners in our field use, even if they are messy, somewhat unwieldy, not foolproof, and even a little embarrassing (see Geisler, 1994, pp. 210–231).

My previous research (Wilder, 2012; Wilder & Wolfe, 2009) has demonstrated the benefits of teaching the *topoi*, or commonplace starting points for arguments, to students in literary studies. Topoi, which were considered central to invention in ancient rhetorical theories, help writers heuristically explore topics and select from among multiple paths to take in their writing. But my research also uncovered how invisible such topoi tend to be to already established experts in a field and how these experts may be reluctant to name and make accessible this messy and seemingly inexpert knowledge to outsiders and newcomers. But restricting student writers' choices or giving them ready-made arguments to support will not increase their access to expertise. We need to demystify the early stages of writing, notably around the generation of topics and arguments useful in our fields. This, I think, is the best way to respond to the paradoxical request that we provide more guidance while granting greater freedom. Give and maintain that freedom, but pull back the curtain and show students how we and others in similar circumstances have dealt with the work of invention as roadmaps for what is possible. Doing so may help students identify as writers in the fields they wish to enter, engage

198 : CONCLUSION

more deeply in the processes of writing in these fields, and transfer what they learn about invention in these fields to new, appropriate contexts.

Guiding students at this crucial early writing stage no doubt takes more work and time than simply assigning topics to them. Instructors, too, then, need the resources of time and attention to help students with the processes of rhetorical invention appropriate to their field. Small class sizes are thus crucially necessary in both introductory and advanced disciplinary course-work, not just in one first-year writing course taught outside the context of students' majors. WAC/WID workshops, which fall by the wayside when institutional resources are tight, are also needed, with incentives for attending them beyond voluntary goodwill.

CUE PAST WRITING KNOWLEDGE TO ENABLE TRANSFER

Substantive support for WAC coordinated with a campus's first-year writing program could help implement what my findings and so much of the transfer literature in writing studies has already made clear: What students learn about writing in first-year writing and elsewhere needs to be cued later. We can see in Student 45's interviews that when knowledge gained about writing wasn't cued in later contexts, he stopped consciously trying to apply that knowledge. Considering the audience of his medical school personal statement surely would have helped him see that he need not describe the school's features to someone already there, he needed to describe himself, the applicant they didn't already know. But his appreciation of audience as a useful concept for a writer faded in the years after his high school AP Lang course. Preliminary findings from the longitudinal study of student writers at Northeastern University point to the important role that a second writing course within students' major played in supporting students' testing and extending their theories of writing (Smith et al., 2021, p. 22). In particular, this course picked up and used again rhetorical terminology from their first-year course such as *exigence* and *audience* (Smith et al., 2021, p. 15), an experience that Student 45 notably lacked.

TEACH TOWARD CULTURAL INCLUSION AND SUSTAINABILITY

Anson (2012) and Poe (2013) have called for WAC faculty support to confront thorny issues related to race and cultural diversity enmeshed in the teaching of writing along with the customary professional development that assists disciplinary faculty in accessing their own tacit genre knowledge and in teaching writing as a process. While even the older, traditional WAC faculty professionalization models would be a welcome addition to the culture of teaching at my research site, the diverse student population there amplifies the need to infuse culturally inclusive and culturally sustaining antiracist teaching practices across the disciplines.

I and other WID researchers (Falconer, 2022; Geisler, 1994; Wilder, 2012) have called on disciplinary faculty to explicitly teach the genre conventions and tacit rhetorical and procedural writing knowledge of their fields in order to stop the insidious hidden rhetorical curriculum of academia that favors those whose home discourses are closer to academic discourses and whose prior preparation exposed them to more genres and opportunities to rehearse them—in short, to stop shutting the gate on students of color and working-class students by simply doing nothing. I hoped also that such explicit instruction would make disciplinary discourse practices apparent and available for critique and even change and that welcoming more diverse students into the disciplines would have the effect of diversifying the views and sources of lived knowledges upon which disciplines draw (see also Falconer, 2019, p. 31). However, Kareem (2020) argues that such approaches to WAC, in their tendencies toward accommodation of the disciplinary status quo and student assimilation, do not go far enough and that we have to demand the disciplines make space for students' discourse varieties. As Kareem (2020) puts it, rather than merely seeking to support students' "competence with established ecosystems of written discourses," a culturally sustaining WAC aims for "the social transformation of these ecosystems" (p. 299). I hear in this critique what I now see as the glacially slow pace of true, socially just change in my vision of inclusion first, transformation second. WAC scholars and facilitators may have worried too long about seeming to impose our values on disciplines (see, for example, Kaufer & Young, 1993; Segal et al., 1998). We may now find we have receptive allies within disciplines to begin to enact transformative change to not only work to include diverse students in the discursive practices of the disciplines but also change the discursive practices of the disciplines to reflect students' and society's diversity.

ASK STUDENTS TO WRITE (MORE)

Many participants had few opportunities to learn and engage through writing, in part because little was asked of them by their college curriculum and by their overburdened instructors and in part because their financially precarious lives left them with few resources for writing. As much as my participants asked for support and empathy, they also recommended that instructors ask more of them as writers and intellectuals. With important exceptions, participants in my study did not tend to encounter increasingly more rigorous and challenging writing assignments over their college years like those documented in longitudinal studies of the writing cultures at places like Harvard and Stanford. If we are to make good on the social promise that a college education will mean something, regardless of which institution a student attends, we must work collectively toward greater parity in making writing meaningful across curricula and across campuses.

APPENDIX

Open-Ended Interview Question Script

Unless otherwise noted, these questions were used in each of the six interviews held over 5 years.

Questions about writing process
- What kinds of writing do you do most typically these days? For school, what kind of papers? What kinds of writing do you typically do outside of school?
- How do these kinds of writing compare to what you remember writing most frequently in high school/in your first year of college?
- What kinds of writing do you expect you will do most frequently when you leave UA?
- What advice would you give beginning college students about writing their first paper during their first semester of college? How should they get started? What do you think they should pay special attention to?
- Describe the process you typically go through in responding to a writing assignment. How do you prepare? How do you begin writing a typical paper for a class? What are the first things you do? How do you get your ideas? How do you get started? Do you outline, for example, or just start? Do you typically revise? How much? What kinds of things do you

https://doi.org/10.7330/9781646426584.c007

do when you revise? Is there anything about that process you might like to change?

- Do other people help or hinder that process?
- If I had a picture of your writing at home or at school, what would it look like? Where do you write, when, how, and with what?
- If you had a problem completing a writing assignment, what would you do?
- Describe your most successful writing experience this past year. Why was it so successful? Compare it to a less successful writing experience. Why was it unsuccessful or unsatisfying?
- How have you used visual elements (images, graphs, charts, maps, clip art, etc.) in your writing?
- Have you done peer review work on writing assignments? If so, was it done inside or outside of the classroom? Was the experience useful to you?
- Have you done any collaborative writing or group projects? How does writing change when it's done collaboratively? What did you think about the experience?
- Have you done any writing outside of what is required for class recently? What kinds of writing? How do your out-of-class activities affect the way you think about writing?

Questions about perceptions of writing ability and instruction
- Do you see yourself as a writer now?
- Do you think you can write well? Tell me what that means to you—what is "being a good writer"? And what is "good writing"?
- What about your writing are you most satisfied with and why? What about your writing would you most like to improve and why?
- Do you see yourself as a writer in the field you have chosen as a major? How would you describe the range of genres and styles in your anticipated major?
- How well prepared do you feel for the writing you will be asked to do in your classes? What might have better prepared you?
- In your high school/college work what is writing used for? What purposes does it serve? Why are you asked to do it?
- What could your previous instructors do to improve their instruction in terms of writing? What advice would you give instructors who assign writing?

Open-Ended Interview Question Script : 203

- What has been the most useful writing assignment you have been assigned? Can you describe it? What made it useful?
- How does the reading and writing you are being asked to do in college differ from the reading and writing you were asked to do in high school?
- Is writing changing for you in terms of its difficulty? In what ways?
- Have you ever received some really useful writing advice or feedback? Can you describe it?
- Did you feel you could disagree with your high school teachers in your writing? How? Do you expect to be able to disagree with your college professors in your writing?
- If you were advising the university on how to assist students in becoming better writers, what types of classes or experiences would you recommend we design?
- Anything I haven't asked that you would like to say about your experience with writing or expectations for writing in college?

Questions about the writing sample provided by the student
- What paper did you bring with you today? What class did you write this for? What was the assignment?
- Why do you feel this paper is representative of the kinds of writing you have been asked to do as a high school student?
- How long is the paper? Is this a typical length for this semester? How long was the longest paper you wrote this semester?
- What do you think you did best in this paper?
- Where/how did you learn this particular writing strategy/technique?

Questions about the first-year course asked during the first interview of those who took it
- What are your expectations for [the first-year course]? What do you think you will learn? And how do you think you will learn it?

Questions about the first-year course asked in interviews 2–6 of those who took it
- What do you most remember from [the first-year course]? What do you see as the main purposes or goals of the course?
- How was [the first-year course] different from your experiences in other college courses?
- How was [the first-year course] similar to your experiences in other college courses?

204 : APPENDIX

- Looking back, is there anything you learned in [the first-year course] that you are now applying in your other courses?
- Were the professor's expectations for writing in [the first-year course] similar to or different from the expectations in your other classes?
- Was there anything you learned in [the first-year course] that made it difficult to write papers for your other classes? Or that conflicted with advice you received in other classes?
- Did you ever have opinions and insights that didn't make it into your papers for [the first-year course]? Your other classes? Why or why not?
- Do you see any connections between what you learned in [the first-year course] and other areas of your studies, life, or future plans?
- Do you think your writing improved as a result of having taken [the first-year course]? Why or why not?
- How did you learn to generate ideas in this course?
- Did you enjoy writing in this course?
- What was writing meant to do in this course? What was its purpose?
- Did anything you learned in [the first-year course] help you to write the paper you brought with you today?

Questions about writing-intensive courses asked of participants who did not take the first-year course

- What writing-intensive courses did you take? What were/are your expectations for your writing-intensive courses?
- What do you most remember from your writing-intensive courses? What do you see as the main purposes or goals of these courses?
- Were your writing-intensive courses different from your experiences in other college courses? If so, how?
- How were your writing-intensive courses similar to your experiences in other college courses?
- Looking back, is there anything you learned in your writing-intensive courses that you are now applying in your other courses?
- Were the professor's expectations for writing in your writing-intensive courses similar to or different from the expectations in your other classes?
- Was there anything you learned in your writing-intensive courses that made it difficult to write papers for your other classes? Or that conflicted with advice you received in other classes?

- Did you ever have opinions and insights that didn't make it into your papers for your writing-intensive courses? Your other classes? Why or why not?
- Do you see any connections between what you learned in your writing-intensive courses and other areas of your studies, life, or future plans?
- Do you think your writing improved as a result of having taken your writing-intensive courses? Why or why not?
- How did you learn to generate ideas in this course?
- Did you enjoy writing in this course?
- What was writing meant to do in this course? What was its purpose?

Notes

Introduction

1. As Kaufer and Young (1993) and Wardle (2009) have noted, disciplines like biology show few qualms about introducing students to a discipline they may never fully enter in their most introductory courses, while composition has routinely kept open for debate the relationship between its introductory course and disciplinarity.
2. Chiseri-Strater's (1991) ethnography tells a very similar story, but with an advanced-level prose writing course serving as the stepping-stone rather than a first-year writing course. Likewise, the rich case studies by Rounsaville (2017) and Roozen (2009a, 2009b, 2010), while not focused on their participants' experience of a first-year writing course, similarly demonstrate the entwined and layered workings of their participants' personal and academic writing with each practice informing, sustaining, and motivating the other.
3. One study suggests that changes in students' writing may emerge before they do in students' conscience awareness: Delacambre and Donahue's (2012) research indicates signs of disciplinary enculturation may be more readily apparent in longitudinal samples of students' writing than in their conscious awareness expressed in longitudinal interviews.
4. See Yancey et al. (2014) and Rounsaville et al. (2022) for more thorough reviews of the theory and literature on transfer.
5. While some institutions allow students to "test out" of a required first-year writing course, either by completing an AP or college equivalent course in high school or by taking a placement test, the students who thus bypass the requirement would clearly not constitute a random and representative sample.
6. Ruecker's (2014) study of seven Latinx students and their journeys from their final year of public high school to either the nearby public research university or the nearby community college as well as Nordquist's (2017) study of minority and immigrant students navigating

208 : NOTES

different public high school English tracks, including some college dual-enrollment courses, join Sternglass (1997) in the concern for students who do not come from privilege and who attend publicly funded institutions, tracking how they face the many obstacles in the way of their educations. Unlike Sternglass (1997), they do not longitudinally examine students' entire college experience, even as they shed important light on a pivotal transition experience for potentially at-risk students. More studies such as these are needed.

7. Indeed, as Swofford (2019) makes the important point that not all entering University of Michigan students fit the profile of a "typical" University of Michigan student, she also reveals that the vast majority of University of Michigan students come from home neighborhoods best described as affluent with numerous resources and opportunities for preparation and support for students as they transition to college.

8. I have long seen the recommendations for pedagogy informed by WAC and WID research as calling to disrupt the status quo of traditional discursive pedagogy in the disciplines by creating and persuading allies in the disciplines to radically change their pedagogies in order to make visible and accessible traditional (and unchanged) disciplinary discursive practices. Such changes seek to help allow students to consciously accommodate rather than blindly or painfully assimilate to disciplinary discourse (Villanueva, 2001) and support the goal of diversifying the disciplines. Another approach articulated by LeCourt (1996) and more recently amplified is a call to persuade disciplinary allies to change the discursive practices of the disciplines to make room for students' code meshing and alternative discourses (Kareem, 2020).

9. The committee's original proposal was for a required two-course sequence. The requirement as implemented reduced this to one first-year course while calling on majors to identify writing experiences for their students that need not be housed within a particular course, thus making the satisfaction of this requirement open to interpretation of departments—departments that were not, it should be noted, provided additional resources to accomplish these goals.

10. As I was a pre-tenure faculty member during these developments, my colleagues with greater seniority shielded me from participation in this work, which they rightly recognized could prove contentious.

11. I must thank the CCCC Research Initiative for providing these necessary funds. Research participants were compensated with a $25 Amazon gift card for every interview they participated in.

12. The random sample was stratified based on students' major and sex.

13. One student who took the first-year course joined the study as a sophomore, and another who took a comparable course at another college before transferring to my research site joined as a junior.

14. It is not uncommon for longitudinal studies of college writers to see such attrition in participation over time. For example, Sternglass (1997) began her study with 53 participants but only nine stuck with the study to provide her with complete data (p. xvi).

15. Participants were reminded of their rights as a volunteer research participant, prompted to ask questions, and signed an IRB-approved consent form before each interview.

16. Each semester some additional sections of the course are taught by doctoral students in English who are compensated either as part of their graduate funding or, if that funding had expired for them, as adjunct instructors paid by the course. Students from these sections were not invited to participate in this study.

17. I assisted the director in drafting the common course objectives and assignments as an appointed "provost fellow" to support the launch of the new writing program in its first year only, before this study began.

18. Ruecker's (2014) work shows how in one geographic area a research university pursues a writing curriculum rooted in more recent research and theory in rhetoric and composition

while a community college remains rooted in a modes-based writing curriculum with roots in the 19th century.

Chapter 1: "They Write A Lot More Than I Am Writing at My School"

1. I assigned each participant a student number that I used consistently across interviews to identify them while keeping their identify confidential, as promised in the consent form I used. In my citations of quotations from interviews, I list first the unique student number, then the student's year in school at the time of the interview ("first-year," "soph" for sophomore, "jr" for junior, "sr" for senior, and "post" for one year after graduation). The number at the end of each citation is the number of the interview I conducted with that participant, with options ranging from 1 to 6. Interview transcriptions included many repetitions and common verbal tics such as "um" and "like" that I largely removed when preparing this manuscript, but otherwise quotations are verbatim.
2. Some of these, especially the genres named in many first interviews conducted just as they embarked on their first semester of college, are genres participants wrote in high school (such as personal statements for applying to college or a "critical lens essay" that is a form unique to the English Regents exam in New York State).
3. Lerner and Poe (2014) describe how a biology student similarly found that reading published professional texts helped her understand the rhetorical purposes and genre constraints of the genres she was asked to write in (p. 51).
4. See Nordquist (2017) for an example of high school students similarly seeking out clandestine peer review amid enormous obstacles (p. 109).
5. He was not alone in naming the personal statement for college admissions as his successful experience—32% of the first-year students I interviewed named this genre as their successful experience during their first interview and shared it with me as their writing sample.
6. Falconer's (2022) study of undergraduates pursuing science degrees at an urban Hispanic-serving institution similarly documents financial pressures materially impinging on students' studies and long-term career choices, most notably in the experience of "Ruben," who opted not to pursue further graduate study or employment in a criminalistics laboratory as had been his intended goal in pursuing an undergraduate degree and instead committed fully to his job in construction in order to meet his family's financial needs.
7. Light's (2001) assessment of how much students at Harvard write also points to their copious production. The data he collected indicate 83% hand in at least 60 pages in an academic year, some considerably more (p. 58).
8. Financial aid requirements that students in my study faced often necessitated they take at least 15 credit hours each semester, and some were financially penalized for taking electives that did not fulfill general education requirements.

Chapter 2: "If There Was a Class That Could Make Them Confident"

1. The terms students used for these seven genres are: paper, blog post, lab report, email, literary criticism, presentation, and case study.
2. The terms students used for these 15 genres are: paper, research paper, literary criticism, lab report, journal reflection, discussion post, movie review, observation, personal experience essay, presentation, scientific writing, summary, treatment plan, advocacy letter, and zine.
3. The terms students used for these seven genres are: paper, book review, compare and contrast, research paper, literary analysis, short story, and website.

210 : NOTES

4. The terms students used for these seven genres are: paper, journal reflection, 50-page thesis for business, compare and contrast, court observation, hypothesis, summary, and personal statement.

5. 51.61% claimed "writer" as an aspect of their identity during the first interview in the early weeks of the first-year course, 50% during the second at the end of this course, and 42.11% during their second year of college.

6. Unlike Sommers's (1980) students, students in this study could and did refer to relying on computer-assisted grammar- and spelling-error-detection tools. The tendency to consult a thesaurus to avoid superficial repetition that Sommers documented can now be updated by a student describing using an online thesaurus (Student 30.jr.4). One student who did not take the first-year course also described using a text-to-speech program to have his draft read to him to better detect "egregious grammar things that don't make sense that Microsoft Word doesn't pick up on" (Student 16.sr.1).

7. One participant described two transfer incidents: one from high school and one from the first-year course.

8. One participant described two transfer incidents: one from high school and another from other college coursework.

Chapter 3: "In Every Part of Your Writing, You Should Be Inside of It"

1. When I report percentage of participants' responses coded, I am reporting the percentage of the total number of interviews conducted in that set of interviews. For example, for Interview 1, conducted at the start of the first-year course, I spoke with 31 participants, so 31 is 100% of participants in this interview. I report percentages so readers can see more clearly how responses trended during a given year of the study. I also consistently report the raw number of respondents offering each coded response so that readers can see more clearly when and how trending responses changed over time. Though a few participants left the study each year, and some returned and joined in later years, my claims in the analysis that follows about types of responses that grew or receded in frequency are based on participants offering different responses to the same questions than those they gave in past years of the study.

2. It should be noted that an international student participant from southern China shared how a similar comment from his first-year writing instructor about abandoning what students know about writing in the five-paragraph form was for him acutely anxiety-provoking rather than liberating since he had just learned that form for the first time in the summer intensive English-language program he had just completed days earlier, a program that promises applicants conditional admission to the university upon successful completion of an 8-week course of study.

3. Of course, it makes sense that so many participants would identify the first-year course as the context for their failed writing experience during the second interview at the end of this course since this course was often the only course that assigned many participants writing assignments in that semester. It is worth noting that nine participants (40%) identified the first-year course as the source of their successful writing experience that semester.

Chapter 4: "You Should Write to Know What You Don't Know"

1. Student 39 was clear to indicate he enjoyed reading the literary works assigned to him in high school; it was only the focus on responding to them in writing with literary

analysis that he found both perplexing and unhelpful. In his final year of college, Student 39 expressed enthusiastic support for wide reading, including literature, as a way to help improve one's writing.

2. In his senior-year interview, Student 39 shared a story of transfer of learning on writing, but not from his first-year course. Instead, the transfer was from his experience in his genetics professor's lab to a paper he wrote on Galileo for a history course. He transferred the concept of exigency, or articulating to readers why what one is writing about is important. As Student 39 put it,

> In the lab that I work in . . . our professor's always stressing to us to explain why it's important. Why does it matter? Because he says you can go on for an hour or so about a topic, but if you can't explain why it matters, then it's not really going to relate to anyone. So, when I was writing this [history paper], I wanted to explain why this matters, why it's important, why it's remembered . . . because not everyone can relate to Galileo, but at least they can understand why it's remembered. Like, why this is in history books and stuff like that. (Student 39.sr.5)

3. Student 39 was very aware that medical schools often require applicants to take two writing courses, so he may have found his way to such a course even if not required, but clearly this is not the case with all students.

Chapter 5: "Being Able to Write Things Quickly, Easily"

1. In some instances, I could detect issues in the writing samples they provided me that suggested evidence of some of the writing challenges these writers may have regularly faced, such as issues with lack of paragraphing, transition phrases misidentifying the content that followed, stating inaccurate information, or addressing stasis issues inappropriate to the genre or assignment as I understood them. But in other instances, their writing samples were of similar quality with similar rates of convention lapses as in samples shared by participants in the wider study.

2. Interestingly, these eight students are nearly evenly divided in their assessment of their own earlier preparation of college-level writing, with each year about half saying their high school writing experience was good preparation for them and half complaining they were asked to write very little in high school, with their longest papers no more than two to three pages, and mainly in preparation for timed writing assessments (their experience thus conforming to trends described by Applebee & Langer, 2011). Some of their views on the adequacy of their preparation changed over time in reassessments that left them sometimes more critical and sometimes more appreciative of their high school experiences. Some of these students completed college-preparatory and even college-equivalency high school coursework in English language arts, such as AP English courses, while others did not. In the wide range of these experiences and perceptions, they do not differ from the other participants in the wider study. It thus does not seem appropriate to conclude that the quality of their previous preparation wholly determined their perception of their abilities as writers in college.

3. Two participated in interviews during their junior and senior years, and one participated in her senior year and in the year following her graduation.

4. One only participated in the first interview at the start of that first-year writing course. The others participated in at least two more interviews at the end of that course and in their sophomore year. Two participated over the entire duration of the study, participating in six interviews that concluded in the year after they graduated.

5. These defining qualities came up 11 times over all 5 years of the study.

212 : NOTES

6. These writers named these qualities only four times: three times in second interviews by participants as they just finished a semester of the first-year course and one time in the junior year interviews. This means that those four participants who did identify as good or decent writers who defined good writing with these qualities each did so only once; the majority just as they concluded an intensive semester of writing in the first-year course, and they went on to define good writing using other terms in later interviews.

7. This year he explained that he was beginning to see the writing his biology professors produced as writing because they were performing, recording, and sharing authentic, groundbreaking science, as opposed to his classes that asked him to perform verification labs for learning purposes (see Baird & Dilger, 2018). This signaled a big shift for Student 45, who previously seemed to exclude all scientific writing from the category of writing. His experience working as a lab technician after graduating solidified this new view of scientific writing:

> STUDENT 45: So right now, in the lab that I'm doing, there is—we are working on a paper. I'm not—I don't really have too much to do with the paper. I'm just doing the experiments. But I realize how important writing is to these Ph.D. students. It's like one of the most important things to them, the publications and stuff. So—
>
> LAURA: Yeah. So, you're participating in that process in a small way, right?
>
> STUDENT 45: Yeah. Yeah. So, for those people who are interested in a Ph.D. in some science, they're going to have to do a lot of writing and read. (Student 45.post.6)

8. When I asked him during this interview what he could recall from his first-year writing course, we had a conversation that showed his confusion with whether his MSA ethnography and the group assignment he did comparing commuting and dorm life were papers or only presentations:

> STUDENT 45: I remember we did a ethno—ethnography. But I don't know if that was an essay. I think it was more of a PowerPoint.
>
> LAURA: Okay. Was that—I'm remembering from past years you did a project on the Muslim Student Association. Was that the ethnography?
>
> STUDENT 45: Yeah, I did that, too.
>
> LAURA: Was that that paper, or maybe it was something else? Maybe it was a different paper.
>
> STUDENT 45: It was in the same class.
>
> LAURA: Yeah.
>
> STUDENT 45: I don't—I remember I did one about that, and I did one about, like, um, commuters versus, uh, like, dorm—
>
> LAURA: Living on campus?
>
> STUDENT 45: Yeah. I don't remember what the assignment was, but I remember that's what I talked about. Uh, I don't—I don't think we did that much writing, actually, in the class.
>
> LAURA: Okay.
>
> STUDENT 45: Um, yeah. That was a long time ago.
>
> LAURA: Yes, I know. I'm asking you to—
>
> STUDENT 45: I think that was my first semester—or second, first or second.
>
> LAURA: Yeah.
>
> STUDENT 45: Um, I don't—I think we had to write a story maybe.
>
> LAURA: Okay.

Notes : 213

STUDENT 45: I don't know, but—or, a narrative or something like that.

LAURA: Yeah.

STUDENT 45: Um, yeah. There was—I think there was a narrative, the ethnography, and then yeah, that—but I—I don't remember what we were—the whole assignment was.

LAURA: Okay. Yeah, and that—that last one was the one about the MSA?

STUDENT 45: The MSA, yeah.

LAURA: Okay, yeah.

STUDENT 45: But I don't even remember what I had to do.

LAURA: And so, maybe the ethnography was about the commuter versus, um . . .

STUDENT 45: Yeah. I—actually I did write something. I did write something for the MSA.

LAURA: Okay.

STUDENT 45: Um, I think it was just, like, about, like, different communities or something.

LAURA: Okay.

STUDENT 45: But that ethnography was I went out. I interviewed some people.

LAURA: Yeah.

STUDENT 45: That one wasn't writing at all. That was, like, I recorded video. There was a PowerPoint.

LAURA: Oh, okay, so no paper associated with it.

STUDENT 45: There was no writing for that one. (Student 45.sr.5)

As we wrapped up the interview, I brought up his MSA ethnography again, curious as I was about its disappearance from his memory when it was so clear in my own:

LAURA: I remember you were pretty invested. At least you were years ago in—in your Muslim Student Association paper.

STUDENT 45: I completely forgot about that [laughter].

LAURA: Yeah, that's so funny.

STUDENT 45: Yeah.

LAURA: Was that an organization that you got involved with in your time as an undergrad?

STUDENT 45: Yeah, I was on the [executive] board for 2 years.

LAURA: Are you still involved in that?

STUDENT 45: This—I mean, I am, but I'm not on the [executive] board anymore. But yeah, I still go to events and stuff.

LAURA: Yeah. Yeah. That was interesting.

STUDENT 45: Yeah.

LAURA: So that sounds like a project that meant a lot to you because of—

STUDENT 45: Yeah, I need to find that paper. (Student 45.sr.5)

9. Forgetting past writing experiences, finding them inaccessible to speak of during our interviews, was a noteworthy feature of the transcripts of interviews with other students who did not identify as capable writers. Student 2 presented his forgetfulness to me as a protective coping mechanism (in his case for his learning disability), which may be another way to frame Driscoll and Jin's (2018) box under the bed metaphor for some students.

214 : NOTES

10. Student 31's comments about how instructors at times praised her writing voice and at other times were critical of it made me wonder if, as a Black student, she may at times use Black English in her academic writing and experienced racist reactions to this choice. However, I saw no evidence of this in the writing samples she shared with me. In her first writing sample I did see evidence of occasional issues usually described as "sentence boundary" issues, such as run-on sentences and comma splices, which are issues of punctuation that pertain only to written English and which an English professor later seemed to flag for her in a way she understood and learned to address (discussed below).

11. See Beaufort (2007) for discussion of procedural and genre knowledge as components of discourse community knowledge students need to write effectively within a specific discipline.

12. Peer mentors played a role in several sections of the first-year writing course. A particularly successful graduate of the course could apply to work as a mentor to students in a section while receiving concurrent mentorship training for course credit.

13. Only once, during the semester she took the course, did she acknowledge when I directly asked about the role of writing in the audio diaries that producing the audio diaries technically required some writing: "We had to like come up with a script" (Student 58.first-year.2).

14. She was not the only graduate of the first-year writing course to recommend the university implement a course devoted to writing instruction. In fact, 12 (54%) of the graduates interviewed just as they finished the course recommended such a course. While sometimes these recommendations were simply underscoring the importance of the required course they just took, sometimes, like in the case of Student 58, students recommended a writing course because they either did not recognize the required first-year writing course they just took as being such a course or because they did not think the section they took adequately fulfilled this goal.

15. Artificial intelligence technologies for writing were released to the wider public as I put the finishing touches on this manuscript, raising many concerns associated with the teaching of writing. One can easily imagine students who embrace a view that writing should be easy and quick being drawn to using these technologies as the answer to their prayers. Some may argue these technologies are well-suited for individuals who struggle with and dislike writing. While we may figure out the best uses of these technologies in the years ahead, I worry that student writers—and all writers—turning to them early in the writing process will be shortchanged—and will shortchange the rest of us—of their opportunity to use writing epistemically and creatively and invent new knowledge—new to themselves and to us all.

Conclusion

1. I say this while well aware that from the perspective of faculty and students at other 2-year and smaller 4-year public institutions, the conditions for writing at my research site, such as instructor course load, likely offer greater support for writing than at their institutions. These levels of disparity, deprivation, and injustice are relative, and all warrant investigation and exposure of their consequences.

2. It is important to note, as Falconer (2022) demonstrates, that systemic biases that materialize in professors' faulty assumptions about discourse practices and "motivated" student behaviors can prevent women and minorities from being perceived as showing exceptional promise in the sciences, thus foreclosing for them this crucial opportunity for learning science's rhetoric and writing practices.

Notes : 215

3. Lindquist and Halbritter (2019) argue against teaching toward "excellence in genre production" (p. 432) in the personal literacy narrative with "genre modeling" (p. 421), and thus advocate instructors should "collect it, don't correct it" (p. 435). They posit the assignment is better repurposed later in the semester as a source of evidence in the inquiry students undertake to produce an "experiential-learning documentary" (p. 417) than as a stand-alone text. This approach stands in contrast to the one advocated by K. P. Alexander (2015), who argues that instructors should explicitly articulate the goals of the assignment and teach invention strategies to help students develop the analytic components of the genre that the term "narrative" may misdirect students away from but which their instructors expect in it, especially because middle-class white students are more likely than minority and working-class students to have been schooled to see analysis as the hidden goal of the assignment.

4. While never to my knowledge previously discouraged as an approach to teaching the first-year course on this campus, the second director of this writing program, hired after my study had concluded, made it her mission to make culturally sustaining pedagogy central to professional development for instructors in the program.

5. The developing literature on antiracist college writing pedagogies present many ways for instructors to incorporate culturally inclusive and sustaining actions and structures in their teaching. As someone new to but eagerly reading this literature, I admit to having questions about Inoue's (2015, 2019) strong advocacy for labor-based grading contracts as an ideal antidote to the white supremacy historically embedded in classroom writing assessments. On the one hand, it would seem such contracts would encourage the kind of deep engagement with writing as a process that a number of my participants identified as connected to their successful and useful writing experiences. On the other hand, so many of the participants at my study site were overcommitted to multiple jobs and obligations, suggesting that extended time for academic labor is for them one of the greatest markers of privilege, and thus labor contracts run the risk of further advantaging those so privileged. I also wonder if they could contribute to the discouraging suspicions voiced by the business students in my study that their instructors are not reading their writing.

References

Addison, J., & McGee, S. J. (2010). Writing in high school/writing in college: Research trends and future directions. *College Composition and Communication*, 62(1), 147–179.

Adler-Kassner, L. (2012). The companies we keep or the companies we would like to try to keep: Strategies and tactics in challenging times. *WPA: Writing Program Administration*, 36(1), 119–140.

Adler-Kassner, L., & Wardle, E. (Eds.). (2015). *Naming what we know: Threshold concepts of writing studies* (1st ed.). Utah State University Press.

Adsit, J., & Wilder, L. (2020). Borders crossed: A nationwide survey on the influence of rhetorical theory on creative writing. *Pedagogy*, 20(3), 401–429. https://doi.org/10.1215/15314200-8544487

Alexander, J., Lunsford, K., & Whithaus, C. (2020a). Affect and wayfinding in writing after college. *College English*, 82(6), 563–590.

Alexander, J., Lunsford, K., & Whithaus, C. (2020b). Toward wayfinding: A metaphor for understanding writing experiences. *Written Communication*, 37(1), 104–131. https://doi.org/10.1177/0741088319882325

Alexander, K. P. (2011). Successes, victims, and prodigies: "Master" and "little" cultural narratives in the literacy narrative genre. *College Composition and Communication*, 62(4), 608–633.

Alexander, K. P. (2015). From story to analysis: Reflection and uptake in the literacy narrative assignment. *Composition Studies*, 43(2), 43–71.

---

https://doi.org/10.7330/9781646426584.c008

218 : REFERENCES

Anderson, J. H., & Farris, C. R. (Eds.). (2007). *Integrating literature and writing instruction: First-year English, humanities core courses, seminars*. Modern Language Association.

Anderson, P., Anson, C. M., Gonyea, R. M., & Paine, C. (2015). The contributions of writing to learning and development: Results from a large-scale multi-institutional study. *Research in the Teaching of English, 50*(2), 199–235.

Anson, C. M. (2012). Black holes: Writing across the curriculum, assessment, and the gravitational invisibility of race. In A. B. Inoue & M. Poe (Eds.), *Race and writing assessment* (pp. 15–28). Peter Lang.

Anson, C. M. (2015). Habituated practice can lead to entrenchment. In L. Adler-Kassner & E. Wardle (Eds.), *Naming what we know: Threshold concepts of writing studies* (1st ed., pp. 77–78). Utah State University Press.

Anson, C. M., Chen, C., & Anson, I. G. (2020). Talking about writing: A study of key writing terms used instructionally across the curriculum. In L. Adler-Kassner & E. Wardle (Eds.), *(Re)considering what we know: Learning thresholds in writing, composition, rhetoric, and literacy* (1st ed., pp. 313–327). Utah State University Press.

Applebee, A. N., & Langer, J. A. (2011). A snapshot of writing instruction in middle schools and high schools. *The English Journal, 100*(6), 14–27.

Arum, R., & Roksa, J. (2011). *Academically adrift: Limited learning on college campuses*. University of Chicago Press. https://press.uchicago.edu/ucp/books/book/chicago/A/bo10327226.html

Baird, N., & Dilger, B. (2017). How students perceive transitions: Dispositions and transfer in internships. *College Composition and Communication, 68*(4), 684–712.

Baird, N., & Dilger, B. (2018). Dispositions in natural science laboratories: The roles of individuals and contexts in writing transfer. *Across the Disciplines, 15*(4), 21–40.

Baird, N., & Dilger, B. (2023). Writing transfer strategies of first-generation college students: Negotiation as a metaphor for adaptive transfer. In K. Ritter (Ed.), *Beyond fitting in: Rethinking first-generation writing and literacy education* (pp. 211–232). Modern Language Association.

Baker-Bell, A. (2020). *Linguistic justice: Black language, literacy, identity, and pedagogy* (1st ed.). Routledge.

Baker-Bell, A., Willians-Farrier, B. J., Jackson, D., Johnson, L., Kynard, C., & McMurtry, T. (2020, July). *This ain't another statement! this is a DEMAND for Black linguistic justice!* Conference on College Composition and Communication. https://cccc.ncte.org/cccc/demand-for-black-linguistic-justice/

Banks, A. J. (2011). *Digital griots: African American rhetoric in a multimedia age*. Southern Illinois University Press.

Banks, A. J. (2016). Dominant genre emeritus: Why it's time to retire the essay. *CLA Journal, 60*(2), 179–190.

Bawarshi, A. (2003). *Genre and the invention of the writer: Reconsidering the place of invention in composition*. Utah State University Press.

Beaufort, A. (2007). *College writing and beyond: A new framework for university writing instruction*. Utah State University Press.

Bereiter, C., & Scardamalia, M. (1987). *The psychology of written composition*. Lawrence Erlbaum Associates.

Bergmann, L. S., & Baker, E. M. (Eds.). (2006). *Composition and/or literature: The ends of education*. National Council of Teachers of English.

Bergmann, L. S., & Zepernick, J. (2007). Disciplinarity and transfer: Students' perceptions of learning to write. *Writing Program Administration*, 31(1–2), 124–149.

Berlin, J. A. (1988). Rhetoric and ideology in the writing class. *College English*, 50(5), 477–494.

Beyer, C. H., Gillmore, G. M., & Fisher, A. T. (2007). *Inside the undergraduate experience: The University of Washington's study of undergraduate learning*. Anker Pub.

Blaauw-Hara, M. (2014). Transfer theory, threshold concepts, and first-year composition: Connecting writing courses to the rest of the college. *Teaching English in the Two-Year College*, 41(4), 354–365.

Boice, B. (1997). Which is more productive, writing in binge patterns of creative illness or in moderation? *Written Communication*, 14(4), 435–459.

Brannon, L. (1995). (Dis)missing compulsory first-year composition. In *Reconceiving Writing, Rethinking Writing Instruction* (pp. 239–248). Lawrence Erlbaum.

Brent, D. (2012). Crossing boundaries: Co-op students relearning to write. *College Composition and Communication*, 63(4), 558–592.

Brooks, K. (2002). Composition's abolitionist debate: A tool for change. *Composition Studies*, 30(2), 27–41.

Brown, T. (2020). What else do we know? Translingualism and the history of SRTOL as threshold concepts in our field. *College Composition and Communication*, 71(4), 591–619.

Bryson, K. (2012). The literacy myth in the digital archive of literacy narratives. *Computers and Composition: An International Journal for Teachers of Writing*, 29(3), 254–268. https://doi.org/10.1016/j.compcom.2012.06.001

Carey, T. L. (2016). *Rhetorical healing: The reeducation of contemporary Black womanhood*. State University of New York Press.

Carroll, L. A. (2002). *Rehearsing new roles: How college students develop as writers*. Southern Illinois University Press.

Carter, M. (1990). The idea of expertise: An exploration of cognitive and social dimensions of writing. *College Composition and Communication*, 41(3), 265.

Charmaz, K. (2006). *Constructing grounded theory: A practical guide through qualitative analysis* (1st ed.). SAGE Publications.

Charney, D. (1993). A study in rhetorical reading: How evolutionists read "The Spandrels of San Marco." In J. Selzer (Ed.), *Understanding scientific prose* (pp. 203–231). University of Wisconsin Press.

Chiseri-Strater, E. (1991). *Academic literacies: The public and private discourse of university students*. Boyton/Cook.

Cleary, M. N. (2013). Flowing and freestyling: Learning from adult students about process knowledge transfer. *College Composition and Communication*, 64(4), 661–687.

Connors, R. J., & Lunsford, A. A. (1988). Frequency of formal errors in current college writing, or Ma and Pa Kettle do research. *College Composition and Communication*, *39*(4), 395–409. https://doi.org/10.2307/357695

Corkery, C. (2005). Literacy narratives and confidence building in the writing classroom. *Journal of Basic Writing*, *24*(1), 48–67.

Crowley, S. (1998). *Composition in the university: Historical and polemical essays*. University of Pittsburgh Press.

Delacambre, I., & Donahue, C. (2012). Academic writing activity: Student writing in transition. In *University writing: selves and texts in academic societies* (pp. 129–149). Emerald.

Devitt, A. J. (2004). *Writing genres*. Southern Illinois University Press.

Dipardo, A. (1994). Stimulated recall in research on writing: An antidote to "I don't know, it was fine." In P. Smagorinsky (Ed.), *Speaking about writing: Reflections on research methodology* (pp. 163–181). SAGE Publications.

Donahue, C., & Foster-Johnson, L. (2018). Liminality and transition: Text features in postsecondary student writing. *Research in the Teaching of English*, *52*(4), 359–381.

Downs, D., & Robertson, L. (2015). Threshold concepts in first-year composition. In L. Adler-Kassner & E. Wardle (Eds.), *Naming what we know: Threshold concepts of writing studies* (1st ed., pp. 105–121). Utah State University Press.

Downs, D., & Wardle, E. (2007). Teaching about writing, righting misconceptions: (Re)envisioning "first year composition" as "introduction to writing studies." *College Composition and Communication*, *58*(4), 552–584.

Driscoll, D. L. (2011). Connected, disconnected, or uncertain: Student attitudes about future writing contexts and perceptions of transfer from first year writing to the disciplines. *Across the Disciplines*, *8*(2). https://wac.colostate.edu/docs/atd/articles/driscoll2011.pdf

Driscoll, D. L., & Cui, W. (2021). Visible and invisible transfer: A longitudinal investigation of learning to write and transfer across five years. *College Composition and Communication*, *73*(2), 229–260.

Driscoll, D. L., & Jin, D. (2018). The box under the bed: How learner epistemologies shape writing transfer. *Across the Disciplines*, *15*(4), 1–20. https://doi.org/10.37514/atd-j.2018.15.4.19

Driscoll, D. L., Paszek, J., Gorzelsky, G., Hayes, C. L., & Jones, E. (2020). Genre knowledge and writing development: Results from the writing transfer project. *Written Communication*, *37*(1), 69–103. https://doi.org/10.1177/0741088319882313

Driscoll, D. L., & Powell, R. (2016). States, traits, and dispositions: The impact of emotion on writing development and writing transfer across college courses and beyond. *Composition Forum*, *34*. http://compositionforum.com/issue/34/states-traits.php

Driscoll, D. L., & Wells, J. (2012). Beyond knowledge and skills: Writing transfer and the role of student dispositions. *Composition Forum*, *26*. http://compositionforum.com/issue/26/beyond-knowledge-skills.php

Dryer, D. B. (2015). Writing is not natural. In L. Adler-Kassner & E. Wardle (Eds.), *Naming what we know: Threshold concepts of writing studies* (1st ed., pp. 27–29). Utah State University Press.

Eodice, M., Geller, A. E., & Lerner, N. (2016). *The meaningful writing project: Learning, teaching, and writing in higher education*. Utah State University Press.

Eodice, M., Geller, A. E., & Lerner, N. (2019). The power of personal connection for undergraduate student writers. *Research in the Teaching of English*, 53(4), 320–339.

Faigley, L. (1986). Competing theories of process: A critique and a proposal. *College English*, 48(6), 527–542.

Falconer, H. M. (2019). "I think when I speak, I don't sound like that": The influence of social positioning on rhetorical skill development in science. *Written Communication*, 36(1), 9–37. https://doi.org/10.1177/0741088318804819

Falconer, H. M. (2022). *Masking inequality with good intentions: Systemic bias, counterspies, and discourse acquisition in STEM education*. The WAC Clearinghouse; University Press of Colorado. https://wac.colostate.edu/books/practice/masking/

Falconer, H. M. (2023). Playing the expectation game: Negotiating disciplinary discourse in undergraduate research. In K. Ritter (Ed.), *Beyond fitting in: Rethinking first-generation writing and literacy education* (pp. 267–281). Modern Language Association.

Fife, J. (2018). Can I say "I" in my paper?: Teaching metadiscourse to develop international writers' authority and disciplinary expertise. *Across the Disciplines*, 15(1), 61–70.

Fishman, J., Lunsford, A., McGregor, B., & Otuteye, M. (2005). Performing writing, performing literacy. *College Composition and Communication*, 57(2), 224–252.

Flower, L. (1989). Taking thought: The role of conscious processing in the making of meaning. In E. P. Maimon, B. F. Nodine, & F. W. O'Connor (Eds.), *Thinking, reasoning, and writing* (pp. 185–212). Longman.

Flower, L., & Hayes, J. R. (1980). The cognition of discovery: Defining a rhetorical problem. *College Composition and Communication*, 31(1), 21–32.

Flower, L., Hayes, J. R., Carey, L., Schriver, K., & Stratman, J. (1986). Detection, diagnosis, and the strategies of revision. *College Composition and Communication*, 37(1), 16–55.

Freedman, A. (1993). Show and tell? The role of explicit teaching in the learning of new genres. *Research in the Teaching of English*, 27(3), 222–251.

Fulkerson, R. (2005). Composition at the turn of the twenty-first century. *College Composition and Communication*, 56(4), 654–687.

Geisler, C. (1994). *Academic literacy and the nature of expertise: Reading, writing, and knowing in academic philosophy*. Lawrence Erlbaum Associates.

Gere, A. R. (Ed.). (2019). *Developing writers in higher education: A longitudinal study*. University of Michigan Press.

Gere, A. R., Curzan, A., Hammond, J. W., Hughes, S., Li, R., Moos, A., Smith, K., Van Zanen, K., Wheeler, K. L., & Zanders, C. J. (2021). Communal justicing: Writing assessment, disciplinary infrastructure, and the case for critical language awareness. *College Composition and Communication*, 72(3), 384–412.

Gilyard, K. (1991). *Voices of the self: A study of language competence*. Wayne State University Press.

Gonsalves, L. M. (2002). Making connections: Addressing the pitfalls of white faculty/ Black male student communication. *College Composition and Communication*, 53(3), 435–465. https://doi.org/10.2307/1512133

Haas, C. (1994). Learning to read biology: One student's rhetorical development in college. *Written Communication, 11*, 43–84.

Hall, A.-M., & Minnix, C. (2012). Beyond the bridge metaphor: Rethinking the place of the literacy narrative in the basic writing curriculum. *Journal of Basic Writing, 31*(2), 57–82.

Hansen, K., Jackson, B., McInelly, B. C., & Eggett, D. (2015). How do dual credit students perform on college writing tasks after they arrive on campus? Empirical data from a large-scale study. *WPA: Writing Program Administration, 38*(2), 37.

Haswell, R. H. (1991). *Gaining ground in college writing: Tales of development and interpretation.* Southern Methodist University Press.

Haswell, R. H. (2000). Documenting improvement in college writing: A longitudinal approach. *Written Communication, 17*(3), 307–352. https://doi.org/10.1177/07410 88300017003001

Hayes, C., Jones, E., Gorzelsky, G., & Driscoll, D. L. (2018). Adapting writing about writing: Curricular implications of cross-institutional data from the writing transfer project. *WPA: Writing Program Administration, 41*(2), 65–88.

Hendrickson, B., & Garcia de Mueller, G. (2016). Inviting students to determine for themselves what it means to write across the disciplines. *The WAC Journal, 27*, 74–93.

Herrington, A. J., & Curtis, M. (2000). *Persons in process: Four stories of writing and personal development in college.* National Council of Teachers of English.

Hesse, D., & O'Neill, P. (2020). Writing as practiced and studied beyond "writing studies." In L. Adler-Kassner & E. Wardle (Eds.), *(Re)considering what we know: Learning thresholds in writing, composition, rhetoric, and literacy* (pp. 76–93). Utah State University Press.

Hilgers, T. L., Bayer, A. S., Stitt-Bergh, M., & Taniguchi, M. (1995). Doing more than "thinning out the herd": How eighty-two college seniors perceived writing-intensive classes. *Research in the Teaching of English, 29*(1), 59–87.

Hilgers, T. L., Hussey, E. L., & Stitt-Bergh, M. (1999). "As you're writing you have these epiphanies": What college students say about writing and learning in their majors. *Written Communication, 16*(3), 317–353.

Hinojosa, Y. I., & de León-Zepeda, C. (2019). Rhetorical tools in Chicanx thought: Political and ethnic inquiry for composition classrooms. In I. Baca, Y. I. Hinojosa, & S. W. Murphy (Eds.), *Bordered writers: Latinx identities and literacy practices at Hispanic-serving institutions* (pp. 77–103). State University of New York Press.

Horner, B., & Tetreault, E. (Eds.). (2017). *Crossing divides: Exploring translingual writing pedagogies and programs* (1st ed.). Utah State University Press.

Howard, R. M. (1995). Plagiarisms, authorships, and the academic death penalty. *College English, 57*(7), 788–806. https://doi.org/10.2307/378403

Inoue, A. B. (2015). *Antiracist writing assessment ecologies: Teaching and assessing writing for a socially just future.* Parlor Press.

Inoue, A. B. (2019). Classroom writing assessment as an antiracist practice: Confronting white supremacy in the judgments of language. *Pedagogy, 19*(3), 373–404.

Jarratt, S. C., Mack, K., Sartor, A., & Watson, S. E. (2009). Pedagogical memory: Writing, mapping, translating. *WPA: Writing Program Administration, 33*(1/2), 46–73.

Johnson, J. P., & Krase, E. (2012). Articulating claims and presenting evidence: A study of twelve student writers, from first-year composition to writing across the curriculum. *The WAC Journal, 23*, 31–48.

Kareem, J. M. (2018). Transitioning counter-stories: Black student accounts of transitioning to college-level writing. *Journal of College Literacy & Learning, 44*, 15–35.

Kareem, J. M. (2019). A critical race analysis of transition-level writing curriculum to support the racially diverse two-year college. *Teaching English in the Two-Year College, 46*(4), 271–296.

Kareem, J. M. (2020). Sustained communities for sustained learning: Connecting culturally sustaining pedagogy to WAC learning outcomes. In L. E. Bartlett, S. L. Tarabochia, A. R. Olinger, & M. J. Marshall (Eds.), *Diverse approaches to teaching, learning, and writing across the curriculum: IWAC at 25* (pp. 293–308). The WAC Clearinghouse; University Press of Colorado.

Kaufer, D., & Young, R. (1993). Writing in the content areas: Some theoretical complexities. In L. Odell (Ed.), *Theory and practice in the teaching of writing: Rethinking the discipline* (pp. 71–104). Southern Illinois University Press.

Keating, B. (2019). "A good development thing": A longitudinal analysis of peer review and authority in undergraduate writing. In A. R. Gere (Ed.), *Developing writers in higher education: A longitudinal study* (pp. 56–79). University of Michigan Press. https://doi.org/10.3998/mpub.10079890

Keels, M. (2019). *Campus counterspaces: Black and Latinx students' search for community at historically white universities*. Cornell University Press. https://doi.org/10.7591/j.ctvq2w2c6

Kerr, J.-A. (2020). Teaching for transfer in the first-year composition course: Fostering the development of dispositions. In A. N. Amicucci & J.-A. Kerr (Eds.), *Stories from first-year composition: FYC pedagogies that foster student writing identity and agency* (1st ed., pp. 105–119). The WAC Clearinghouse; University Press of Colorado. https://wac.colostate.edu/docs/books/stories/chapter6.pdf

Kitzhaber, A. R. (1963). *Themes, theories, and therapy: The teaching of writing in college*. McGraw Hill.

Knutson, A. V. (2019). Grace: A case study of resourcefulness and resilience. In A. R. Gere (Ed.), *Developing writers in higher education: A longitudinal study* (pp. 193–216). University of Michigan Press. https://doi.org/10.3998/mpub.10079890

Lammers, J. C., & Marsh, V. L. (2018). "A writer more than . . . a child": A longitudinal study examining adolescent writer identity. *Written Communication, 35*(1), 89–114. https://doi.org/10.1177/0741088317735835

LeCourt, D. (1996). WAC as critical pedagogy: The third stage? *Journal of Advanced Composition, 16*(3), 389–406.

Lerner, N., & Poe, M. (2014). Writing and becoming a scientist: A longitudinal qualitative study of three science undergraduates. In M. J. Curry & D. I. Hanauer (Eds.), *Language, literacy, and learning in STEM education: Research methods and perspectives from applied linguistics* (pp. 43–63). John Benjamins.

Light, R. J. (2001). *Making the most of college: Students speak their minds*. Harvard University Press.

Lindquist, J., & Halbritter, B. (2019). Documenting and discovering learning: Reimagining the work of the literacy narrative. *College Composition and Communication*, 70(3), 413–445.

Lunsford, A. A. (2010). *Stanford study of writing*. Stanford Web Archive Portal. https://swap.stanford.edu/was/20220129004722/https://ssw.stanford.edu/about

Lunsford, A. A., Fishman, J., & Liew, W. M. (2013). College writing, identification, and the production of intellectual property: Voices from the Stanford Study of Writing. *College English*, 75(5), 470–492.

Lunsford, A. A., & Lunsford, K. J. (2008). "Mistakes are a fact of life": A national comparative study. *College Composition and Communication*, 59(4), 781–806.

Mack, N. (2023). From literacy narrative to identity-conflict memoir: Agency in representation. In K. Ritter (Ed.), *Beyond fitting in: Rethinking first-generation writing and literacy education* (pp. 282–299). Modern Language Association.

Macrorie, K. (1988). *The I-search paper: Revised edition of searching writing* (revised ed.). Heinemann.

Martins, D. S., & Van Horn, S. (2017). "I am no longer sure this serves our students well": Redesigning FYW to prepare students for transnational literacy realities. In S. K. Rose & I. Weiser (Eds.), *The internationalization of US writing programs* (pp. 151–167). Utah State University Press. https://doi.org/10.7330/9781607326762

McCarthy, L. P. (1987). A stranger in strange lands: A college student writing across the curriculum. *Research in the Teaching of English*, 21(3), 233–265.

Melzer, D. (2014). *Assignments across the curriculum: A national study of college writing*. Utah State University Press.

Neely, M. E. (2014). Epistemological and writing beliefs in a first-year college writing course: Exploring shifts across a semester and relationships with argument quality. *Journal of Writing Research*, 6(2), 141–170.

Nelms, R. G., & Dively, R. L. (2007). Perceived roadblocks to transferring knowledge from first-year composition to writing-intensive major courses: A pilot study. *WPA: Writing Program Administration*, 31(1/2), 214–240.

Nelson, J. (1990). This was an easy assignment: Examining how students interpret academic writing tasks. *Research in the Teaching of English*, 24, 362–396.

Newman, B. M., & García, R. (2019). Teaching with bordered writers: Reconstructing narratives of difference, mobility, and translingualism. In I. Baca, Y. I. Hinojosa, & S. W. Murphy (Eds.), *Bordered writers: Latinx identities and literacy practices at Hispanic-serving institutions* (pp. 125–146). State University of New York Press.

Nordquist, B. (2017). *Literacy and mobility: Complexity, uncertainty, and agency at the nexus of high school and college*. Routledge.

Nowacek, R. S. (2011). *Agents of integration: Understanding transfer as a rhetorical act* (16578298). Southern Illinois University Press.

Odell, L., Goswami, D., & Herrington, A. (1983). The discourse-based interview: A procedure for exploring the tacit knowledge of writers in non-academic settings. In P. Mosenthal, L. Tamor, & S. A. Walmsley (Eds.), *Research on writing* (pp. 221–236). Longman.

Olinger, A. R. (2021). Self-contradiction in faculty's talk about writing: Making and unmaking autonomous models of literacy. *Literacy in Composition Studies, 8*(2), 1–38. https://doi.org/10.21623/1.8.2.2

Ortmeier-Hooper, C., & Ruecker, T. C. (Eds.). (2017). *Linguistically diverse immigrant and resident writers: Transitions from high school to college*. Routledge.

Pajares, F. (2003). Self-efficacy beliefs, motivation, and achievement in writing: A review of the literature. *Reading & Writing Quarterly, 19*(2), 139–158.

Penrose, A. M. (2002). Academic literacy perceptions and performance: Comparing first-generation and continuing-generation college students. *Research in the Teaching of English, 36*(4), 437–461.

Penrose, A. M., & Geisler, C. (1994). Reading and writing without authority. *College Composition and Communication, 45*(4), 505–520.

Perkins, D. N., & Salomon, G. (1988). Teaching for transfer. *Educational Leadership, 46*(1), 22.

Perryman-Clark, S. (2013). *Afrocentric teacher-research: Rethinking appropriateness and inclusion*. Peter Lang.

Petraglia, J. (1995). Writing as an unnatural act. In J. Petraglia (Ed.), *Reconceiving writing, rethinking writing instruction* (pp. 79–100). Lawrence Erlbaum.

Poe, M. (2013). Re-framing race in teaching writing across the curriculum. *Across the Disciplines, 10*(3). https://wac.colostate.edu/docs/atd/race/poe.pdf

Prior, P. (2018). How do moments add up to lives: Trajectories of semiotic becoming vs. tales of school learning in four modes. In R. Wysocki & M. P. Sheridan (Eds.), *Making future matters*. Computers and Composition Digital Press. https://ccdigital press.org/book/makingfuturematters/prior-conclusion.html#content-top

Regidor, M. P. C. (2023). "I'm a bad writer": Latina college students' traumatic literacy experiences. *College English, 86*(1), 9–35.

Reiff, M. J., & Bawarshi, A. (2011). Tracing discursive resources: How students use prior genre knowledge to negotiate new writing contexts in first-year composition. *Written Communication, 28*(3), 312–337.

Richardson, E. B. (2004). Coming from the heart: African American students, literacy stories, and rhetorical education. In E. B. Richardson & R. L. Jackson (Eds.), *African American rhetoric(s): Interdisciplinary perspectives* (pp. 155–169). Southern Illinois University Press.

Robillard, A. E. (2007). We won't get fooled again: On the absence of angry responses to plagiarism in composition studies. *College English, 70*(1), 10–31. https://doi.org /10.2307/25472248.

Roozen, K. (2009a). "Fan fic-ing" English studies: A case study exploring the interplay of vernacular literacies and disciplinary engagement. *Research in the Teaching of English, 44*(2), 136–169.

Roozen, K. (2009b). From journals to journalism: Tracing trajectories of literate development. *College Composition and Communication, 60*(3), 541–572.

Roozen, K. (2010). Tracing trajectories of practice: Repurposing in one student's developing disciplinary writing processes. *Written Communication, 27*(3), 318–354.

226 : REFERENCES

Roozen, K. (2016). Reflective interviewing: Methodological moves for tracing tacit knowledge and challenging chronotopic representations. In K. B. Yancey (Ed.), *A rhetoric of reflection* (pp. 250–267). Utah State University Press.

Rose, M. (1980). Rigid rules, inflexible plans, and the stifling of language: A cognitivist analysis of writer's block. *College Composition and Communication, 31*(4), 389–410.

Rose, S. K., & Weiser, I. (Eds.). (2017). *The internationalization of US writing programs.* Utah State University Press. https://doi.org/10.7330/9781607326762

Rounsaville, A. (2014). Situating transnational genre knowledge: A genre trajectory analysis of one student's personal and academic writing. *Written Communication, 31*(3), 332–364. https://doi.org/10.1177/0741088314537599

Rounsaville, A. (2017). Genre repertoires from below: How one writer built and moved a writing life across generations, borders, and communities. *Research in the Teaching of English, 51*(3), 317–340.

Rounsaville, A., Leonard, R. L., & Nowacek, R. S. (2022). Relationality in the transfer of writing knowledge. *College Composition and Communication, 74*(1), 136–163.

Ruecker, T. (2014). Here they do this, there they do that: Latinas/Latinos writing across institutions. *College Composition and Communication, 66*(1), 91–119.

Russell, D. R. (1995). Activity theory and its implications for writing instruction. In J. Petraglia (Ed.), *Reconceiving writing, rethinking writing instruction* (pp. 51–77). Lawrence Erlbaum.

Rymer, J. (1988). Scientific composing processes: How eminent scientists write journal articles. In D. Jolliffe (Ed.), *Advances in writing research* (vol. 2, pp. 211–250). Ablex.

Saldana, J. (2015). *The coding manual for qualitative researchers* (3rd ed.). SAGE Publications.

Sánchez, Y., Nicholson, N., & Hebbard, M. (2019). Familismo teaching: A pedagogy for promoting student motivation and college success. In I. Baca, Y. I. Hinojosa, & S. W. Murphy (Eds.), *Bordered writers: Latinx identities and literacy practices at Hispanic-serving institutions* (pp. 105–124). State University of New York Press.

Segal, J., Paré, A., Brent, D., & Vipond, D. (1998). The researcher as missionary: Problems with rhetoric and reform in the disciplines. *College Composition and Communication, 50*(1), 71–90.

Sitler, H. C. (2020). Becoming a person who writes. In A. N. Amicucci & J.-A. Kerr (Eds.), *Stories from first-year composition: FYC pedagogies that foster student writing identity and agency* (pp. 71–90). The WAC Clearinghouse. https://wac.colostate.edu/docs/books/stories/chapter4.pdf

Smit, D. W. (2004). *The end of composition studies.* Southern Illinois University Press.

Smith, K. G., Girdharry, K., & Gallagher, C. W. (2021). Writing transfer, integration, and the need for the long view. *College Composition and Communication, 73*(1), 4–26.

Sommers, N. (1980). Revision strategies of student writers and experienced adult writers. *College Composition and Communication, 31*(4), 378–388.

Sommers, N. (2008). The call of research: A longitudinal view of writing development. *College Composition and Communication, 60*(1), 152–164.

Sommers, N., & Saltz, L. (2004). The novice as expert: Writing the freshman year. *College Composition and Communication, 56*(1), 124–149.

Sternglass, M. S. (1997). *Time to know them: A longitudinal study of writing and learning at the college level.* Lawrence Erlbaum.

Swales, J. M. (1990). *Genre analysis: English in academic and research settings.* Cambridge University Press.

Swofford, S. (2019). Reaching back to move beyond the "typical" student profile: The influence of high school in undergraduate writing development. In A. R. Gere (Ed.), *Developing Writers in Higher Education: A Longitudinal Study* (pp. 255–280). University of Michigan Press. https://doi.org/10.3998/mpub.10079890

Tate, G., Rupiper Taggart, A., Schick, K., & Hessler, H. B. (2014). *A guide to composition pedagogies.*

Thaiss, C., & Zawacki, T. M. (2006). *Engaged writers and dynamic disciplines: Research on the academic writing life.* Boyton/Cook Heinemann.

Thonney, T. (2016). "In this article, I argue": An analysis of metatext in research article introductions. *Teaching English in the Two-Year College, 43*(4), 411–422.

Tomlinson, B. (1984). Talking about the composing process: The limitations of retrospective accounts. *Written Communication, 1*(4), 429–445. https://doi.org/10.1177/0741088384001004003

Villanueva, V. (2001). The politics of literacy across the curriculum. In S. H. McLeod, E. Miraglia, M. Soven, & C. Thaiss (Eds.), *WAC for the new millennium: Strategies for continuing writing-across-the-curriculum programs* (pp. 165–178). NCTE.

Wardle, E. (2007). Understanding "transfer" from FYC: Preliminary results of a longitudinal study. *WPA: Writing Program Administration, 31*(1/2), 65–85.

Wardle, E. (2009). "Mutt genres" and the goal of FYC: Can we help students write the genres of the university? *College Composition and Communication, 60*(4), 765–789.

Wardle, E. (2012). Creative repurposing for expansive learning: Considering "problem-exploring" and "answer-getting" dispositions in individuals and fields. *Composition Forum, 26.* http://compositionforum.com/issue/26/creative-repurposing.php

Warren, J. E. (2011). "Generic" and "specific" expertise in English: An expert/expert study in poetry interpretation and academic argument. *Cognition and Instruction, 29*(4), 349–374.

Weese, K. L., Fox, S. L., & Greene, S. (1999). *Teaching academic literacy: The uses of teacher-research in developing A writing program.* Routledge.

White, E. M. (1990). The damage of innovations set adrift. Change for the worst. *American Association for Higher Education Bulletin, 43*(3), 3–5.

Wilder, L. (2002). "Get comfortable with uncertainty": A study of the conventional values of literary analysis in an undergraduate literature course. *Written Communication, 19*(1), 175–221.

Wilder, L. (2006). "Into the laboratories of the university": A rhetorical analysis of the first publication of the Modern Language Association. *Rhetoric Review, 25*(2), 162–184.

Wilder, L. (2012). *Rhetorical strategies and genre conventions in literary studies: Teaching and writing in the disciplines.* Southern Illinois University Press.

Wilder, L., & Wolfe, J. (2009). Sharing the tacit rhetorical knowledge of the literary scholar: The effects of making disciplinary conventions explicit in undergraduate writing about literature courses. *Research in the Teaching of English*, 44(2), 170–209.

Wolfe, J. (2010). Rhetorical numbers: A case for quantitative writing in the composition classroom. *College Composition and Communication*, 61(3), 452–475.

Wolfe, J., Olson, B., & Wilder, L. (2014). Knowing what we know about writing in the disciplines: A new approach to teaching for transfer in FYC. *The WAC Journal*, 25, 42–77.

Yancey, K. B. (1998). *Reflection in the writing classroom*. Utah State University Press.

Yancey, K. B. (Ed.). (2016). *A rhetoric of reflection* (1st ed.). Utah State University Press.

Yancey, K. B., Davis, M., Robertson, L., Taczak, K., & Workman, E. (2018). Writing across college: Key terms and multiple contexts as factors promoting students' transfer of writing knowledge and practice. *The WAC Journal*, 29, 42–63. https://doi.org/10.37514/wac-j.2018.29.1.02

Yancey, K. B., Davis, M., Robertson, L., Taczak, K., & Workman, E. (2019). The teaching for transfer curriculum: The role of concurrent transfer and inside—and outside—school contexts in supporting students' writing development. *College Composition and Communication*, 71(2), 268–295.

Yancey, K. B., Robertson, L., & Taczak, K. (2014). *Writing across contexts: Transfer, composition, and sites of writing* (1st ed.). Utah State University Press.

Young, V. A., Barrett, R., Young-Rivera, Y., & Lovejoy, K. B. (2014). *Other people's English: Code-meshing, code-switching, and African American literacy*. Teachers College Press.

Zwagerman, S. (2008). The scarlet P: Plagiarism, panopticism, and the rhetoric of academic integrity. *College Composition and Communication*, 59(4), 676–710.

Index

academic inquiry, 84, 142, 187
academic voice, breaking from, 112
academic writing, 87, 92, 109–10, 114, 187, 193; challenges of, 192; criteria for, 132; engagement in, 141; home identity in, 186; outlet for, 142–43; personal writing and, 134, 138–48; productive, 174
Academically Adrift (Arum and Roksa), 60
ACT exam. *See* timed reading exams
Adler-Kassner, L., 111, 177–78, 179
advocacy letters, 68, 209n2
agency, 7, 21, 50, 59, 142; sense of, 51, 74, 128
Alexander, J., 10, 59, 152
Alexander, K. P., 187, 215n3
analysis, 16, 23, 120, 143, 154, 168; film, 164; genre, 125; interview transcript, 20–21, 26, 89, 101, 167; literary, 30, 116, 172, 209n3, 210n1; quantitative, 21; rhetorical, 105, 119
analysis papers, 131; rhetorical, 105, 119
Animal Farm (Orwell), 118
Anson, C. M., 11, 162, 198
answer-getting, problem-solving versus, 6
anticipatory thoughts, describing, 166
AP courses, 28, 67, 131, 198, 207n5, 211n2
AP English Language and Composition, 87, 161, 163

AP exams, 28, 67, 129
APA, 107; citation format, 30, 101
Applebee, A. N., 29
apprenticeships, 114, 127
argumentation, 32, 77, 92, 94, 119, 123; debate-style, 105; implicit, 166; researched, 117; specific, 104; starting point for, 197
Aristotle, 197
arrangement, 93, 97, 100, 131, 132, 142, 162, 197
Arum, R., 60
assessments, 8, 22, 28, 60, 91, 134, 169, 183; alternative, 90; instructor, 169; standardized, 183; timed, 211n2
assignments, 62, 75, 142, 167–68, 185; boredom with, 81; caring about, 59; challenging, 83, 182–83, 200; completing, 50, 202; describing, 47, 142; emphasis on, 32; engagement in, 138; guidelines for, 15, 137, 142; identifying, 115; increasing, 199–200; length of, 37; meaningful, 52, 129, 194, 196; nature of, 39; with page counts, 137; parameters of, 59, 196; prompting from, 40; purpose of, 91–92; starting, 59, 78, 83; successful, 50, 157–58; types of, 112; useful, 52, 163, 166, 203
audience, 6, 100, 162, 179, 188, 198
audio diaries, 175, 176, 190, 214n13

230 : INDEX

autonomy, 22, 31, 88, 121; instructor, 8, 24
awareness, 121, 124, 150; conscience, 207n3;
critical language, 194; genre, 7, 21, 189–90,
194; metacognitive, 64; increased, 66, 115

Baird, N., 69, 158
Baker-Bell, A., 12, 193
Banjo (McCay), 77
Banks, A. J., 189
Bawarshi, A., 5–6, 190; boundary guarders
and, 6; literacy and, 187
Beaufort, A., 4, 5, 181, 185, 190, 214n11
Bergmann, L. S., 4, 65, 111
Beyer, C. H., 60
binary oppositions, developing, 143
biology, 41, 61, 115, 123, 124, 127, 128, 132, 133,
158, 160, 162, 164, 167; writing, 58, 121, 122
Black English, 193, 194, 214n10
Black students, overrepresentation of, 19
blank pages, offering, 196–98
blog posts, 68, 209n1
Boice, B., 174
book reports, 42, 209n3
boundary crossers/boundary guarders, 6
brainstorming, 39, 75, 88, 173
Brave New World, A (Huxley), 131, 134, 136
Brett, D., 77
Bryson, K., 187
business, 37, 44, 75, 109, 141, 145, 147, 181

capstone paper, 37, 40, 44, 45, 108
Carroll, L. A., 4, 5, 60, 151, 186; research databases and, 83
case studies, 68, 113, 114, 149, 150, 179, 209n1;
descriptive, 5
CCCC Research Initiative, 208n11
Charney, D., 126
Chicago Manual of Style, citation format, 30
Chiseri-Strater, E., 147, 181, 207n2
citation format, 38, 121; APA/MLA, 101; Chicago, 30
class size, differences in, 90
coding, 12, 16, 20, 21, 26, 66, 91, 92, 93, 98, 138,
154, 196, 208n8, 210n1; tallies of, 113
collaboration, 38, 40–41, 83, 130–31, 137, 202;
benefits of, 20; encouraging, 76; experiences with, 39, 75–76, 104; self-sponsored,
71; views on, 74–76, 131
college application essay, 116, 129, 139
communications, 42, 114, 131; cross-cultural,
149; successful, 126–27; visual, 132
comparative studies, 8, 15, 66, 183
complaint letters, 129, 132

composition, 75, 122, 123, 208n18; teaching, 3;
theory, 21; traditional, 24. *See also* first-year
writing course
composition courses, 8, 14, 23, 84
conceptual framework, 179, 188
conclusions, 102, 113, 130
connections, 43, 106; emotional, 59; personal,
185
control groups, comparison to, 7–11
Corkery, C., 187
Council of Writing Program Administrators
(CWPA), 38
COVID-19, 19, 119–20
creative writing, 7, 63, 139, 146; training in,
242
criminal justice, 40, 108, 115, 117, 118, 119, 120,
121, 177, 182
critical thinking, 149; developing, 113, 114–28
Cui, W., 100
cultural inclusion, teaching, 193–94, 198–99
culture, 146; teaching, 99; writing, 8, 28, 89,
200; youth, 189
curriculum, 24, 47, 154; business, 45; changes
in, 84; college, 199; common, 22; introductory, 22; rhetorical, 122
Curtis, M., 5, 61, 134, 147, 185, 196

data, 67, 85, 101; collecting, 65; quantitative, 21;
research, 83, 163
de León-Zepeda, C., 186
Dead Presidents, The (film), 106, 164
Delacambre, I., 207n3
demographics, racial/ethnic, 19
development, 12, 111, 127; longitudinal, 89; professional, 23, 198, 215n4
Devitt, A. J., 190
differences, 71–81, 89; cultural, 184; disciplinary, 121; racial, 184; stylistic, 122
Dilger, B., 69, 158
Dipardo, A., 17
disciplinary, 111, 160, 181, 192, 199, 207n1; conventions, 120–21; personal, 128–38
disciplinary courses, 108, 184, 198, 208n8
disciplining, personal, 128–38
discourse, 17, 100; academic, 12, 190; alternative, 208n8; disciplinary, 199; oral, 11, 22;
writing and, 187–88
discourse community, 6, 11, 12, 179, 188, 190,
191, 192, 194
discovery, process of, 41, 178, 196
discussion, 72, 81, 121, 122, 140; class, 75, 90;
course, 116; participation in, 90; peer, 70;
posts, 209n2

Index : 231

dispositions, 5, 16, 52, 65, 82, 88; different, 71; "disconnected," 111

Dively, R. L., 181

diversity, 8, 31, 34, 66, 74, 82, 189, 194; cultural, 198; racial, 198; social, 199

Donahue, C., 5, 207n3

Downs, D., 179, 188

drafts, 38, 51, 117, 129; discovery, 107; initial, 93; major paper, 156; rough, 97; sharing, 138; submitting, 93

Driscoll, D. L., 4, 7, 41, 69, 100, 102, 158, 160, 176, 190, 213n9; "disconnected" disposition and, 111; self-efficacy and, 161; unidirectional disposition and, 52

Dryer, D. B., 178

dual-enrollment courses, 28, 208n6

economic hardships, 9, 182

editing, freewriting and, 173

education, 62; early, 28; experiential, 127; higher, 24, 147, 149, 183; rhetorical, 133, 149. *See also* general education

ELA. *See* English language arts

emotional reactions, 59, 152, 174, 191–92

engagement, 51, 52, 59, 138, 194, 196, 199; civic, 21; deep, 69; epistemic, 83; increasing, 197; lack of, 58, 148; social, 83

English, 58, 165, 167, 170, 172, 174, 210n2; variants of, 193; writing, 122, 123

English language arts (ELA), 87, 109, 183, 211n2

Eodice, M., 52, 59, 185, 196

epistemic process, 25, 77, 84, 85, 184

essay exams, 29

essays: academic conventions for, 88; focus of, 23

ethnography, 4, 51, 142, 190, 192, 207n1, 212n8, 213n8; MSA, 162, 163, 164

evaluations, 11; negative, 47, 50, 149; positive, 47

expectations, 2–3, 87, 182, 203, 204; cultural, 72; increased, 170

experiences, 16–17, 28, 65, 85, 88, 114, 115, 122, 127; autonomy from, 31; collaborative, 39, 75–76; college, 8, 9, 39–47, 50–52, 54–55, 58–59, 62, 80, 140, 184; comparing, 43, 64, 66, 68, 81, 89; designing, 63; disconnected, 39; educational, 31, 82, 182; eye-opening, 105–6; failed, 105, 210n3; first-year writing course, 10, 64, 90; high school, 91, 99, 211n2; impersonal, 39; interactive, 39–41, 181–82; learning, 5–6, 45, 105, 153; less successful, 56–57t, 59, 105, 117, 139; meaningful, 39, 47, 50–52, 54–55, 58–59; negative, 18, 153; personal, 105, 108, 109, 186; positive,

18, 153; previous, 67, 71, 87; recent, 37, 43, 53, 68, 105, 117, 119, 121, 129, 131, 132, 141, 145; reflecting on, 153, 154; successful, 47, 48–49t, 50–51, 52, 54, 59, 60, 69, 119, 121, 129, 135, 202, 210n3; thinking/learning/communicating and, 62; writing, 28–31, 67, 80, 82, 111, 119, 132, 139, 141, 153, 156, 162, 186, 190

expression, 84, 92, 147, 191

failure, 54; learning from, 104–5

Falconer, H. M., 149, 192, 209n6, 214n2

feedback, 31, 38, 40, 44, 51, 62, 81, 95, 107, 108, 115, 122, 124, 129, 130, 139, 166, 171, 182, 203; cheerleading, 178; draft, 24, 39; good writing and, 169; individualized, 157; information and, 45; instructor, 39, 45, 110, 116, 119, 148; peer, 45, 61, 69–71, 82, 110; providing, 121, 177; receiving, 90, 133; responding to, 96; seeking, 70, 138; useful, 39, 143. *See also* peer review

50-page paper, 44, 46, 210n4; drafts of, 45

financial aid, 9, 15, 209n8

financial hardships, 22, 58, 59, 62

first-person pronoun, using, 100, 103

first sentences, 97

first-year writing course, 4, 41–42, 64, 68, 78, 114; enrollment in, 19; hindrances to transfer from, 105–9; impact of, 10, 24–25, 66, 113, 174–77; knowledge gained in, 80; new, 21–24; participation in, 14; questions about, 87, 203; required, 13, 18; taking, 28, 72, 74, 77–78, 79, 80, 82; transfer from, 100–104. *See also* composition

five-paragraph form, 87, 95, 102, 210n2; breaking from, 112

Floyd, George, 120

fluency, 95, 98, 110

Foster-Johnson, L., 5

freewriting, 83, 172, 176; editing and, 173; epistemic exploration and, 77

Fulkerson, R., 24

Galileo, 211n2

Garner, Eric, 117

general education, 3, 127, 158, 183, 209n8

general education courses, 22, 64, 70, 81, 92, 158

genres, 6, 15, 23, 40, 65, 116, 119, 122, 158, 159, 162, 164, 173, 183, 186, 196, 199, 202; academic, 32, 187; affordances/constraints of, 190; analysis of, 125; conventions of, 189; different, 107–8; disciplinary, 192; diversity of, 34, 189; identified, 33–34t, 35-36t; media

232 : INDEX

and, 82, 189; range of, 31–32, 34, 37–39, 68; reading practices for, 45; relevance of, 174; rhetorical, 8; scientific, 106, 150, 165; target, 79; terms used for, 209n1, 209n2, 209n3; work of, 194
Gere, A. R., 18, 64, 194
Gilyard, Keith, 194
Gladwell, Malcolm, 159
Global Englishes, 193
good writer, being, 155, 156
good writing, 140, 152, 188, 202; defining, 155–56, 157t, 158–66, 174, 177, 178; feedback on, 169; revising definitions of, 167–74; theory of, 158–66; understanding, 156, 158, 167
grammar, 24, 54, 155, 170
guidelines, 129, 134, 136, 137, 142, 157–58, 159; highlighting, 135

Haas, C., 4
habits, 5, 104; general-purpose, 84
Halbritter, B., 214n3
Hansen, K., 4, 64, 65
Harvard University, 8, 15, 28, 60, 62, 183, 200
Haswell, R. H., 5
Hemingway, Ernest, 77
Herrington, A. J., 5, 61, 134, 147, 185, 196
Hesse, D., 72–73
heuristics, 78, 95, 110, 177, 190, 197
high-stakes tests, preparation for, 29
Hilgers, T. L., 65
Hinojosa, Y. I., 186
history, 70, 118, 120, 123, 141, 144, 164, 211n2
history paper, 119, 211n2
Hobbes, Thomas, 141
humanities, 61, 109, 114, 123, 128, 165

I-search papers, 22
identity, 26, 84, 138, 152, 185; academic, 148; developing, 5, 73–74, 177; embracing, 82; home, 140, 186; marginalized, 149; novice, 6, 149; transfer and, 149–50; writing, 9, 71–74, 85, 149, 153, 188, 193
IMRAD. See Introduction, Methods, Results and Discussion
inequities, 24, 28, 43, 183
information: background, 55, 97; double, 131; factual, 117; feedback and, 45; gathering, 126
inquiry, 22, 23, 41, 79, 88, 121, 143, 185, 187, 196; academic, 84, 142; disciplined, 4, 194; genre, 194; language, 194
Inside the Undergraduate Experience (Beyer et al.), 60
insights, 4, 41, 73, 76, 127, 131, 204, 205, 206

institutional review board (IRB), 14, 20
instruction, 12, 31, 39, 76, 197; apprentice-style, 127; disciplinary, 181; discounting, 112; experiencing, 96; genre, 11; high school, 29, 30, 115; improving, 202; informing, 84; interactive, 42, 182; perceptions of, 202–3; quantity/quality of, 181; strategy, 143, 191; timed essay exams and, 29; training in, 13
instructors, 3, 83; advice for, 195t; blaming, 105; feedback from, 39, 45, 110, 116, 119, 148; guidelines from, 135; improvements for, 121
internships, 32, 141, 142, 158; applications for, 148; experiencing, 55; financial need and, 58
interview questions, 18, 20, 89, 152
interview transcripts, 17, 19, 138, 144, 154, 209n1; analysis/coding of, 20–21, 26, 89, 101, 167
interviews, 4, 25, 42–43, 51, 64, 69, 75, 80, 90–94, 96, 98, 99, 102, 106, 108; conducting, 20, 180, 210n1; described, 209n1; differences in, 71; discourse-based, 17, 100; labor-intensive, 66; limitations of, 16, 66; number of, 20; personal, 163, 187; protocols for, 18, 65; responses to, 65, 67; student, 86–87; tendencies/changes in, 89
Introduction, Methods, Results and Discussion (IMRAD), 121, 135, 160, 190
introductions, 77, 102, 130; ending with, 96; starting with, 78; struggling with, 78
introductory writing course, 80, 81, 92, 207n1
invention, 83, 182; strategies for, 159, 197; teaching, 196–98
IRB. See institutional review board

Jarratt, S. C., 17, 65, 66
Jin, D., 52, 213n9
Johnson, J. P., 5
journals, 133, 209n2, 210n4

Kareem, J. M., 12, 147–48, 186, 196, 199
Kaufer, D., 207n1
Keating, B., 70
Keels, M., 148
King, Stephen, 152
knowledge: building, 7, 14, 80, 81, 110, 166; genre, 7, 61, 162, 172, 189, 190, 191, 214n11; procedural, 172, 190–93, 214n11; repurposing, 102, 164; rhetorical, 97, 190; superficial, 30; testing, 90, 92; transfer of, 6, 7, 84, 108, 149, 158, 160, 161, 162, 184, 191; writing-process, 81, 183. See also writing knowledge
knowledge writing studies, 179
Knutson, A. V., 10, 170
Krase, E., 5

Index : 233

lab reports, 68, 122, 149, 209n1, 209n2; writing, 41, 121, 159–60
Langer, J. A., 29
Latinx, 186, 207n6; identifying as, 15; under-representation of, 19
learning, 149, 196; deep, 39, 43; higher-order, 38; integrative, 38; outcomes, 89; process of, 196; reflective, 38; transfer of, 7, 79–80, 100, 113, 128, 177, 211n2; verification of, 89–90; writing and, 16, 79–80, 182
learning disabilities, 59, 213n9
LeCourt, D., 208n8
Lerner, N., 62, 209n3
Light, R. J., 209n7
Lindquist, J., 214n3
linguistic traditions, Latinx/Black, 12
literacy: digital/multimodal, 21; information, 22; myth of, 187, 193; skills, 192
literacy trauma, 149, 185
literary studies, 12, 24
literary writing, 146, 210n1
long papers, 68, 82, 130, 135
longitudinal studies, 7–11, 16, 25–26, 28, 97, 151, 152, 180, 181, 186, 200, 208n14; impor-tance of, 128; interview-based, 15, 18, 65; large-scale, 8, 14, 15; participants in, 66; student writing, 5, 15

Macrorie, K., 22
Marx, Karl, 146
McCarthy, L. P., 4, 10, 106
McKay, Claude, 77
Meaningful Writing Project, The (Eodice et al.), 47, 52, 59
medical school, 115, 124, 126, 128, 150, 166, 178, 187; application for, 165; personal statement for, 184
Melzer, D., 9, 61, 91
mental health, writing and, 174
mentorship, 125, 128, 190, 192, 194; peer, 88, 214n12
methodologies: discourse-based, 100; inter-view, 15–20, 100; research, 4, 16, 154
mindsets, 98, 99; change in, 104, 110; general-purpose, 84; transfer of, 102
minorities, 186, 187, 207n6; racial/ethnic, 15, 19
MLA, 30, 42, 68; citation format, 101
Morrison, Toni, 152
motivation, 16, 65, 99, 187
Muslim Student Association (MSA), 162, 163, 212–13n8

Naming What We Know (Adler-Kassner and Wardle), 111, 177–78, 179
narratives, 122, 165, 215n3; master, 67; per-sonal, 114, 116; skills for, 186; writing, 124, 134. *See also* personal narratives
National Survey of Student Engagement (NSSE), 38
Neely, M. E., 83
Nelms, R. G., 181
Nelson, J., 142, 196
Nordquist, B., 207–8n6, 209n4
not writing, 34, 41, 61, 160, 176, 189
NYS Department of Corrections and Commu-nity Supervision, 55

O'Neill, P., 72–73
opening sentences, 95
opinion essay, 32
opinions, 92, 109, 116, 117, 119, 120, 204, 205; sharing, 108
opportunities, impoverished/limited, 42–46
Orwell, George, 118
outcomes, 3, 13, 41, 174, 184; learning, 12, 22, 89
outlining, 45, 93, 96, 133, 142, 201

page counts, 15, 69, 137; statistics on, 37t
paper length, 68, 82, 130, 135
participants, 96, 100; researchers and, 180; responses from, 91, 92; revision, 93; transfer-prone, 101
participation, 32, 37–38, 43, 44, 90, 154, 211n4; compensation for, 153
pedagogy, 6, 22, 23, 88, 183, 194; antiracist, 215n5; differences in, 90; discursive, 208n8; writing, 12, 193
peer review, 24, 39, 51, 76, 83, 84, 93, 101, 116, 125, 202; clandestine, 45; experiencing, 70, 130; pedagogical practice of, 133; usefulness of, 130; using, 102; writing assignment, 202. *See also* feedback
Pepperdine, 8, 18, 60, 62, 151, 183; longitudinal studies at, 186
perfectionism, 140, 158, 168, 171, 172
personal information, 185; sharing, 143, 175, 176, 186
personal interest, 99; academic inquiry and, 142
personal narratives, 122, 164, 165, 166, 186, 187, 188, 193, 194, 214n3; writing, 133, 134
personal statements, 38, 165, 166, 187, 209n5, 210n4; medical school, 198

234 : INDEX

personal writing, 111–12; academic writing and, 134, 138–48; beneficial effects of, 185; reconsidering, 184–88
Persons in Process (Herrington and Curtis), 147
perspectives, 11; alternate, 127; experiences and, 118
philosophy, 108, 141, 144, 160
physical health, writing and, 174
plagiarism, 135, 136, 137, 180
Plato, 141
Poe, M., 11, 62, 198, 209n3
poetry, writing, 73–74
point-of-view, 70, 102–3
political science, 106, 109, 141, 144
posting, email/social media, 32
preparation, 29, 71, 112, 152, 201, 202, 211n2; college, 28; writing, 67–68
prewriting process, 50, 83
Prior, P., 7
problem-solving, answer-getting versus, 6
procrastination, 55, 76, 141, 142, 148, 153, 167, 168, 169, 174, 177; avoiding, 94, 172; tendencies for, 171
psychology, 43, 61, 181
public health, 40, 41, 115, 120, 182
Purdue OWL web resource, 101

qualitative studies, 9, 23, 84, 149

racism, 118, 199, 214n10
reading: professional, 45; scientific, 124
recognition, 12, 13, 121, 122, 128
recommendations, 25, 45, 166, 178, 214n14; for first-year writing, 183–94; for university, 80–81; for WAC/WID, 194, 196–200, 208n8
reflection, 16, 28, 66, 81, 92, 179, 181, 192; developing skills in, 186; journal, 209n2, 210n4; literacy, 187; self-, 194; on writing, 153–54
Regents exams. *See* timed reading exams
Regidor, M. P. C., 187
Reiff, M. J., 5–6
research, 21, 23, 84, 127, 162, 166, 197; composition, 8; documents, 183; empirical, 11, 181; exploratory, 79; methods, 16, 154, 193; participation in, 14; presenting, 133; primary, 125, 132; qualitative, 23, 149; quasi-experimental, 64; secondary, 121, 132; writing, 114, 117, 178, 190, 191, 192
research papers, 31, 32, 117, 119, 133, 134, 162, 163, 209n2, 209n3; legal, 101; writing, 51–52
research process, 31, 38, 52, 59

research questions, overarching, 10–11
research site, 12–15
resources, 43, 79; academic, 199; institutional, 198; minimal, 181; supportive, 152; writing, 199
restrictions, 196, 198; breaking from, 103
revision, 24, 105, 110, 182, 197; descriptions of, 76; process, 38, 93, 148; substantive, 76, 93, 94, 96, 97
rhetoric, 12, 24, 97, 114, 133, 149, 158, 160, 197, 208n18, 209n3, 214n2; potential, 184–85; writing process and, 182
Rhetoric (Aristotle), 197
rhetorical activity, 102, 109, 111
rhetorical process, 83, 182, 198
Rogerian argument, 94, 105, 144
Roksa, J., 60
Roozen, K., 7, 147, 207n2
Rose, M., 78, 83, 97, 103, 167; fluency problems and, 95
Rounsaville, A., 7, 185, 207n2, 207n4
Rousseau, Jean-Jacques, 146
Ruecker, T., 207n6, 208n18
Russell, D. R., 84, 190
Rymer, J., 93, 188

Saltz, L., 6, 60, 185
samples, 32, 33–34t, 34, 38, 41, 44, 68, 144, 145, 160, 162–63, 211n1; page counts of, 37, 37t; providing, 203; sources cited in, 38t
SAT exams. *See* timed reading exams
scaffolding, 45, 61, 97, 143, 196
science, 83, 89, 106, 133, 149, 159, 165, 182, 192; as rhetorical, 114–28; writing, 124, 160–61
scientific writing, 121, 122, 124, 125–26, 133, 159, 209n2, 212n7; understanding, 127
Scantron exam answer sheets, 183
self-efficacy, 16, 65, 78, 83, 84, 129, 151, 161; low, 170, 174, 177, 189
self-sponsored writing, 71, 114, 138, 145
sense of self, developing, 177
"sentence boundary" issues, 214n10
sentence length, 172
Sitler, H. C., 184
skills, 13; developing, 185; improving, 40
Smith, K. G., 178
social activity, 102, 109, 111
social circumstances, 11, 12
social issues, 116, 118
social process, 25, 85
social science, 43, 61, 164
sociology, 101, 107, 128, 131, 132, 148
Socratic seminar, 131

Sommers, N., 6, 60, 76, 83, 185, 210n6
sources: number of, 38; statistics on, 38t; tallies of, 69
Spanglish, 193
Standard English, 193
Stanford Study of Writing, 37
Stanford University, 8, 9, 18, 183, 200
STEM, 43, 109
Sternglass, M. S., 15, 28, 59, 60, 208n6, 208n14; economic hardships and, 9; longitudinal study of, 8, 27
strategies, 76, 148, 177, 204; developing, 143; genre, 178; instruction for, 29; procedural, 191; rhetorical, 6, 161; writing process, 171–72
structural difficulties, 62, 80, 99
style, 81, 87, 99, 197, 202; conversational, 172; differences in, 88; modifying, 169; one certain, 123; teaching, 89
subheadings, 126, 142, 160
subtopics, 21, 129, 130
success: defining, 54; luck and, 156–58; sense of, 50
Sun Also Rises, The (Hemingway), 77
support, seeking, 159, 181–83
sustainability, teaching, 193–94, 198–99
Swales, J. M., 125
Swofford, S., 208n7

technology, 18, 76
term paper, 32
test scores, supplementing, 91
text correctness, emphasizing, 99
text-to-speech program, 210n6
texts, 131, 160; starting, 95
Thaiss, C., 65, 181
timed writing exams: ACT, 29; Regents, 28, 29, 67, 209n2; SAT, 28, 29, 67
time limits, 29, 65, 129
Time to Know Them (Sternglass), 27
timed-examination preparation, breaking from, 112
topics, 96; academic, 141; exploration of, 23; selecting, 196–97; writing assignment, 186
topoi, 197
transfer, 9, 11, 25, 83, 85, 113, 122, 158, 160, 162, 165, 177, 179, 185, 191; barriers to, 101; engaging in, 161, 198; hindrances to, 105–9; identity and, 149–50; incidents, 101, 102, 106, 210n7, 210n8; invisible, 100; opportunities for, 114; productive, 115; teaching for, 188; term, 7; visible, 100, 101, 107
transformation, 7, 167, 171, 199

transitions, 42, 80, 88, 122, 208n6
Tufts University, 43, 62, 81

University of Denver, writing program at, 22
University of Michigan, 8, 18, 28, 183, 208n7
University of Wisconsin, composition program at, 23

viewpoints, 119, 144
visuals, 34, 121, 131, 139, 189, 202

WAC. *See* writing across the curriculum
Wardle, E., 6, 111, 177–78, 179, 188, 189, 207n1
wayfinding, 7, 147
Wayfinding Project, 147
Wells, J., 69, 158, 161
WI courses. *See* writing-intensive courses
WID. *See* writing in the disciplines
Wolfe, J., 190
writers: broadening, 7–11; capable, 188; embracing, 189–90, 193; good/defining, 157t; identifying as, 9, 71–74, 72f, 85, 149, 153, 188, 193; minority, 114
writer's block, 78, 97, 167, 191; avoiding, 130; overcoming, 98, 159
writing: about self, 108; analytic, 119; appreciating own, 99–100; attitudes about, 88–89; challenges of, 158, 160, 191, 192; college-level, 31–32, 34, 37–39, 80, 92, 146, 196; definition of, 68, 166, 173, 179, 188; disciplinary, 127, 160; as epistemic, 16, 25, 96, 179; first, 148, 201; formal, 103, 193; framework for, 179, 188; future, 111–12; high school, 80, 92, 101, 102, 161, 201; improving, 143, 211n1; interactive, 41–42; interest in, 138, 152; purposes of, 90–92, 103; recent, 34, 35–36t; rhetorical nature of, 16, 115; successful, 69, 71, 141, 148, 153, 156–58; teaching, 6, 173, 199; theories of, 6, 18, 179, 188–89; understanding, 133, 167, 178, 179; writing about, 188, 194
writing across the curriculum (WAC), 9, 11–12, 24, 39, 62, 91, 181, 182, 183, 189, 198, 199, 200; commitment to, 14; developmental goals of, 13; findings relevant to/recommendations for, 194, 196; professionalization of, 13; structure, 13–14
writing courses: college-equivalent, 4, 5, 64; conducting, 19, 211n3; high-school, 79; recollections from, 66; required, 92
writing in general, term, 81
writing in the disciplines (WID), 11, 12, 122, 123, 127, 198, 199

236 : INDEX

writing-intensive (WI) courses, 13, 18, 42, 61, 63, 64, 66, 81, 127, 172, 212n7; designation of, 39–40, 182; questions about, 204–5

writing knowledge, 16, 26, 82, 100, 150; cuing past, 198; developing, 162, 185; procedural, 199; rhetorical, 199; transfer of, 11, 25, 83, 107; types of, 79

writing practices, 82, 83, 96, 100, 109, 118, 131, 150, 188; acquisition of, 14; origin of, 103–4; regular, 100; types of, 79

writing process, 18, 21, 26, 50–51, 52, 67, 69, 82, 83–84, 97, 111, 116, 129, 138, 142, 149; applying/ developing, 60; automaticity of, 17; beginning, 77, 93, 95, 143; challenges of, 179, 184; current, 94–95; descriptions of, 76–79, 93–94, 96, 201–2; effortlessness of, 155; engaging in, 54, 55, 58, 59, 196; experimenting with, 177; feelings about, 152, 153; first stages of, 197; guidance on, 191; helping/ hindering, 202; ineffectual/ unhealthy, 178; interactive, 39, 61; judging, 178; modifying, 100, 110, 169, 171–72; planning, 54–55; questions about, 201–2; rhetorical functions and, 182; social/collaborative, 110; strategies for, 171–72; typical, 76, 97, 171

writing studies, 7, 8, 31, 111, 189, 190, 198; conducting, 181; introduction to, 6, 179, 188, 191; undergraduate, 15

writing theories, 6, 18, 146, 179, 188–89, 190, 198; metacognitive awareness of, 64; questioning, 191

Yancey, K. B., 6, 64, 179, 207n4; conceptual framework and, 188

Young, V. A., 193, 207n1

Zawacki, T. M., 65, 181

Zepernick, J., 4, 65, 111

zines, 74, 131, 209n2

About the Author

LAURA WILDER is an associate professor of English at the University at Albany, SUNY. Her first book, *Rhetorical Strategies and Genre Conventions in Literary Studies* (SIUP 2012), was awarded the 2014 CCCC Research Impact Award. Her articles have appeared in journals such as *Written Communication*, *Research in the Teaching of English*, *The WAC Journal*, and *Pedagogy*. She has been recognized with the SUNY Chancellor's Award for Excellence in Teaching.